The significant role of Scottish missionaries in the nurture and growth of Christian faith worldwide particularly the global south, during the past three hundred years, which culminated in the World Missionary Conference, Edinburgh 1910, is legendary. This book, which deepens our knowledge of the history, methodology and theology of this important epoch in mission studies, has lessons to teach the development of mission in the contemporary worldwide church. It clearly opens up lessons that can be applied to the development of mission thinking and practice in different contexts, specifically the contemporary heartlands of the Christian Church in Africa and Asia.

Professor Cephas N. Omenyo, Dean, Faculty of Arts
University of Ghana, Legon, Ghana.

Kenneth Ross and a distinguished list of scholars have offered a seminal text that celebrates and critiques three hundred years of Scottish mission history. Their scholarly contours offer deep insights into the unique understanding and practice of mission fashioned by competent, committed, compassionate and consistent leadership whose immeasurable contribution can best be summarised as 'evangelization through education'. This publication will serve as a valuable missiological resource. I therefore commend this book as a necessary text for all missional practitioners and scholars.

Professor Roderick R. Hewitt, Academic Leader - Theology and Ethics
Director – Systematic Theology, School of Religion, Philosophy and Classics
University of KwaZulu-Natal, South Africa

This compendium on Scotland's vital and colourful roles in the most recent half-millennium's transformation of Christianity is both instructive in its broader analyses of the modern missions movement and moving in its specific accounts of individuals and organizations. More than simply stirring up 'Scotland the Brave' in the reader's breast, the volume delivers essential components of what the title ambitiously promises: 'Retrieving Scotland's Missionary Story' as part of the worldwide drama of Christian mission.

Dr Nelson Jennings, Executive Director, Overseas Ministries Study Center,
New Haven, Connecticut, USA;
Editor, *International Bulletin of Missionary Research*

The fruits of the Scottish missionary labours in India, especially in the field of education, are too visible to be ignored. The 177 year-old Madras Christian College is one such fruit. This book, is an inspiring missionary story, which I am sure would motivate pastors, theologians and teachers, especially the young ones, to take steps to strengthen Christian witness in a world where the very word 'mission' is seen as unwelcome. This book should adorn the shelves not only of the seminaries and churches, but also of Christian educational institutions.

Dr Joshua Kalapati, Associate Professor of Philosophy, Madras Christian College, India; co-author of *Life and Legacy of Madras Christian College*

If reading means nodding and sighing, it is especially true for this sophisticated but enjoyable mission history. A collection of articles written by the Scots themselves, this book vividly depicts how the Scottish Church had emerged as a disproportionately vibrant centre of missions, contributing to empire and boosting national pride; how she went through the turbulent but rewarding transition experience from missions to mission, realizing that mission is learning and receiving; and how she has grown in partnership in the dramatically changed landscape of mission such as reverse mission and ecumenical engagement. Summarizing the characteristics of Scottish mission as social concern, church-centeredness, theology, extensive engagement, long-term perspective, and glocality, this book reminds us how many national churches owe their origins to the Scots, in the list of which the Korean Church is not to be excluded.

Rev. Professor Kyo Seong Ahn,
Presbyterian University and Theological Seminary, Seoul, Korea

REGNUM STUDIES IN MISSION

Roots and Fruits:
Retrieving Scotland's Missionary Story

Series Preface

Regnum Studies in Mission are born from the lived experience of Christians and Christian communities in mission, especially but not solely in the fast growing churches among the poor of the world. These churches have more to tell than stories of growth. They are making significant impacts on their cultures in the cause of Christ. They are producing 'cultural products' which express the reality of Christian faith, hope and love in their societies.

Regnum Studies in Mission are the fruit often of rigorous research to the highest international standards and always of authentic Christian engagement in the transformation of people and societies. And these are for the world. The formation of Christian theology, missiology and practice in the twenty-first century will depend to a great extent on the active participation of growing churches contributing biblical and culturally appropriate expressions of Christian practice to inform World Christianity.

Series Editors

Julie C. Ma	Oxford Centre for Mission Studies, Oxford, UK
Wonsuk Ma	Oxford Centre for Mission Studies, Oxford, UK
Doug Petersen	Vanguard University, Costa Mesa, CA, USA
Terence Ranger	University of Oxford, Oxford, UK
C.B. Samuel	Emmanuel Hospital Association, Delhi, India
Chris Sugden	Anglican Mainstream, Oxford, UK

A full listing of titles in this series
appears at the end of this book

REGNUM STUDIES IN MISSION

Roots and Fruits:
Retrieving Scotland's Missionary Story

Edited by Kenneth R Ross

British Library Cataloguing in Publication Data
A catalogue record for this book is available from the British Library

ISBN: 978-1-908355-29-4

Typeset by Words by Design
Printed and bound in Great Britain
for Regnum Books International
by TJ International Ltd, Padstow, Cornwall

MIX
Paper from
responsible sources
FSC® C013056

CONTENTS

PREFACE

This book owes its origins to a series of conferences and seminars which was prompted by the approach of the centenary of the Edinburgh 1910 World Missionary Conference. While it was anticipated that this notable milestone in missionary and ecumenical history would be celebrated on a global basis, it was considered important that Scotland, as the host nation of Edinburgh 1910, should pay particular attention to the centenary. So much so that a mission studies community came together under the banner of "Towards 2010" to run a series of day conferences from 2002 to 2007, each focussed on one of the Commissions which prepared Reports for the 1910 Conference. In due course, this was published as David A. Kerr and Kenneth R. Ross eds., *Edinburgh 2010: Mission Then and Now* (Oxford: Regnum, 2009) as a contribution to the international preparations being made to celebrate the centenary.

Within the global network which formed around the Edinburgh 1910 centenary a question recurrently asked was: "why Scotland?" Why was it that Scotland came to host the most celebrated and most influential missionary conference of modern times? Three day conferences, held by "Towards 2010" between October 2008 and October 2009 under the title "Roots and Fruits", set out to answer this question and generated the material which forms the basis of this book.

The Edinburgh 1910 World Missionary Conference therefore forms an integral point of reference for the book as a whole. As the event which constituted the most concentrated expression and summation of the modern missionary movement it sheds light both on the history which preceded it and on that which followed. It is therefore employed to open up a history which extends across three hundred years – from the formation of Scotland's first mission agency, the Society in Scotland for the Propagation of Christian Knowledge, in 1709, right up to the present day.

As is apparent in the bibliography, there have been many studies of particular people, places and periods which feature in Scotland's missionary movement. Much less common has been the effort to take a comprehensive and synchronic view of the movement as a whole. It is this which is attempted in the essays brought together in this volume.

Sincere thanks are due to the bodies which combined to form the Towards 2010 Council which conceived and organised the conference series on which the book is based: Action of Churches Together in Scotland; the Church of Scotland World Mission Council; Edinburgh University's Centre for the Study of World Christianity; the International Christian College, Glasgow; the Missionary Representatives Fellowship, Scotland; Scottish Churches World Exchange; the Scottish Roman Catholic Church; Tearfund; Scottish Catholic International Aid Fund (SCIAF); and

Christian Aid. This book owes much to the members of the Council, not least its indefatigable secretary David Miller; and Jack Thompson who suggested "Roots and Fruits" as an appropriate title.

Heartfelt thanks are recorded also to the bodies which contributed financially to the work undertaken by "Towards 2010": the Alexander Duff Missionary Lectureship Trust, the Church of Scotland World Mission Council, the Pollock Trust and the Society in Scotland for the Propagation of Christian Knowledge (SSPCK).

Above all, thanks are due to those who participated in the conferences. Samples of their contributions are found in the chapter on 'Edinburgh 1910 and Scottish Experience of Serving in Mission 1950-2000' which reveals the calibre of the discussion and debate which took place. This has served to significantly strengthen all the chapters as the original conference papers have been reworked to take account of questions raised and challenges posed. "Theology begins at sunset," suggested Gustavo Gutierrez. After an action-packed "day" of mission the "Towards 2010" community sat down to reflect on what it all had meant. Not as a matter of nostalgia or sentimentality but to stimulate the next missionary impetus as the action-reflection cycle continues.

An earlier version of 'Edinburgh 1910 and Scottish Experience of Serving in Mission 1950-2000' appeared in Vol. 38 No. 1 (April 2010) of *Missionalia*, the Southern African Journal of Missiology, and I am grateful to the editor for permission to include this material. An earlier version of the Conclusion was published online in *Transformation: An International Journal of Holistic Mission* in May 2014 and again I am grateful to the editor for permission to include it in this book.

Kenneth R. Ross
Chair, Towards 2010 Council 2001-09

INTRODUCTION

Despite being a small nation on Europe's northwestern seaboard, or perhaps because of it, Scotland has had a remarkable width and depth of international engagement. As Michael Fry has remarked: "… the nation's historical, political and economic circumstances have always made its sense of itself strangely intangible, compelling Scots to search elsewhere for promises of fulfilment."[1] The extent of the Scots diaspora and the influence which it has had in commerce, industry, politics and culture has been the subject of a great many studies. One strand in this wide-ranging engagement which has not always enjoyed the attention it merits is the missionary movement in which Scotland played a disproportionately prominent role. As Dugald Mackichen observed: "The cosmopolitan outlook for which Scotland is noted has been fostered not merely by the far-reaching commercial interests of its inhabitants, but also and perhaps in a manner more intense and more fruitful of benefit to the world, by its missionary enterprise."[2]

For those who have seen at first hand the influence and the extent of Scottish missionary engagement with other parts of the world, it is clear that this is an important part of Scotland's story. For others, it remains something of a Cinderella subject. John Fairbank, former president of the America History Society, observed that, "the missionary in foreign parts seems to be the invisible man of … history."[3] We may add that the women missionaries, though not less influential, are even more invisible. This book aims to give visibility to the Scottish missionary movement by considering some of its leading themes in a rounded and comprehensive way.

Andrew Walls begins the book by offering a three hundred year retrospect on Scotland and mission, taking his starting point from the establishment of the Society in Scotland for the Propagation of Christian Knowledge in 1709. The global reach and comprehensive range of his analysis allows him to reveal the salient features of Scotland's missionary engagement with the wider world.

The Edinburgh 1910 World Missionary Conference is widely employed in this book as a prism through which to examine various dimensions of the Scottish missionary movement. Kenneth Ross examines the Scottish provenance of the Conference, suggesting that the influence of Scotland

---

[1] Michael Fry, *The Scottish Empire* (Edinburgh: Tuckwell Press & Birlinn, 2001), viii.

[2] Dugald Mackichan, *The Missionary Ideal in the Scottish Churches* (London: Hodder & Stoughton, 1927), 129-30.

[3] John K. Fairbank, "Assignment for the '70s", *American Historical Review*, 74/3 (1969), 877.

went much further than simply providing the venue. Scots played leading roles in all of the Commissions which reported, influenced the ethos of the conference itself and ensured that it broke new ground in terms of its engagement with the intellectual and theological mainstream. A great deal of the character of the missionary movement in Scotland is revealed through consideration of all that was involved in hosting the 1910 Conference.

Esther Breitenbach focuses on the influence of the missionary movement not in the far-flung mission fields which were its primary concern but rather on the population at home in Scotland. She is careful not to overplay the extent of the missionary enthusiasm in Scotland but, working from empirical data, shows how wide was its reach, particularly when it was at the height of its influence in the late 19th and early 20th century. During this period it attained a high public profile and became a source of national pride in Scotland.

Rose Dowsett offers an original account of a strand of missionary activism which emerged from the evangelistic drive apparent at the Edinburgh 1910 conference: one which was self-consciously "evangelical" and which shared an experience of formation at the Bible Training Institute in Glasgow. Though largely unheralded, this movement of evangelical witness has had a major impact in situations as diverse as China and Australia. A number of vignettes give us the flavour of the movement and a sense of the pioneering part which it played in Christian mission from Scotland to the wider world.

John McCracken offers an even more tightly focussed essay, examining a succession of four Scottish missionaries in southern Africa: John Philip, David Livingstone, David Clement Scott and Andrew Ross. There is a poignancy to this chapter in that, in the original plan for the conference series, this topic would have been covered by Andrew Ross. His death, in July 2008, meant that this was not to be. However, John McCracken stepped up to write a chapter in which Ross is subject rather than author, with his own life being considered in the context of the three 19th century missionaries about whom he wrote. Passionate commitment to social justice is the common thread, with the role of the missionary movement in fostering Scottish national identity as a sub-theme.

A particularly memorable conference in the series which underlies this book, was one held in Glasgow in April 2009 at which no less than thirty-three former missionaries brought reflections on their overseas service. They gave not so much a narrative account as an attempt to interpret what their missionary service had really been all about. Tears were shed as people spoke of lands and people they had loved. Kenneth Ross and James Wilkie provide a digest of the reflection which was offered, organised under the five themes which they found to be most prominent. This provides a rare glimpse into the inner purpose and motivation which drove the missionary movement as it entered what may prove to be its twilight years at the end of the 20th century.

Mission and unity have proved over history to be two sides of the same coin. Discussion of one invariably leads to the other. Hence the Edinburgh 1910 Conference which could not have been clearer about its missionary purpose also had such a strong emphasis on unity that it became the celebrated birthplace of the Ecumenical Movement. Through a series of interviews with selected key players, Stephen Smyth offers an analysis of Scotland's current experience of ecumenism. Though realistic about the difficulties faced by the Ecumenical Movement, it celebrates how far we have come and is upbeat in identifying approaches which hold promise for further advances to be made.

A final chapter by Chris Wigglesworth considers the missionary movement in relation to internationalism. In a wide-ranging essay which sweeps across a great variety of people, times and places, Wigglesworth traces the part played by missionary thinking in fostering internationalism in Scotland, particularly in relation to combating poverty and countering environmental threat. He concludes with a sharp analysis of the need for the spirit of internationalism to be deployed in the contemporary world in the quest for peace among the religions.

No claim is made that this book says all that could be said about the Scottish missionary movement. Both at the level of detailed studies and at that of comprehensive, overall assessment, there is much more to be done. What is offered here is a contribution to the discussion, based on the exploration of a number of carefully selected themes, each of which sheds light on what this prolific movement has meant, both for Scotland and for the world.

It is necessarily a backward-looking book, taking account of a particular history. Inasmuch as it engages the question of Christian mission, however, its field of reference cannot be confined to the past. For each new age brings new impulses of mission, our own being no exception. Consideration of the various dimensions of the Scottish missionary movement as they are traced across three centuries may prove instructive to new movements emerging to engage today's global context.

THREE HUNDRED YEARS OF SCOTTISH MISSIONS

Andrew F. Walls

The Missionary Movement from the West

The story of the missionary movement covers five hundred years and has Catholic and Protestant chapters. The early chapters are essentially Catholic, beginning as Europe, as a result of the trans-oceanic voyages of the late fifteenth and early sixteenth centuries, moved out of hundreds of years of isolation from most of Africa and Asia, and total ignorance of the Americas. Spain and Portugal led the explorations; the missionary aspect of the story came out of the movements of religious renewal within the Catholic Church in the century that brought the Protestant Reformation.

The true nature of the missionary movement has been obscured by the fact that it originated at a time when European Christians were already propagating their faith by other means. The European experience of Christianity may be summed up in the word "Christendom." Christendom is Christianity geographically expressed: the concept of Christian territory where Christian peoples live under Christian law. This meant that the Christian faith could be propagated by expanding Christian territory; and in its military aspect this produces the idea of crusade. In many ways the Spanish conquest of Mexico and Peru can be seen (though it was not so called at the time) as the last of the crusades, bringing new territories under Christian law so that Mexico could be called New Spain. But in Asia, and in much of Africa, conquest and crusade were alike impossible for such a small power as Portugal. In China, India, Japan compulsion (outside some small enclaves) was out of the question; if Christianity was to take root, it must be by persuasion. And persuasion required a new order of Christians, people prepared to live within an alien society on that society's terms, learning its language and finding a place within it. Missionaries formed this new order; and it was within Catholic southern Europe that such people were first found; people not only with zeal, such as Francis Xavier, but with patience and application, such as Matteo Ricci, Roberto de Nobili and Alexandre de Rhodes, who set themselves to understand the languages and cultures of China, India and Vietnam.[1]

Protestants, occupied by the struggle for reformation of the church in Europe and with the theological and pastoral revolution which that involved, were generally slower to become aware of the new worlds

---

[1] Cf. Andrew F. Walls, *The Cross-Cultural Process in Christian History* (Maryknoll NY: Orbis, 2002), 27-48.

beyond Europe. The evangelization of the world, the preaching to all nations, was most easily conceived in eschatological terms, as an event of the last times, rather than as a present concern. It is in this light that we should probably understand the citation of Matthew 24:14 on the title page of the Scots Confession of 1560. It is not a call to a programme for world evangelization, but a reminder of the final outcome of proclaiming the "glaid tydinges of the Kingdom." The nature of that Gospel was being spelled out in the Confession, and was being proclaimed in Scotland; it would be vindicated in the Last Times.[2]

The first signs of a Protestant missionary movement beyond Europe appear, in a very small way, in North America, where for the first time a Protestant community lived as neighbours of a community that was not Christian at all.[3] The Puritan settlers in New England, religious refugees or self-exiles from Old England, were radical Christians; and it has been at the radical end of the Christian spectrum, whether Protestant or Catholic, that those most formative in the missionary movement have been found. It was another radical movement in Protestantism, German Pietism, that led in 1706 to the first Protestant overseas mission, that directed to the Danish colony of Tranquebar in India. Another branch of the Pietist movement, the Moravians, took up the cause, and became the most dynamic Protestant mission force of the eighteenth century.[4]

During that same century England, Scotland and North America were visited by a series of movements of radical Christianity which shared many of the features of Pietism. Taken together these movements constitute the Evangelical Revival, which deeply affected the Protestant Christianity of the nineteenth century. Protestants, like Catholics, had commonly professed a desire for the Christian faith to be universally proclaimed; the Evangelical movement, with its radicalizing of Christian commitment, brought a new urgency to bring the Christian message to the whole world, especially where it was hitherto unknown.

Scotland's Entry into the Missionary Movement

Scotland's involvement in this missionary movement has two sources, which in the course of the eighteenth century came to flow together. Each began with domestic efforts directed to Scotland; each took on a wider aspect through contact with the new world of America. The Evangelical

---

[2] Conveniently available in *The Scots Confession 1560,* edited by G.D. Henderson, together with a rendering into modern English by James Bulloch (Edinburgh: St Andrew Press, 1960).

[3] See S.H. Rooy, *The Theology of Missions in the Puritan Tradition* (Grand Rapids: Eerdmans, 1965).

[4] On Moravian influence on the later Protestant missionary movement, see J.C.S. Mason, *The Moravian Church and the Missionary Awakening in England* (Woodbridge, Suffolk: Boydell Press for Royal Historical Society, 2001).

Revival was one of these sources, but not the first; an earlier development arose from the urge to complete the Reformation process in Scotland.

Scotland had embraced the Reformation in a more radical form than that adopted by its southern neighbour, and seventeenth century events gave added emphasis to this. But in some areas of the country that Reformation had barely taken hold. The distinctively Scottish expression of the Reformed faith had developed alongside a vigorous programme of public education, fired by the conviction that all should be able to read the Bible. But large tracts of the Highlands, and many of the islands, had been little affected by either the religious or the educational revolutions that were now shaping Scottish identity; and by the beginning of the eighteenth century it was clear that the parish system as it then functioned was ill equipped to address the situation. In Highland parishes, often vast in extent, a small number of ministers, usually working entirely in English, had pastoral responsibility for a scattered, mostly unlettered and predominantly Gaelic-speaking population. In some areas Catholicism (though the actual number of practising Catholics was probably exaggerated by contemporary commentators) remained entrenched, and while Jacobitism continued, this was seen as a political threat. But even leaving aside this residual Catholicism (and the effect of later Catholic missions), Reformed Christianity in much of the Highlands and Islands was at the beginning of the eighteenth century shallow and fragile.

Around this time, earnest English High Churchmen were becoming alarmed at the irreligion of post-Restoration England, and in particular the ignorance, both religious and secular, of the urban population. In response, a group of such people formed in 1699 a "Society for Promoting Christian Knowledge." Influenced by Pietist practice in Germany, the Society funded charity schools and the preparation and distribution of Christian literature. Many of the group were also concerned for the spiritual needs of the English colonies in America,[5] and the aims of the SPCK included promoting Christian knowledge abroad as well as at home.[6] In 1709 a group of Scottish churchmen drew on this English model by forming a "Society in Scotland for Propagating Christian Knowledge."[7] As with the English society, the stated aims included "the advancement of the Christian religion in heathen countries"; but the immediate and always primary aim was to provide for the population of the Highlands and Islands instruction in "the Christian Reformed Protestant Religion." Again in emulation of the English SPCK (which itself was here following a model developed by the Geman Pietists), schools were seen as the principal instrument for the purpose. The Society aimed to recruit and oversee "men of loyalty,

---

[5] The Society for the Propagation of the Gospel, with the supply and equipment of clergy for the colonies as its main aim, owed its origin to the same constituency.
[6] See W.K. Lowther Clarke, *A History of the SPCK* (London: SPCK, 1959).
[7] See *An Account of the Rise, Constitution and Management of the Society in Scotland for Propagating Christian Knowledge* (Edinburgh: William Brown, 1720).

prudence, gravity, competent knowledge, and literature" who would propagate truth, foster piety and eradicate error, thereby lifting an illiterate population out of "barbarity, incivility, and superstition."[8]

The Society was, in effect, aiming at a cultural revolution in the Highlands and Islands, with religious change effected by educational means. Schools were to be open to all, Catholic or Protestant, and free to the poor. The teachers were bidden to catechize their pupils twice a week, and to pray with them twice a day.

After a slow start, (only five schools were started in the first two years), the Society's schools expanded across the Highlands; by 1795 the number of schools had reached 229. Schoolmasters were often called "missionaries," and by the end of the century there were signs that a religious and cultural revolution in the Highlands had indeed taken place.[9]

A revolution had also taken place in the way that the Society operated. It had seemed axiomatic to the founding fathers that the medium of transformation would be English, and that Gaelic had no place in vital Christianity. In the Society's early days, teachers and pupils were forbidden to use the Gaelic language; but this proved unrealistic. Led by the experience of its teachers, themselves native Gaelic speakers, the Society gradually modified its stand, initially authorizing use of the "comparative method", whereby Gaelic might be used to explain English words, then setting one of its ablest teachers to compile a Gaelic-English vocabulary. By 1767, the Society had published a translation of the New Testament in Gaelic, and one which made use of the best contemporary scholarship on the Greek text, even occasionally diverging from the text used by the Authorized Version.

The Gaelic Bible became a potent instrument in the transformation of the religion in the Highlands; it recognizably belonged to the soil. The Gaelic language, instead of being an obstacle for the Gospel to overcome, became the vehicle by which it was conveyed. And in this way the cultural revolution did come to the Highlands and Islands, bringing with it a literary deposit of books and libraries, both English and Gaelic, as well as a literate constituency to use them. And the revolution came about, not through the abolition of the language and existing culture of the Highlands, as the pioneers intended, but through the revitalization and expansion of that culture, as the scriptures were absorbed through the medium of the principal indigenous cultural resource of the Highlands, the Gaelic language.[10]

---

[8] On the establishment of the SSPCK, see Nathan Philip Gray, "A Publick Benefite:" The Charitable and Religious Origins of the Society in Scotland for Promoting Christian Knowledge, 1695-1715", PhD, University of Glasgow, 2011.

[9] See Douglas Ansdell, *The People of the Great Faith: The Highland Church 1690-1900* (Stornoway: Acair, 1998).

[10] See Donald E. Meek, "Gaelic Bible, Revival and Mission: Spiritual Rebirth of the Nineteenth Century Highlands" in James Kirk ed., *The Church in the Highlands*

The eighteenth century experience of Scottish home missions, which reinforced and expanded the earlier experience of the Scottish Reformation, underlies some features of subsequent Scottish missions overseas. The idea of a literate, enlightened community, well-grounded in Christian understanding, fitted well with Scottish beliefs about the nation's history. This is already reflected in the work of Robert Millar (1672-1752), the first Scottish writer to attempt a comprehensive history of Christianity in terms of the history of its propagation.[11] Millar traces the parallel themes of the spread of Christianity and the downfall of paganism, depicting one phase of this history as ending with the christianization of Europe. Other forms of paganism had arisen since; but Millar sees a new phase of Christian expansion at hand, heralded – as the Reformation had been – by "the reviving of arts and sciences, knowledge and learning."

Such a vision could be endorsed by Scottish churchmen of different theological viewpoints. Moderates and Evangelicals could alike conscientiously support the work of SSPCK; and such a Moderate as William Robertson, who expounded so vigorously the view that Christ came "in the fullness of time" to a world intellectually prepared for that event,[12] could, evoking Millar, envisage that a suitable programme of education might prepare the way for the coming of Christianity to India.[13] And an Evangelical Scottish missionary such as Henry Brunton, at the beginning of the nineteenth century, could invoke the example of the Scottish Highlands to justify a programme of long-term trans-generational

---

(Edinburgh: Scottish Church History Society, 1998), 114-145; John MacInnes, *The Evangelical Movement in the Highlands of Scotland, 1688-1800* (Aberdeen: Aberdeen University Press, 1951).

[11] Robert Millar, *The History of the Propagation of Christianity and the Overthrow of Paganism, wherein the Christian religion is confirmed, the rise and progress of heathenish idolatry is considered, the overthrow of paganism and the spreading of Christianity in the several ages of the New Testament Church are explained, the present state of the heathens is enquired into and methods for their conversion offered* (Edinburgh, 1723; 2nd ed. London, 1726). See also John Foster, "A Scottish Contributor to the Missionary Awakening: Robert Millar of Paisley," *International Review of Missions* Vol. 37 (1948), 138-145.

[12] William Robertson, *The Situation of the World at the Time of Christ's Appearance and its connection with the success of his religion considered* (Edinburgh, 1755). It is interesting to note that this was originally a sermon preached for the SSPCK.

[13] William Robertson, *An Historical Disquisition concerning the Knowledge which the Ancients had of India, and the progress of trade in that country prior to the discovery of the passage to it by the Cape of Good Hope; with an appendix containing observations on the civil polity – the laws and judicial processes – the arts – the sciences – and the religious beliefs of the Indians* (London, 1701). On this work see Stewart J. Brown, "William Robertson, Early Orientalism and the Historical Disquisition on India", *Scottish Historical Review* Vol. 88 (2009), 289–312.

vernacular Christian literature for West Africa.[14] In the Highlands, he declared, the seed sown in vernacular literacy based on the Bible had come to fruition in the vital religion of the children and grandchildren of those who received it. In the new century, a similar process in Africa could bring a similar result.

We have seen that the SSPCK had from the beginning included in its aims, if not in its practice, provision for promoting Christian knowledge overseas. The first step towards this came about, naturally enough, through the Highland diaspora.[15] In 1735 the Society sent a newly-ordained Skye-born minister, John Macleod, to accompany a colony of would-be colonists from Skye to Georgia. Another initiative was facilitated by a legacy from an English Dissenter, Dr. Daniel Williams.[16] The money was used, not to send a missionary from Scotland, but to enable a young colony-born minister, David Brainerd, to address a Native American population in New England. Through his journals, published, with some commentary, by Jonathan Edwards,[17] Brainerd came to have an immense influence on the Protestant missionary movement, becoming an iconic figure, the model of the missionary, for generations to come.

In this indirect and almost incidental fashion, Scottish official involvement in overseas missions began. Brainerd never saw Scotland, but after his death the SSPCK continued to support missions to the Native Americans.[18] The connection was cemented when, between 1766 and 1768, a Native American minister, Samson Occom, whom the SSPCK had been supporting, toured Scotland preaching and raising missionary consciousness. The General Assembly of the Church of Scotland took

---

[14] Henry Brunton, *Grammar and Vocabulary of the Susoo Language* (Edinburgh: J. Ritchie, 1802).

[15] See Henry R. Sefton, "The Scotch Society in the American Colonies in the Eighteenth Century," *Scottish Church History Society Records*, Vol. XVII (1972), 169-84.

[16] Williams was the founder of the theological library in London that still bears his name. His bequest to the SSPCK, when he had no clear connection with Scotland, is noteworthy; as a Dissenter from the Church of England, he could not even be a member of the English SPCK, which at this time was supporting the work being carried on by Halle Pietists in the Tranquebar mission in India. There was a considerable gap between the receipt of the legacy by the SSPCK and its application to mission in America.

[17] A scholarly edition is available in *The Works of Jonathan Edwards Vol. 7: The Life of David Brainerd*, ed. Norman Pettit (New Haven CT: Yale University Press, 1984).

[18] See Margaret Connell Szasz, *Scottish Highlands and Native Americans: Indigenous Education in the Eighteenth Century* (Norman, OK: University of Oklahoma Press, 2007); Rusty Roberson, "Scottish Missions and Religious Enlightenment in Colonial America: the SSPCK in Transatlantic Context", PhD, University of Edinburgh, 2012.

cognizance of this by approving a collection for missionary work in North America.[19]

The Evangelical Revival and Missionary Consciousness in Scotland

In undertaking support for Brainerd, the SSPCK had linked Scotland with both overseas mission and the Great Revival which had begun in America. The second important series of developments shaping the Scottish missionary movement originated in a Scottish outcrop of the Evangelical Revival, connected to America in a way that had ecumenical consequences.

In the "Cambuslang Wark" of 1742, a Lanarkshire parish witnessed scenes of spiritual renewal that paralleled what was happening in the ministry of Jonathan Edwards in America and of Wesley and Whitefield in England.[20] One feature of the Cambuslang revival was the frequency of meetings for prayer, with believers interceding for the spread of the knowledge of Christ throughout the world. The influential Scottish Evangelical John MacLaurin promoted the idea of a covenant for prayer that God would "fill the whole earth with His glory." Jonathan Edwards, inspired by reports of the Cambuslang praying groups, called for a "concert of prayer" among Christians everywhere for the extension of Christ's Kingdom. In 1748 Edwards, with his customary comprehensive vision, united the topics of the Scottish prayer meetings, Biblical eschatology and the now widespread contemporary evidence of the revival of vital religion, in a single short book. It was called, *A Humble Attempt to Promote Explicit Agreement and Visible Union of God's People in Extraordinary Prayer for the Revival of Religion and the Advancement of God's Kingdom on the Earth.*[21] It depicted the revivals as pointers to a coming day when the earth would be filled with the knowledge of God, calling for "extraordinary" prayer for the coming Kingdom. The eminent Evangelical John Erskine of Greyfriars sent the book to an English Baptist correspondent,[22] and as a result the group of Baptists in Northamptonshire that included Andrew Fuller and later, William Carey, initiated regular prayer meetings. A direct outcome was Carey's proposal in 1792 that his Baptist brethren form a missionary society and send missionaries to the non-Christian world. The

---

[19] On Occom, see Joanna Brooks ed., *Collected Writings of Samson Occom, Mohegan: Leadership and Literature in 18th Century Native America* (New York: Oxford University Press, 2006).
[20] See Arthur Fawcett, *The Cambuslang Revival of the Eighteenth Century* (London: Banner of Truth, 1971).
[21] A scholarly edition in *The Works of Jonathan Edwards Vol. 5: Apocalyptic Writings,* ed. Stephen J. Stein (New Haven: Yale University Press, 1977).
[22] John Sutcliff, who produced a cheap abridged version of the work. On the significance and consequences of Edwards' book, see John Foster, "The Bicentenary of Jonathan Edwards' *Humble Attempt,*" *International Review of Missions* Vol. 37/4 (1948), 375-381.

event marked a new stage in mission commitment and in mission organization in England.[23]

The Early Missionary Societies

David Bogue, a Scottish minister then pastoring an Independent congregation in England, forcefully drew the attention of "Evangelical Dissenters who practiced infant baptism" in an article in the *Evangelical Magazine* challenging his colleagues to emulate the Baptist initiative. His hope was realized in the founding in 1795 of what was at first called simply the Missionary Society, but soon became known as the London Missionary Society (LMS).[24] Independents (or Congregationalists) were its backbone, but the Society attracted a broad spectrum of Evangelicals, including some maverick Anglicans, with its stated aim to send the Gospel to the heathen, leaving church government to the decision of the churches that would arise from mission activity. The ministers of the Scottish churches in London, both of the Church of Scotland and of the Secession, were enthusiastic supporters; one of them, John Love, became the Society's secretary, and Bogue, after the early years, undertook the preparation of the Society's missionaries. An auxiliary of the Society was soon formed in Scotland. Over the years Scotland was to provide a significant proportion of the Society's missionary candidates. Many came from Congregational or Evangelical Union backgrounds, but there were numbers of Presbyterians also. Local missionary societies mushroomed in Scottish cities and towns and those in Edinburgh and Glasgow emulated the LMS in recruiting and sending missionaries.

In the absence of action through the official structures of the churches on either side of the border, the voluntary society was now becoming the organ through which missionary concern was expressed. In England this remained the situation into the twentieth century; neither the established Church of England nor the dissenting churches could readily accommodate overseas mission within their polity and structure.[25] In Scotland, the

---

[23] See Brian Stanley, *A History of the Baptist Missionary Society, 1792-1992* (Edinburgh: T and T Clark, 1992).

[24] See Richard Lovett, *History of the London Missionary Society 1795-1895*, Vol. 1 (London: Henry Frowde, 1899).

[25] Methodism offers a partial exception to this statement. Wesley sent missionaries to America and the Caribbean; and after his death preachers for Africa and Asia were sent by Thomas Coke or by the Methodist Conference. Coke, in particular pressed the cause of overseas mission; but only in 1814 was a Wesleyan Methodist Missionary Society formed, and then only on a local basis; it was extended to the whole Wesleyan connexion in 1818. The formation in 1932 of the Methodist Church from the union of the Wesleyan, Primitive Methodist and United Methodist connexions saw the inauguration of the Methodist Missionary Society, of which every member of the Church was *ipso facto* counted a member. The society was

SSPCK had so far provided an umbrella for missionary activity, but Presbyterian polity offered possibilities absent from eighteenth century Anglican and Congregational models of governance.[26] Various proposals for the support of missions were put before the Church of Scotland and the secession churches. Motions relating to missions were brought to the General Assembly of the Church of Scotland of 1796 from two synods. One called on the Assembly to appoint a committee with a view to establishing a mission; the other for financial support for the existing mission societies. Many churchmen distrusted the societies as not subject to Assembly control, and open to manipulation by politically unreliable people. As to mission activity directed by the Church, though missions were generally an Evangelical cause, we have seen that a Moderate such as William Robertson could envisage the conversion of India by means of Christian education. In the end the Assembly voted for cautious inaction, passing a motion which approved missions in principle while preventing their furtherance in practice.[27]

Nor was the response from the Secession churches overwhelming. The Relief Church and the Burgher (Associate) Synod offered encouragement, but no funds; many church leaders doubtless saw the provision of ministers

---

eventually replaced by an Overseas Division of the Church. See John A. Vickers, *Thomas Coke, Apostle of Methodism* (London: Epworth Press, 1969); John Pritchard, *Methodists and their Missionary Societies* (Farnham, Surrey: Ashgate, 2014).

[26] The Society for the Propagation of the Gospel (SPG), founded by royal charter, had official standing in the Church of England; but its charter limited it to possessions of the British Crown, and its activities at this time lay mainly in the North American colonies. In practice (with some important exceptions, including Thomas Thompson's foray to West Africa in the 1740s) those activities (as the unsuccessful SPG missionary John Wesley found to his cost) mainly concerned the pastoral care of settlers of English origin. On the SPG see Daniel O'Connor and others, *Three Centuries of Mission: the United Society for the Propagation of the Gospel 1701-2000* (London: Continuum, 2004). The (English) SPCK was, strictly speaking, a voluntary society, though including the bishops and irreproachable in churchmanship. From an early date it had helped and supported the mission in Tranquebar, accepting its missionaries as ordained clergy of a sister national Protestant church; and when the mission extended its operations into East India Company, and thus British, territory, it took on direction. Occasional attempts to find English clergy for the mission were unsuccessful. Anglican Evangelicals, committed both to the Gospel as Evangelicals understood the Gospel and to the Church as Anglicans understood the Church, formed in 1799 the Church Missionary Society for Africa and the East (CMS), as a voluntary society directed to areas where the SPG did not then operate.

[27] Cf. the well-known account in [Robert Heron], *Account of the Proceedings and Debate in the General Assembly of the Church of Scotland respecting the Propagation of the Gospel to the Heathen...*(Edinburgh: Lawrie, 1796); see also Hugh Watt, "Moderator, Rax me that Bible", *Scottish Church History Society Records*, Vol. X (1950), 54.

for Scottish migrants to North America as a higher priority. It was thus left to the voluntary societies to channel the growing enthusiasm in Scotland for overseas missions. Such concern was not only an urban phenomenon; prayer meetings for missions noticeably flourished in the north of Scotland.

The societies brought together members of different churches linked by evangelical concern and enthusiasm for missions. But traditional tensions did not always disappear: what began as the Glasgow Missionary Society, for instance, split into two societies, one supporting establishment and the other voluntarist principles.

Missionary concern was one major component of the burgeoning Evangelical movement in Scotland, the desire for overseas mission interacting with the pursuit of more vigorous evangelism at home. Robert Haldane attempted to establish a mission to Bengal in the 1790s; his known radical political opinions ensured that it was blocked. Thereafter he and his brother, James Alexander Haldane, concentrated their energies on Scotland, using itinerant preachers and furthering the emergence of Scottish Congregational, and later Baptist, churches.

The Edinburgh and Glasgow Missionary Societies instituted missions in the hinterland of Sierra Leone, Jamaica, South Africa and India in their early days. The societies survived the disasters that befell the early missions: one missionary became a slave trader, another a lecturer in the cause of atheism, yet another fell to armed robbers. Presbyterians quarrelled with Congregationalists, and the catholicity of the LMS fell apart when a long sea voyage opened the issue of the extent of the Atonement. The Edinburgh Society transferred Henry Brunton from the Susu in West Africa to a new mission to the Tartar peoples in the Russian empire, along with his African assistant, Jellorum Harrison.[28] As we have seen, Brunton developed a mission theory centering on vernacular education, heavily influenced by the experience of the Scottish Highlands; he imparted this to the (Anglican) Church Missionary Society who had resumed the Susu mission that the Edinburgh Society had begun.[29] The Presbytery of Jamaica, a fruit of the Edinburgh Society's work, initiated its own mission to Calabar in West Africa, despite Scottish church reluctance. The Glasgow Society's work in South Africa included establishing the highly influential Lovedale Institution;[30] among its early students was the remarkable Xhosa minister, Tiyo Soga, who went on to seven years of study in Scotland and a

---

[28] See M.V. Jones, "The Sad and Curious Story of Karass, 1802-1835," *Oxford Slavonic Papers* No. 8 (1975), 53-81.

[29] See Andrew F. Walls, "West African Languages and Christian Proclamation: The Early Years"," *Bible Translator Technical Papers* Vol. 55/3 (2004), 389-400.

[30] See Graham A. Duncan, *Lovedale: Coercive Agency* (Pietermaritzburg: Cluster Publications, 2003); Leon de Kock, *Civilising Barbarians: Missionary Narrative and African Textual Response in Nineteenth Century South Africa* (Johannesburg: Witwatersrand University Press, 1996).

many-sided ministry of preaching, translation, and writing.[31] The Scottish Missionary Society (SMS)[32] mission to Western India included among its members the redoubtable John Wilson, an energetic translator engaging busily with Hindu, Parsi, and Muslim scholars.[33] And Scots, notably those influenced by the Haldane movement, were prominent among those enrolling with the London Missionary Society.

There were unexpected developments: the Congregationalists John Paterson and Ebenezer Henderson, diverted from their original intention of serving in India, became notable for Bible translation and distribution and evangelism across Northern Europe, from Iceland through Scandinavia to Russia, working with the British and Foreign Bible Society and, in Paterson's case, the Russian Bible Society.[34] The enthusiasts who supported the societies were sustained by the "missionary intelligence" received through the magazine *Scottish Missionary Register* and other publications, including, of course, those of the LMS. Vigorous church congregations, such as Thomas Chalmers' charge in Glasgow, held regular meetings where such intelligence was read and shared and prayed over.

No survey should overlook the presence of missionary societies in each of the Scottish universities, fostering missionary interest and becoming a source of graduate missionary candidates for which England (save for Charles Simeon's circle of Cambridge undergraduates, where the claims of East India Company chaplaincy were paramount) had no equivalent until much later in the nineteenth century. The St Andrews University Missionary Society, under the patronage of Thomas Chalmers while Professor of Moral Philosophy in the University, produced not only the seminal figure of Alexander Duff, but a series of other notable missionaries.[35]

In England, missionary societies long continued to be the main mode of operation for the missionary movement, developing relationships with denominational structures but retaining their identity. From the second half

---

[31] See J.A. Chalmers, *Tiyo Soga: A Page of Missionary History* (Edinburgh: Elliot, 1873); Donovan Williams, *Ufumdisi: A Biography of Tiyo Soga* (Alice: Lovedale Press, 1978); and Donovan Williams ed., *The Journal and Selected Writings of the Rev Tiyo Soga* (Cape Town: Balkema for Rhodes University, 1983).

[32] The body founded as the Edinburgh Missionary Society later took the name Scottish Missionary Society.

[33] On Wilson, see George Smith, *The Life of John Wilson, DD, FRS* (London: John Murray, 1878).

[34] See *Extracts of Letters from the Rev. John Paterson and the Rev. Ebenezer Henderson during their respective tours through the East Sea provinces of Russia, Sweden, Denmark, Jutland, Holstein, Swedish Pomerania etc, to promote the objects of the British and Foreign Bible Society* (London: Tilling and Hughes, 1817).

[35] See Stuart Piggin and John Roxborogh, *The St Andrews Seven: The Finest Flowering of Missionary Zeal in Scottish History* (Edinburgh: Banner of Truth, 1985).

of the nineteenth century onwards, these denominational societies[36] were joined by many non-denominational and inter-denominational societies.[37] Scottish Baptists, Methodists, and Episcopalians commonly joined their denominational mission societies, with their bases in England; significant numbers of Scots also went to the new non-denominational mission societies and to specialist agencies such as the Mission to Lepers (later known as the Leprosy Mission). Scotland produced its own specialist agencies: societies for sending female teachers to India flourished in the days before the concept of women as missionaries in their own right had developed; and the Edinburgh Medical Missionary Society (EMMS), established in 1841, long maintained a service to other missions by training doctors for missionary service through the Edinburgh University medical school.[38]

Scottish Church Missions

The Church of Scotland was brought to review its ideas on overseas mission partly as a result of increasing Christian concern over India. A Scot, Claudius Buchanan, who had received Anglican ordination and become a chaplain of the East India Company, wrote a series of influential works on the religious needs of India, appealing for "an ecclesiastical establishment" there. Buchanan also established annual prizes in the Scottish universities for essays on Christianity in India.[39] Another Scot, Charles Grant, who had come to evangelical conversion while serving as a

---

[36] The LMS never lost its openness to any denomination, but the growth of denominational societies made it by default the particular resort of Congregationalists.

[37] See Klaus Fiedler, *The Story of Faith Missions* (Oxford: Regnum, 1996).

[38] John Lowe (1835-1892) was the long-serving secretary of the EMMS. His book *Medical Missions, Their Place and Power* (London: T. Fisher Unwin, 1886), often reprinted, is an outstanding early discourse on the topic.

[39] See Claudius Buchanan, *Memoir of the Expediency of an Ecclesiastical Establishment for British India: both as the means of perpetuating the Christian religion amongst our own countrymen and as a foundation for the ultimate civilization of the Natives* (London: Cadell and Davies, 1805); and *Colonial Ecclesiastical Establishment, being a brief view of the state of the colonies of Great Britain and of the Asiatic Empire, humbly submitted to the consideration of the Imperial Parliament* (London: Cadell and Davies, 1812). The latter work was written with the legislation for the renewal of the charter of the British East India Company in view. Buchanan also drew the attention of Western readers to the Thomas Christians, the early Indian Christian communities: see his *Christian Researches in Asia, with notices on the translation of the Scriptures into the Oriental languages,* 5th ed. (London: Cadell and Davies, 1812), and his oft reprinted sermon, "The Star in the East". On Buchanan see Allan K. Davidson, *Evangelicals and Attitudes to India, 1785-1813: Missions, Publicity and Claudius Buchanan* (Abingdon, Berks: Sutton Courtenay Press, 1990).

Company official in India and become a Member of Parliament and a close associate of Wilberforce and the Clapham Sect, pressed the case in official circles. When the East India Company charter was renewed in 1813, Wilberforce and others secured the inclusion of the so called "pious clauses," one of which set up chaplaincies of the established church in Bengal, Madras, and Bombay.[40]

The Church of Scotland quickly moved to secure the recognition of its own status as one of the established churches of the Kingdom alongside the Church of England. One of the chaplains appointed, James Bryce in Bengal, argued for an educational mission in India and prepared a memorial for the 1824 General Assembly of the Church of Scotland.[41] The Assembly appointed a committee under the convenership of the distinguished Moderate John Inglis. The committee eventually recommended a central school in India, with branch schools, each under the leadership of an ordained minister. It was a measure on which Moderates and Evangelicals could unite;[42] in effect, it extended to India the ideas and ideals of the SSPCK. The Church was not however able to proceed further until 1829, when Alexander Duff,[43] a recent graduate of St Andrews, an Evangelical moulded by the missionary society at his university, was appointed to take charge. Duff arrived in India in 1830, and thereafter the Church remained committed to the mission.

When the Disruption came in 1843 the serving missionaries of the Church opted for the Free Church, providing it with a ready-made mission force in India; the established Church recruited other missionaries to enter into their work. From this time onwards the Scottish missionary societies faded. As early as 1835 the Scottish Missionary Society had transferred its missionaries in Western India to the Church of Scotland, with a financial subsidy; in 1847 the Presbytery of Jamaica established by the SMS was transferred to the United Secession Church. The following year the SMS disbanded. In 1843, the missionaries of the Glasgow Missionary Society Adhering to Established Church Principles joined the Free Church, and in 1847 its voluntarist counterpart identified with the newly formed United

---

[40] See Kenneth Ingham, *Reformers in India: An Account of the Work of Christian Missionaries on Behalf of Social Reform* (Cambridge: Cambridge University Press, 1956).

[41] Bryce (1785-1866) later proved supportive in India too. See his *Sketch of Native Education in India under the Superintendence of the Church of Scotland; with remarks on character and condition of the Hindus as they bear on the question of conversion to Christianity* (London: W.H. Allen and Edinburgh: Blackwood, 1839).

[42] See Don Chambers, "The Church of Scotland's nineteenth century Foreign Mission Scheme: Evangelical or Moderate revival?", *Journal of Religious History* 9/2 (1976), 115-138.

[43] On Duff, see George Smith, *The Life of Alexander Duff* (London: Hodder and Stoughton, 1881). On the Indian background of his project see Michael A. Laird, *Missions and Education in Bengal 1793-1897* (Oxford: Clarendon Press, 1972).

Presbyterian Church.[44] Henceforth, Scottish missionary concern would substantially, though not exclusively, be directed from within the structures of the Scottish churches. The SSPCK gradually faded away;[45] but it had helped to shape Scottish thought about mission.

The Development of Scottish Mission Theory

The ecclesiastical circumstances of Scotland produced a specifically Scottish form of the missionary project. Evangelicals and Moderates could support that project as long as education remained at its centre, and in this regard the experience of the Highlands and Islands offered hope for the future. Its passage to India brought it into contact with the Bengal renaissance.[46]

This intellectual and religious renewal movement had been partly stimulated by Indian responses to Western and Christian influences. Bengal had been long under the rule of the British East India Company. Company policy generally avoided interference in matters of custom and tradition and proclaimed neutrality in religion; but its administration needed educated Indian officials. It had its own "Hindu College", providing a secular education in Western style literary and scientific subjects. Christian missions, working largely in the vernacular, denounced practices such as widow burning and hook swinging.[47] Reform movements arose among Hindus, rejecting these and other traditional practices. A Hindu intellectual, Ram Mohun Roy, a strong monotheist who was enthralled by the teachings of Jesus, was particularly influential.[48] Meanwhile, many young men at the Hindu college became rebellious about traditional customs.

---

[44] A good modern account of the Scottish missionary societies is still needed. William Brown, *History of the Propagation of Christianity among the Heathen since the Reformation,* 2nd ed. (Edinburgh: Fullarton, 1823), and later editions, offers some useful information; Brown had himself served as secretary of the Scottish Missionary Society, and the work is dedicated to the Society's directors.

[45] "The Society in Scotland for Propagating Christian Knowledge" is now the name of the Scottish arm of the SPCK.

[46] For a comprehensive account of Christian life and activity in India, see Robert Eric Frykenberg, *Christianity in India from the Beginnings to the Present* (Oxford: Oxford University Press, 2008).

[47] See Geoffrey A. Oddie, *Popular Religion, Elites and Reform: Hook-swinging and its Prohibition in Colonial India* (New Delhi: Manohar, 1996); and Ingham, *Reformers in India.*

[48] Roy published *The Precepts of Jesus: the guide to peace and happiness, extracted from the New Testament ascribed to the four evangelists,* originally published anonymously. From 1824 editions (Calcutta: Unitarian Press) he added three "appeals to the Christian public" to the text in reply to the criticisms made by the Baptist missionary Joshua Marshman. Roy's place in the development of Hindu-Christian encounter is outlined in M.M. Thomas, *The Acknowledged Christ of the Indian Renaissance* (London: SCM Press, 1969).

Duff had enthused over Chalmers' philosophy lectures, and imbibed along with his Evangelical faith a rational Calvinism, offering a total worldview, shaped by the Scottish Enlightenment – but an Enlightenment in which Chalmers had triumphed over Hume. In this view, science, literature, and political economy all illustrated Biblical truth.[49] Duff, adhering to the spirit, if not the letter, of the instructions drafted by Inglis, departed from the practice of most of the existing missions. Instead of their regular round of vernacular public preaching, while tending little congregations of low caste and out-caste converts, Duff offered the whole curriculum of literature and science desired by those of higher caste aspiring to government service. And it was offered in English, which was increasingly replacing Sanskrit and Persian as the language of official discourse.[50] But, unlike the Company's secular Hindu College, Duff's school offered its intellectual wares in the context of Biblical teaching. Ram Mohun Roy assisted the school's foundation by allaying fears of Hindu parents about the teaching of the Bible.[51]

Duff argued that such an approach looked to the future of India and its church. Rather than chipping small numbers of converts (who would remain dependent on the missions) from the Hindu mass, he proposed would plant a mine that could explode within the fortress of traditional Hinduism. It would also engage the secular rationalism characteristic of the Hindu College, which rejected old Hindu tradition but had nothing of value with which to replace it. For the rest of his life Duff explained and defended this position to the Scottish churches and the missionary movement at large.[52] With the former constituency he was largely successful; Scottish missionaries, more than most others, concentrated on education and, in India, more specifically higher education with English as the medium. India, the first field, long retained its primacy as the centre of Scottish missionary effort. The wider mission constituency was less easily

---

[49] See Ian Maxwell, "Alexander Duff and the Theological and Philosophical Background to the General Assembly's Mission to Calcutta", PhD, University of Edinburgh, 1998.

[50] See, e.g., Alexander Duff, *A New Era of the English Language and English Literature in India; or, An exposition of the late Governor-General's last edict* (Edinburgh: John Johnstone, 1837).

[51] Alexander Duff, *India and Indian Missions* (Edinburgh: John Johnstone, 1840), chapter VI, 497-629, gives Duff's account of the origins and early days of the institution, its aims, methods and educational philosophy. The first pupils came through the recommendation of "a native of rank and influence, who had expressed himself favourable to our design" (p. 549) – that is, Ram Mohun Roy. Duff also stresses the malign influence of European "infidels" in India.

[52] See, e.g., Alexander Duff, *Vindication of the Church of Scotland's India Missions, being the substance of an address, delivered before the General Assembly of the Church...* (Edinburgh: John Johnstone, 1837).

persuaded, especially in the years following the "Indian Mutiny" of 1857.[53] Most missions, in India as elsewhere, included some form of education in their programmes; the Scottish missions were unusual in making education the hub. The reason for this has roots in Scotland's religious history, and not least in the role of the SSPCK.

For some years Duff could claim that the policy was vindicated by results; through it some fifty mostly high caste young men became Christians, intellectually and doctrinally grounded and often spiritually tested in the fires of family rejection. Such people could write and debate and tellingly present the Christian message in Hindu contexts, whether traditional or reformist. But as time went by, the stream of notable converts became a trickle. India was changing as the national movement developed. Increasingly, Hindu intellectuals identified foreign rule, rather than reactionary tradition, as the principal opponent of their nation's progress. Had the fuse for Duff's mine burned out?[54]

But the Scottish theory of mission outlasted Duff. John Anderson, founder of the Madras Mission had insisted "India must be brought to think"; his successor, William Miller, whose missionary career extended over 44 years, developed the fragile institution that he inherited from Anderson until, as Madras Christian College, it reached university standard, and he himself became Vice-Chancellor of the University of Madras. Miller aimed to reach "true Hindus" – those beyond the low caste, non-caste and tribal communities that formed the background of most Christians in India, and to penetrate minds that were shaped by the Vedas and the Indian philosophical tradition.

The aim of the college thus became less immediate conversion (though Miller claimed that more "true Hindus" were converted through the Scots colleges than by all other means combined), but to produce an intellectual climate in which "true Hindus" could hear the gospel in such a way as to require a decision about it. To this end the colleges must "influence the corporate thought of Hinduism"; and engage with elements of Hindu faith

---

[53] The discussion on education at the Liverpool Conference on Missions of 1860 is instructive in this regard. Thomas Smith, of the Free Church of Scotland, (later to be Duff's successor in the chair at Edinburgh), set out an argument for education *as* mission, not merely ancillary to mission; but many of his audience of missionaries and mission executives were unpersuaded. See *Conference on Missions held in 1860 in Liverpool* edited by the Secretaries of the Conference (London: Nisbet, 1860). At another meeting held in 1858 in London to consider the future of Christianity, it is clear that many favoured leaving "the proud Brahmin" aside in favour of the more open-minded masses. See *Christianity in India: proceedings of a public meeting held at Exeter Hall to consider the future relations of the British government to religion in India* (London: Reed and Parden, 1858).

[54] On this section, cf. Andrew F. Walls, "The Scottish Missionary Diaspora", in *The Cross-Cultural Process in Christian History* (Maryknoll NY: Orbis, 2002), 259-272.

now dormant.[55] Such thinking later found fuller expression in John Nicol Farquhar (1861-1899).[56] Farquhar, an Aberdonian who did not belong to a Scottish mission (his background was Evangelical Union and he served with the LMS and the YMCA) maintained Miller's outlook and extended its range. He held that the "Christian" colleges, while properly providing a good education, were now no longer intellectually engaging the young Hindus who identified with the national movement. Such people now espoused neo-Krishnaism, with the Bhagavad-Gita as the normative text.[57] The work that had originally been seen as the province of the Scottish colleges now had to be done in a different way if Christianity was not to remain a foreign element in India. Farquhar invested his life in the study of Indian religious literature, producing works that have continued to be republished in India,[58] expounding the thesis that the aspirations reflected in the Gita are fulfilled in Christ.

The work of Farquhar's younger contemporary, A. G. Hogg (1876 – 1954) resumed the traditional Scots college role from within Madras Christian College, of which Miller's institution had been the nucleus.[59] A philosopher, whose own road to Christian faith had been difficult, he argued that the problem for Christianity in India was that it provoked too *little*, not too much opposition. In the ways in which Christianity was commonly presented, it was too easy to ignore. Many of the common doctrinal formulations in Western Christianity had little relevance in India, and no equivalent in Indian philosophical tradition. They dealt with matters that had never been of interest in India, ignoring issues of vital concern there. Hogg pursued a Christian interaction with Hindu thought focusing not, as Farquhar had, on fulfilment, but on selective contrast. Thus he stressed the Kingdom of God in the teaching of Jesus, and the New Testament promise of cosmic redemption as a message needed in India and not foreshadowed in traditional Hindu quests for individual salvation.[60] He

---

[55] On Miller, see Joshua Kalapati and Ambrose Jeyasekaran, *Life and Legacy of Madras Christian College (1837-1978)* (Chennai: Zha Communications, 2010). Some of his leading ideas are enunciated in William Miller, *Scottish Missions in India: Two Lectures* (Edinburgh: Elliot, 1868).

[56] On Farquhar, see Eric J. Sharpe, *Not to Destroy but to Fulfil: the Contribution of John Nicol Farquhar to Protestant Missionary Thought in India before 1914* (Lund: Gleerup, 1965).

[57] See J.N. Farquhar, G*ita and Gospel,* Madras: Christian Literature Society, 1917.

[58] This is true, for instance of his *Outline of the Religious Literature of India* (London: Oxford University Press, 1920) and his *Modern Religious Movements in India* (London: Macmillan, 1915).

[59] On Hogg, see Eric J. Sharpe, *Alfred George Hogg 1875-1954: An Intellectual Biography* (Chennai: Christian Literature Society, 1999); Eric Sharpe ed., *The Theology of A.G. Hogg* (Chennai: Christian Institute for the Study of Religion and Society, 1971).

[60] See his *Christ's Message of the Kingdom: A Course of Daily Study for Private Students and Bible Circles* (Edinburgh: T and T Clark, 1911).

also sketched a doctrine of atonement designed to address Hindu understandings of suffering, and particularly the idea of *karma*.[61]

Farquhar's writings remain valuable for the study of Indian religious literature and Hogg remains one of the most interesting theologians of the twentieth century working in English; one of the few to wrestle seriously with the issues for Christian theology raised by the intellectual and religious traditions of Asia.[62] Miller, Farquhar and Hogg are all characteristic products of the Scottish missionary tradition, which derives from the instructions given to Alexander Duff and his implementation of them.

The Geographical Spread of Scottish Missions

India was the first field for Scottish church missions and India determined much of their later direction. The initial involvement in Bengal and Western India was followed by other initiatives, as Scottish churches opened work in Southern India (centred on Madras/Chennai), in Central India, (centred on Nagpur), in the Santal tribal homeland in what is now Bihar, and in the Punjab. The roots from which much of Pakistani Christianity would later grow are found in the Punjab Mission with its base at Sialkot. Its first missionaries Thomas and Jane Hunter were killed, along with their infant son, soon after their arrival in 1857 when the "Indian Mutiny" broke out; but by the end of the century the church was growing rapidly.[63] Such variety of location inevitably involved a variety of approach. The commitment to education, and to higher education, remained, but Scottish missions in India participated in almost all the forms of witness and service – from village evangelism to Bible translation, from surgery to savings banks – that other missions developed.

But Scottish missions had begun with the missionary societies. In some fields, such as Sierra Leone and the Russian Empire, their presence was short-lived; but the involvement in the Caribbean and in South Africa which the Scottish societies initiated left a substantial legacy to the Scottish church missions which followed. The later nineteenth century and the first

---

[61] A.G. Hogg, *Karma and Redemption: An Essay Toward the Interpretation of Hinduism and the Restatement of Christianity* (London: Christian Literature Society for India, 1910). This work has also been reprinted recently.

[62] We may note that Professor Sir S. Radhakrishnan, who became a major interpreter of the Hindu philosophical tradition to the Western academic world, studied with Hogg. See Joshua Kalapati, *Dr S. Radhakrishnan and Christianity: an Introduction to Hindu-Christian Apologetics* (Delhi: ISPCK, 2002).

[63] See John F.W. Youngson, *Forty Years of the Punjab Mission of the Church of Scotland 1855-1895* (Edinburgh: R. & R. Clark, 1896); Jeffrey Cox, *Imperial Fault Lines: Christianity and Colonial Power in India, 1818-1940* (Stanford, CA: Stanford University Press, 2002), chapter 5.

part of the twentieth saw the activity of Scottish church missions spread to every continent.[64]

The Jamaica Mission led to a new West African mission in Calabar, which was eventually to extend to a wide area of what later became Nigeria.[65] The need to replace German missionaries deported or interned during World War I brought Scottish missionaries to the Gold Coast, to become a formative influence for the Presbyterian Church of Ghana.[66] The early work of the societies around Sierra Leone was not continued (or, in the case of the Susu mission, was taken over by others); but in the twentieth century the United Pentecostal Mission based in Kilsyth began work in the Sierra Leone interior.[67]

The work in South Africa begun by the two Glasgow societies was inherited, and considerably expanded, by the Free Church and the United Presbyterian Church respectively; while the supply of evangelical Scottish ministers, including the renowned Andrew Murray, to the Dutch Reformed Church in South Africa had important consequences for that Church's spirituality.[68] The Free Presbyterian Church had a mission in what is now Zimbabwe. Both the Church of Scotland and the Free Church sent missions to Central Africa in memory of David Livingstone; the resultant emergence of the Blantyre and Livingstonia Synods has forged a continuing link between Scotland and Malawi.[69] African evangelists from Livingstonia

---

[64] What follows is treated in more detail in A.F. Walls, "Missions" in Nigel M. de S. Cameron (organizing editor), *Dictionary of Scottish Church History and Theology* (Edinburgh: T. and T. Clark, 1993). This article also contains a substantial bibliography of Scottish missions, arranged by region. No attempt is made to reproduce this here. See also Elizabeth G.K. Hewat, *Vision and Achievement 1706–1956: A History of the Foreign Missions of the Churches United in the Church of Scotland* (London: Nelson, 1960).

[65] See Geoffrey Johnston, *Of God and Maxim Guns: Presbyterianism in Nigeria 1846-1946* (Waterloo Ont.: Wilfred Laurier University Press, 1988).

[66] See Noel Smith, *The Presbyterian Church of Ghana, 1835-1960* (Accra: Ghana Universities Press, 1966).

[67] See E. Sinclair, *The Wee Man with the Big Heart: The Story of the Life of Matthew Sinclair and of the United Pentecostal Mission* (Kilsyth: United Pentecostal Mission, 1973).

[68] For the complex interrelationships of piety, theology and ideology among Afrikaner Christians in South Africa, see Richard Elphick, *Equality of Believers: Protestant Missionaries and the Racial Politics of South Africa* (Charlottesville: University of Virginia Press, 2012).

[69] See John McCracken, *A History of Malawi 1859-1966* (Rochester NY: James Currey, 2012); John McCracken, *Politics and Christianity in Malawi 1875-1940: the Impact of the Livingstonia Mission in the Northern Province* (Cambridge: Cambridge University Press, 1977; Zomba, Malawi: Kachere, 3rd edn. 2008); Kenneth R. Ross, *Malawi and Scotland: Together in the Talking Place since 1859* (Mzuzu, Malawi: Mzuni Press, 2013); Andrew C. Ross, *Blantyre Mission and the Making of Colonial Malawi,* (Blantyre, Malawi: CLAIM,1996); T. Jack Thompson,

extended that link to what is now Zambia.[70] After the union of the Church of Scotland and the United Free Church in 1929, the continuing United Free Church set up a Mission in Bechuanaland, now Botswana. The Scottish Episcopal Church became involved in South Africa when Bishop Gray of Cape Town, after his dispute with Bishop Colenso of Natal, appealed to the Scottish Church to supply the needs of a new diocese of "Kaffraria" (eventually named Saint John's). This brought into being the Board of Missions of the Episcopal Church, working in cooperation with the Society for the Propagation of the Gospel; an arrangement closer to that operating in the Scottish Presbyterian churches than with those of the Church of England.

The East Africa Scottish Mission was a creation of Sir William MacKinnon and a group of like-minded Scottish entrepreneurs, who, embracing Livingstone's doctrine of the concomitance of Christianity and commerce in Africa, saw a mission as a necessary accompaniment to the Imperial British East Africa Company. In 1901 the Church of Scotland assumed responsibility for the mission, and established its fateful connection with Kenya.[71] Scottish church involvement in Mauritius arose from the colonial church establishment; but sometimes assumed missionary dimensions – such as setting up Indian congregations and translating the New Testament into Mauritian Krio.

The forcible opening of China to western influence in the 1840s attracted much attention from Western missions; but, despite the heavy Scottish involvement in the tea trade, China came late into the consciousness of the Scottish churches, and Scottish mission involvement there was piecemeal. (The 1840s, that saw the expansion of the Western presence in China, were, of course, a time of ecclesiastical turmoil in Scotland). One early and consistent Scottish Christian influence in China was the National Bible Society of Scotland; its agent, Alexander Williamson, brought China, Japan and Korea to the notice of the Scottish churches at critical junctures. One indirect source of Scottish involvement was the development of a China mission by the Presbyterian Church of England, which recruited most of its missionaries from the Free Church of

---

Christianity in Northern Malawi: Donald Fraser's Missionary Methods and Ngoni Culture (Leiden: Brill, 1996).

[70] A.D. Roberts, *A History of the Bemba: Political Growth and Change in North-Eastern Zambia before 1900* (Longman, London, 1973). On the later developments which brought the church into the United Church of Zambia, see Peter Bolink, *Towards Church Union in Zambia: Church Union Efforts in Central Africa* (Franeker, Netherlands: Wever, 1967).

[71] See R. Macpherson, *The Presbyterian Church in Kenya: An Account of the Origins and Growth of the Presbyterian Church of East Africa* (Nairobi: Presbyterian Church of East Africa, 1973).

Scotland. Among these was William Chalmers Burns,[72] already nationally known in Scotland as an evangelistic preacher when he undertook a major missionary reconnaissance in China. Burns' influence on James Hudson Taylor, and thus on the infant China Inland Mission, is well known. Burns also pressed the claims of Manchuria on the Irish Presbyterian Church at a time when Williamson was engaging the interest of the United Presbyterian Church of Scotland in the same area. A comity agreement avoided competition; it was followed by active cooperation, and North-east China, "China beyond the Wall," with all the invasions, wars, alien occupation and natural disasters that afflicted it in the late nineteenth and early twentieth centuries, became the principal centre of Scottish missionary activity in China.[73] It was not the only commitment; in the 1870s one of the later additions to the "treaty ports", Ichang (Iyang), in Central China became the basis of a Church of Scotland mission. And the English Presbyterian mission in South China and Taiwan[74] was for a long time effectively a Scottish enterprise, since so many of its missionary staff came from the Free Church (which had declined to sponsor Burns in his China reconnaissance).

Korea, held off all foreign influences, missions included, after China and Japan had succumbed to them. A United Presbyterian missionary in Manchuria, John Ross, realizing the significance of the Korean traders who came there regularly through the "Korean Gate," made the first Bible translation into Korean by working with them. Colporteurs brought these scriptures into Korea, and an indigenous church arose before missionaries were formally allowed entrance.[75] Involvement in Manchuria also led to the establishment of a United Presbyterian Mission in Japan, though this was discontinued after the church union of 1900.[76]

Scottish expatriates in Malaya first brought a Scottish church presence there. The closing of China to missions by 1950 led many mission agencies

---

[72] See Islay Burns, *Memoir of the Rev William C. Burns, Missionary to China from the English Presbyterian Church* (London: James Nisbet 1870; reprinted Stoke-on-Trent: Tentmaker, 2006).

[73] See Austin Fulton, *Through Earthquake, Wind and Fire: Church and Mission in Manchuria, 1867-1950* (Edinburgh: St Andrew Press, 1967).

[74] See George A. Hood, *Mission Accomplished? The English Presbyterian Mission in Lintung, South China* (Frankfurt: Peter Lang, 1986); A. Hamish Ion, *The Cross and the Rising Sun, Vol. 2, The British Protestant Missionary Movement in Japan, Korea and Taiwan, 1865-1945* (Waterloo Ont.: Wilfred Laurier University Press, 1993).

[75] See Sung-Deuk Oak, *The Making of Korean Christianity* (Waco TX: Baylor University Press 2013); James H. Grayson, *John Ross: First Missionary to Korea,* published in Korean, *Na Yohan: Han'gug-ui ch'ot son'gyo-sa* (Taegu: Kyemyŏng University Press, 1982); Sung-il Choi, "John Ross (1842-1915) and the Korean Protestant Church", PhD, University of Edinburgh, 1992.

[76] See Ion, *The Cross and the Rising Sun, Vol. 1.*

to increased interest in Malaysia and Singapore; the effect on specifically Scottish missions seems to have been slight.[77]

In the Middle East, Scottish Church missionaries have at different times have been active in Israel-Palestine, Syria, and Lebanon, with medical work especially prominent, as well as in the South Arabian Mission in the Yemen.[78] The earliest, and perhaps the most remarkable single initiative was the "mission of inquiry" in Palestine undertaken on behalf of the Church of Scotland by a party which included the celebrated Evangelical preachers Andrew Bonar and Robert Murray M'Cheyne.[79] The mission had been inspired by the contemporary renewal of interest in prophecy leading to a new concern for the Jewish people. It did not lead to any immediate opening of missionary operations in the Middle East, but an accident to one of the party while on the journey home led to a prolonged stay in Budapest. The eventual outcome of this was a mission to the Jewish community in Hungary on the part of the Free Church, with the eccentric and much loved John ("Rabbi") Duncan as its notable standard bearer. In addition to its importance in the development of missions to Jewish people, the Scottish presence in Budapest is significant for its influence in movements for renewal within the Reformed Church of Hungary.[80]

Scottish missionaries were numerous in the Pacific missions of the LMS; but only one island group in the Pacific was adopted by a Scottish church mission, and that only for a short time. The Reformed Presbyterian Church mission in the New Hebrides, (now Vanautu) had two highly influential writers in John Inglis and John G. Paton, who made the islands and their peoples – and the oppressive and exploitative activities of foreign traders there – well known in Scotland.[81]

The Caribbean was among the earliest fields of specifically Scottish missionary activities. Apart from Jamaica and the Cayman Islands where the SMS began work later taken over by the United Secession and then the United Presbyterian Church, Scottish churches appeared at various times in

---

[77] See George A. Hood, *Neither Bang nor Whimper: The End of a Missionary Era in China* (Singapore: Presbyterian Church of Singapore, [1991]).

[78] On Yemen, see J.M. Ritchie, *The Church of Scotland South Arabia Mission founded by Ion Keith-Falconer's Vision* (Stoke-on-Trent: Tentmaker, 2006).

[79] See [Andrew A. Bonar and Robert Murray M'Cheyne], *Narrative of a Mission of Inquiry to the Jews from the Church of Scotland in 1839* (Edinburgh: William Whyte, 1843).

[80] See Abraham Kovacs, *A History of the Free Church of Scotland's Mission to the Jews in Budapest, and its Impact on the Reformed Church of Hungary* (Frankfurt: Peter Lang, 2006).

[81] See John Inglis, *Bible Illustrations from the New Hebrides, with Notices of the Progress of the Mission* (London: Nelson, 1990); John G. Paton, *Missionary to the New Hebrides: An Autobiography,* edited by his brother, the Rev. James Paton, (London: Hodder and Stoughton, 1903); A.K. Langridge, *John G. Paton: Later Years and Farewell* (London: Hodder and Stoughton, 1910).

other Caribbean islands, and in Belize and Guyana on the mainland.[82] In South America the Bible Society agent, James (Diego) Thomson, a Scot who had inherited the Scottish view of the link between Reformation and education, had considerable influence on the educational policies of several of the republics in the early days of their independence[83] – a tradition continued in the twentieth century by John A. Mackay when the continuing Free Church of Scotland opened a new field in Peru in 1916. Mackay made high class education (Collegio San Andres) the distinctive feature of the mission, studied and taught at a Peruvian university, and engaged in constructive dialogue with both Catholics and Liberals.[84]

The list of Scottish missions above relates only to the missions of the Scottish churches and the antecedent Scottish mission societies, without taking account of Scots serving in other mission agencies. As we have seen, the LMS recruited heavily from Scotland especially in the brief flowering of Scottish Congregationalism following the Haldane movement. David Livingstone, often seen as the archetypal Scottish missionary, was such a recruit,[85] as were James Gilmour[86] (always associated with mission in Mongolia), James Chalmers[87] (equally linked with Papua New Guinea), James Legge[88] the great sinologist and Eric Liddell, the famous athlete. The

---

[82] See F.J. Osborne and G.D. Johnston, *Coastlands and Islands: First Thoughts on Caribbean Church History.* (Kingston, Jamaica: United Theological College of the West Indies, 1972).

[83] See William Mitchell, "James Thomson and Bible Translation in the Andean Languages" *The Bible Translator Technical Papers* Vol. 41/3 (July 1990), 341-45; William Mitchell, "Diego Thomson: Precursor de la Traducción Bíblica en la Época Moderna" *La Biblia en las Américas* Vol. 48/4 (1993), 21-23; also the website maintained by Dr William Mitchell at www.jamesdiegothomson.com , which contains a full bibliography.

[84] See John A. Mackay, *The Other Spanish Christ: A Study in the Spiritual History of Spain and South America.* (New York: Macmillan, 1932). On Mackay's life and influence see John Mackay Metzger, *The Hand and the Road: the Life and Times of John A. Mackay* (Louisville KY: Westminster John Knox Press, 2010). On the wider picture of missions in Peru see J.B.A. Kessler, *A Study of the Older Protestant Churches in Peru and Chile* (Goes, Netherlands: Oosterbaan en Le Cointre, 1957).

[85] Of the innumerable studies of Livingstone, Andrew C. Ross, *David Livingstone: Mission and Empire* (London: Hambledon, 2002) is a recent, rounded and readable account which addresses the Scottish dimension.

[86] See James Gilmour, *James Gilmour of Mongolia: His Letters, Diaries and Reports,* edited and arranged by Richard Lovett, (London: Religious Tract Society, 1895); and James Gilmour, *More about the Mongols,* selected and arranged from the Diaries and Reports of James Gilmour by Richard Lovett (London: Religious Tract Society, 1893).

[87] See James Chalmers, *His Autobiography and Letters,* with a supplementary chapter by A.I. Johnston (London: Religious Tract Society, 1914).

[88] See Norman Girardot, *The Victorian Translation of China: James Legge's Oriental Pilgrimage* (Berkeley: University of California Press, 2002); Lauren F.

immediate successor to William Carey in Bengal was a Scottish Baptist, John Mack. Scottish Methodists have never been numerous, but they contributed to the Wesleyan Methodist Missionary Society such figures as David Cargill,[89] the pioneer linguist in Fiji, and George and Isobel Kerr[90] who developed a celebrated work for leprosy sufferers in India, as well as figures who became prominent in the leadership of the Wesleyan and, later the Methodist Missionary Society, such as D. Goudie and E.W. Thompson.

The first missionary on the roll of the (Anglican) Society for the Propagation of the Gospel, George Keith, was a Scot; and a succession of non-juring Scots followed him as early SPG missionaries in America.[91] The Church Missionary Society also had a number of Scots on its roster: W.J. Elmslie,[92] their first medical missionary, and Duncan Main[93] ("Dr. Apricot of Heaven Below") of Hangchow were recruited through the Edinburgh Medical Mission Society. Scotland was also a natural place to look when a missionary with engineering skills was needed, as happened when the CMS Uganda mission required a lake steamship and recruited Alexander Mackay of the Free Church of Scotland.[94] The East Indian Company chaplain Claudius Buchanan, already mentioned, though never a CMS missionary, was influential in CMS circles, and his writings on India reached a wide circle of readers outside the mission constituency.

The Scottish contribution to the non-denominational and inter-denominational missions, from the China Inland Mission[95] to the Evangelical Union of South America, has been immense; some congregations such as Charlotte Chapel in Edinburgh have produced and supported a long succession of missionaries, and the Bible Training

---

Pfister, *"Striving for the 'Whole Duty of Man'": James Legge and the Scottish Protestant Encounter with China* (New York: Peter Lang, 2004). Legge, after some thirty years as a missionary in Malacca and Hong Kong, became the first Professor of Chinese in the University of Oxford.

[89] See Mora Dickson, *The Inseparable Grief: Margaret Cargill of Fiji* (London: Dobson, 1976).

[90] See C.H. Monahan, *The Lepers of Dichpalli* (London: Methodist Book Room, n.d.).

[91] For Keith, a former Quaker, see Daniel O'Connor, *Three Centuries of Mission*.

[92] See [John Lowe] *Medical Missions as Illustrated by Some Letters and Notices of the late Dr Elmslie* (Edinburgh: Edinburgh Medical Missionary Society, 1874).

[93] See Kingston de Gruchè, *Dr D. Duncan Main of Hangchow, who is known in China as Dr Apricot of Heaven Below* (London: Marshall, Morgan and Scott, 1930).

[94] Mackay proved to be much more than a competent engineer: see Alexina Mackay Harrison, *A.M. Mackay: Pioneer Missionary of the Church Missionary Society to Uganda* (London: Hodder & Stoughton, 1890); D.A. Low, "Alexander Mackay", *Makerere Journal* Vol. 2 (1959), 50-56.

[95] One may cite as an example Alexander Mair, from Portknockie on the Moray Coast, who joined the CIM in 1906. His own account is given in *Unforgettable: Memories of China and Scotland* (London: Epworth Press, 1967).

Institute in Glasgow (later Glasgow Christian College and now merged in International Christian College, Glasgow) became one of the principal centres in Britain for training for the faith missions. Nor should one forget the Scottish presence among the Christian Brethren, with figures as significant as F.S. Arnot[96] in Zambia and the irrepressible Dan Crawford[97] (author of *Thinking Black,* a best-seller in its day) and other independent missionaries. Among these the story of the Glasgow doctor Robert Reid Kalley in Madeira and Brazil is perhaps the most extraordinary.[98] Nor should one forget Scots who served in the missions, particularly Presbyterian, of other nations: for instance John Hogg, the father of A.G. Hogg already mentioned, was a major contributor to the work of the American Presbyterian Mission in Egypt.[99]

Scotland and the Missionary Movement from the West

Within the period covered by this article the face of the Christian world has changed out of recognition, and the cultural and demographic composition of the Christian community has been transformed. In 1709 Christianity (despite the continuing presence of Christians across the Middle East, and in South India and Ethiopia, of which Western Christians knew little), was essentially the faith of Europeans and their descendants in the New World – a Western religion and the religion of the West. By 2009 the majority of Christians were Africans, Asians and Latin Americans. Adherence to the Christian faith was still increasing in Africa and Asia; in the West it was receding, the recession being particularly noticeable in Europe. A century earlier, at the World Missionary Conference in Edinburgh in 1910, it was possible to speak of the "home base" of missions, located, broadly

---

[96] See Frederick S. Arnot, *Garenganze: or, Seven Years' Pioneer Mission Work in Central Africa* (London: J.E. Hawkins, 1889); *Bible and Garenganze; or Four Years Further Work in Central Africa* (London: J.E. Hawkins, 1893); *Missionary Travels in Central Africa,* with an introduction by W.H. Bennet (Bath: Echoes of Service, 1914). The last title is now in a digital version by Bibliobazaar, 2009.

[97] Dan Crawford, *Thinking Black: 22 Years Without a Break in the Long Grass of Central Africa* (London: Hodder and Stoughton, 1912); Dan Crawford, *Back to the Long Grass: My Link with Livingstone.* (London: Hodder and Stoughton, 1923).

[98] On Kalley, see William B. Forsyth, *The Wolf from Scotland: The Story of Robert Reid Kalley – Pioneer Missionary* (Darlington: Evangelical Press, 1988); Joyce E. Winifred Every-Clayton, "The Legacy of Robert Reid Kalley." *International Bulletin of Missionary Research* Vol. 26/3 (2002), 123-127.

[99] See Rena L. Hogg, *Master-Builder on the Nile; Being a Record of the Life and Aims of John Hogg, DD, a Christian Missionary* (Pittsburgh: United Presbyterian Board of Publication, 1934). Another Scot associated with Egypt, who was influential in missions in the Muslim world more widely, was the Anglican W.H. Temple Gairdner of the Church Missionary Society. See Constance E. Padwick, *Temple Gairdner of Cairo* (London: SPCK, 1929).

speaking, in Europe and North America.[100] Today, there is no single identifiable "home base" of missions: Christian initiatives may arise in almost any part of the world, and be directed to almost any other part. The post-Christian West is now a field for cross-cultural mission; and there are signs that African and Asian Christians are increasingly seeing it in these terms.

Many factors have contributed to this transformation. But it is impossible in considering those factors to escape the conclusion that the missionary movement from the West detonated an immense religious explosion. This fact makes the missionary movement one of the most important developments in the whole of Western church history. Enough has been said here to indicate that the Scottish component in the movement was substantial. It is natural also to ask how far was that component distinctive? Were there elements in it that especially reflected specifically Scottish concerns or conditions?

In considering this question, we may begin with an analysis made a century ago, in 1911, with the missionary movement at its peak, by the Aberdeen theologian David Cairns, who had participated prominently in the World Missionary Conference in Edinburgh the previous year.[101] Addressing an audience of Scottish students, Cairns set out three features he believed to be especially characteristic of Scottish missions. The first of these was a concern for the Kingdom of God, which he saw as derived from the theocratic tradition in Scottish religion. The second was the close connection of mission with the idea of the Church; and the third a habit of strong theological thinking. These three themes are worth revisiting after a century.

We have considered the importance of the SSPCK for the way that Scottish Missions developed the close connection of mission overseas with mission at home, and cherished the memory of the Reformation of the Church that shaped the nation and its close link of that Reformation with national education. Scottish writers on Church history tended to stress the link between Renaissance and Reformation, and expected movements of renewal in letters and learning to accompany movements of renewal in religion. As the nineteenth century dawned, Scottish Evangelicals drew encouragement from the developments in the Highlands over the previous

---

[100] "The Home Base of Missions" was the topic allotted to Commission VI of the conference. Its report appears as Vol. VI of World Missionary Conference, 1910, *Reports of Commissions I to VIII and History and Records of the Conference,* Edinburgh: Oliphant, Anderson and Ferrier, 1910.

[101] Cairns was Chairman of the Conference's Commission IV, appointed to consider "The Christian Message in relation to Non-Christian Religions". On the Conference as a whole, see Brian Stanley, *The World Missionary Conference, Edinburgh 1910* (Grand Rapids MI: Eerdmans, 2009). Chapter 8 presents a valuable study of Cairns (and the influence of A.G. Hogg upon his thought) and of the work of the Commission.

century, seeing in it hope for the evangelization of the world beyond
Scotland. This perspective, comprehending the passing of generations, gave
to the early Scottish overseas missions the expectation of a long period of
sowing before a harvest could be expected, a readiness for the long haul. It
also reflected an expectation that the preaching of the Gospel and patient
application to Christian education would bring transformation within
society, not just the rescue of individuals from heathendom and hell. Such
an expectation could co-exist with deep convictions of the necessity for
personal conversion and regeneration. We noted how Henry Brunton, a
Seceder who had served with the Scottish Missionary Society, set out such
a programme for West Africa more than twenty years before Evangelicals
in the Church of Scotland joined with Moderates to inaugurate the
Church's commitment to mission overseas – with an educational mission to
India.

Such a vision reflects a concept of the Kingdom of God brought to
completion in the fullness of God's time. Alexander Duff's articulation of
mission policy fits readily into this. His choice of missionary method and
his aim at a particular segment of Indian society were deliberately made
with a view to the Christian future of India. Those decisions did not of
themselves bring Christian missions into the Bengal renaissance – the
mission presence was already a substantial factor behind that movement.
But it brought the Christian message into vigorous engagement with an
intellectual ferment that was changing Bengal and would change India.
There is an essential continuity in Scottish missionary policy in India over
the following century. Changing circumstances and deepening
understanding moved such people as Miller and Farquhar away from
Duff's idea of the intellectual mine that would simply destroy Hinduism,
and caused them to address movements within Hinduism itself; but
throughout the missionary period the idea of engagement with intellectual
life in India remained a paramount concern of the Scots colleges. The
concern was not uniquely Scottish; other missions were similarly engaged –
but the relatively heavy commitment of Scottish mission resources to
higher education is particularly noticeable. The Scots colleges, and the
intellectual activity associated with them, saw the emergence of Indian
Christian leaders of the stature of Lal Behari Day,[102] Behari Lal Singh,[103]

---

[102] Lal Behari Day, a Professor of English, was an eloquent educationist and a
prolific writer in both English and Bengali, whose works on Bengali folk tales
continue to be reprinted. He wrote accounts of his early life, which include
*Recollections of Alexander Duff DD LLD, and of the Mission College which he
founded in Calcutta* (London: T. Nelson & Sons, 1879). See also G. Macpherson,
Life of Lal Behari Dey: Convert, Pastor, Professor and Author (Edinburgh: T. & T.
Clark, 1900).
[103] On Singh, and especially his part in the Liverpool Conference on Missions of
1860, see Andrew F. Walls, "Distinguished Visitors: Tiyo Soga and Lal Behari
Singh in Europe and at Home," in Judith Becker and Brian Stanley (eds), *Europe as*

Dhanjibhai Nauroji,[104] and Krishna Mohan Banerjea.[105] These were people for whom the Gospel of Christ was addressed to every aspect of human life, who saw Christ as Lord of life, and the kingdoms of this world becoming subject to the Kingdom of our God and of His Christ. The cosmic nature of redemption and the Kingdom of God was a theme constantly articulated by A.G. Hogg, one of the outstanding representatives of the Scottish tradition, for whom the redeeming work of Christ, bringing a new heaven and a new earth, was a distinctively Christian teaching that had peculiar relevance to India. It spoke to India's long tradition of teaching of salvation in terms of individual escape from the endless circle of existence, offering a more splendid hope and a fuller salvation.

The concern to proclaim the gospel across the various dimensions of life, public and private, appears frequently and diversely in the Scottish missionary story. It appears in the work of the Scottish LMS missionary John Philip in the early Cape Colony, as he championed the Khoi against white settler exploitation and transformed the Bethelsdorp settlement into an economically sustainable unit.[106] It appears again in the Calabar mission, opening with the school that, as the Calabar chiefs recognized, would help Calabar in the palm oil trade; nourishing a church of communicants, which for many years was very small, while regularly addressing the leaders of the whole Calabar community, one of the chiefs interpreting. These sessions declared the way of God as regards both salvation and societal reform; denouncing "idolatry", the killing of slaves for the funeral of an

---

the Other: External Perspectives on European Christianity (Goettingen: Vandenhoek & Ruprecht), forthcoming; see also Behari Lal Singh, *Leading Incidents Connected with a Missionary Tour in the Gangetic Districts of Bengal* (Calcutta: J. Thomas, 1853).

[104] Dhanjibhai Nauroji gave his own account of his conversion and subsequent ministry: *From Zoroaster to Christ: An Autobiographical Sketch of the Rev Dhanjibhai Nauroji the first modern convert from the Zoroastrian religion* (Edinburgh: Oliphant, Anderson & Ferrier, 1909). The effect of the conversion of Nauroji and Hormusj Pesonji on their own community is discussed by J.S. Palsetia, "Parsi and Hindu Traditional and Nontraditional Responses to Christian Conversion in Bombay 1839-1843," *Journal of the American Academy of Religion* Vol. 74/3 (2006), 615-645.

[105] Banerjea, a Kulin Brahmin, was not himself a product of the Scots colleges, but a radical anti-traditionalist from the Government's secular education programme. He became a Christian after examination of Christian teaching in dialectical engagement with Duff. He later received Anglican ordination, and was known as educationist, social reformer, opponent of racial discrimination in Government and Christian apologist, commending the Gospel to Hindus, seeing in the Vedas foreshadowings of the Incarnation and atonement. A selection of his writings is included in T.V. Philip, *Krishna Mohan Banerjea: Christian Apologist* (Madras: Christian Literature Society, 1982). See also K.M. Banerjea, *Dialogues on the Hindu Philosophy* (Calcutta: Thacker, Spink & Co, 1861).

[106] See Andrew C. Ross, *John Philip, 1775-1851: Missions, Race and Politics in South Africa* (Aberdeen: Aberdeen University Press, 1986).

important person, the exposure of twins. It is interesting to note the stages of community response: the gradual abandonment of cults and violent practices, decided in each case by the traditional authorities and proclaimed by the traditional ritual means. And such societal reforms took place before the breakthrough years in which, with the scriptures translated into Efik and a fresh infusion of mission workers from Jamaica, large numbers came to faith and the church grew exponentially.[107]

A similar outlook is reflected in those very Scottish Christian commonwealths in the Blantyre and Livingstonia missions in what is now Malawi, with their marriage of church, schools, hospital, agriculture, industry and technology (the sturdily independent Bible-only Dan Crawford confessed that he thought education was no proper part of a missionary's work – until he visited Livingstonia).[108] And that outlook underlies the career of the most celebrated Scottish missionary, David Livingstone, a Congregationalist who served fourteen years with the LMS. His move from missionary to explorer was not a change of life; his vision comprehended the end of the East African slave trade, and a prosperous Africa evangelized by Africans. With these ends in mind, exploration was part of mission.[109] In a later generation and a different context a comparable vision directed the career of J.H. Oldham,[110] who (originally by default) came to organize the World Missionary Conference, Edinburgh 1910, and thereafter to steer many of the developments that followed, including, and for many years, the International Missionary Council. Where some saw only a continuing need for more evangelistic effort, Oldham saw that a World Church had come into being, that the issue of race could blight the life of that Church, and must be tackled within the World Church; and that a perilous international situation demanded international Christian social thinking and action.

In the history of mission there have always been maximalists, whose vision of mission has encompassed the universe, and minimalists, who,

---

[107] On Calabar see Johnston, *Of God and Maxim Guns;* Rosalind Hackett, *Religion in Calabar: The Religious Life and History of a Nigerian Town* (Berlin and New York: Mouton de Gruyter, 1989); W. Harrison Daniel, "Patterns of Mission Preaching: The Representation of the Christian Message and the Efik Response in the Scottish Calabar Mission, Nigeria, 1846-1900", PhD, University of Edinburgh, 1993.

[108] On Livingstonia and Blantyre, see McCracken, *A History of Malawi*; McCracken, *Politics and Christianity*, Ross, *Malawi and Scotland*; Ross, *Blantyre Mission*; Thompson, *Christianity in Northern Malawi*. On the wider issue, see Kenneth R. Ross, *Presbyterian Theology and Participatory Democracy* (Edinburgh: St Andrew Press, 1993).

[109] Livingstone's book *Missionary Travels and Researches in South Africa* (London: John Murray 1857), written in the light of his years of missionary service and his first long walk across Africa, conveys this message.

[110] See Keith Clements, *Faith on the Frontier: A Life of J.H. Oldham* (Edinburgh: T. & T. Clark; Geneva: WCC, 1999).

having identified "one thing needful", single-mindedly pursue that one thing. Each is necessary to the other in the Kingdom of God. Scottish mission history furnishes examples of both; but one can hardly avoid noting in the record the presence of many significant maximalists, concerned to apply the Gospel to every dimension of life, every human activity, and every aspect of society.

Scottish patterns of education may have some relevance to this. In the early nineteenth century the CMS, the leading English missionary society, found it hard to recruit missionary candidates who were ordained or had the educational and social background then required for Anglican ordination; and Dissenters were excluded from the English universities.[111] Early Scottish missions could look for missionaries in the regular sources of the ministry, the universities and divinity halls; even Wesleyan Methodists, so few in Scotland, could, in Peter Cargill, supply a university graduate, rarely found in their earlier missions. Without entering the ongoing debate over the alleged exceptionalism of Scottish education, one cannot but note the intellectual curiosity of many Scottish missionaries. A single example, out of many possible, must suffice. In 1845 Stephen Hislop was recruited for the Free Church Mission in India because John Wilson was looking for a colleague who could teach science as well as theology. Hislop became the architect of the Nagpur Mission, combining itinerant vernacular evangelism with much involvement in education. But he found time to build an internationally recognized collection of fossils, identify the coal seams in the region and discover a mineral new to science – the outcome, arguably, of Scottish education's embrace of the scientific, mechanical and technological as well as the classical.

Cairns' second point, the importance of the church concept in Scottish mission thinking, needs deeper consideration. Integration of overseas mission activity within the structures of the church is certainly a feature of the historic Scottish churches.[112] It is also true that Presbyterian polity, the norm in Scotland, facilitated this in ways that contemporary Anglican and Congregational polity did not. Study of mission history, however, suggests that, as in other missions, policy was often determined by factors quite outside the official structures: certainly new mission initiatives were sometimes due to entrepreneurial missionaries or concerned lay folk with knowledge of particular situations overseas. Further, in principle, integration implies the engagement of all members of the Church in forwarding the mission of the Church. Alexander Duff certainly believed this, and set out a programme of prayer, education and designated personal giving to implement it; but its effectiveness seems to have faded when he

---

[111] See Andrew F. Walls, "Missionary Vocation", in *The Missionary Movement in Christian History* (Maryknoll NY: Orbis, 1996), 160-72.
[112] The church bodies in mind are usefully described by Elizabeth G.K. Hewat in the subtitle of her book *Vision and Achievement: 1796-1956,* already mentioned, as *"the churches united in the Church of Scotland."*

was not present. Even the news of the death of Livingstone in 1873, a media event at the time, did not prove a major incentive to ordinary Scottish church members to provide for the continuation of his work. Though the Church of Scotland and the Free Church established missions in Central Africa in Livingstone's memory, both found the fundraising hard going.[113] In Scotland, as elsewhere, serious missionary concern was, most of the time, the sphere of the enthusiasts – even in times when missions were widely approved and commended.[114]

Nor is the integration of Church and mission a simple, unambiguous concept. From the time of the first positive response to the Gospel, the word "church" applied equally to the body of believers living in Scotland and to each of the diverse bodies of believers living in the various "mission fields." Missionaries had to relate to both entities, and this could rise to endless anomalies and contradictions. And when tension arose between the interest of the church in Scotland and that on the "mission field," (and the long train of Scottish church secessions and unions, with their financial consequences, more than once gave rise to this), the former interest was likely to prevail. Mission work could suffer, or as with that in Japan in 1900, be given up, as a result of a church union in Scotland. An unforeseen consequence of the union of 1929 in Scotland was the organizational division of the church in Kenya along racial lines.[115] In Manchuria, a single indigenous Chinese church arose from the work of Irish and Scottish Presbyterian missions – but the two missions remained rigidly separate. As Dugald Mackichan pointed out in the 1920s, ecumenical issues were often much more readily resolved on the mission field than in Scotland.[116]

Cairns contrasted the Church consciousness he believed to be characteristic of Scotland with the "freelances of the Spirit." He nevertheless recognized the indispensability of the "freelances of the Spirit", and Scottish mission history offers its own evidence of their importance.

The period following World War II gave new urgency to the issue of relations between missions deriving from the churches of the West

---

[113] Andrew C. Ross. "Scottish Missionary Concern 1874-1914: A Golden Era?" *Scottish Historical Review* Vol. 51 (1972), 52-72.

[114] Of the Scottish churches, the United Presbyterian Church seems to have produced the highest per capita giving.

[115] The union created an "overseas presbytery" of the Church of Scotland to include the (overwhelmingly white) congregation of St Andrew's Nairobi and all the missionaries. The establishment in 1943 of the Presbyterian Church of East Africa ended this anomaly.

[116] Dugald Mackichan, *The Missionary Ideal in the Scottish Churches* (London: Hodder and Stoughton, 1927). Mackichan, a United Free Church minister who had been Principal of Wilson College, Bombay, is here referring particularly to the emergence of the Presbyterian Church of India some years earlier, and the fact that the union of the two great Presbyterian churches of Scotland, eventually accomplished in 1929, was still awaited.

(whether or not integrated with the structures of those churches), and the churches across the world that had arisen from or in some other way been associated with them. The pace of political decolonization forced upon the missionary movement from the West the need to decolonize its own structures. Those structures had been designed to bring the Gospel of Christ to the non-Christian world beyond the West, and thus essentially for one way traffic. Yet the same mission agencies were much the strongest, and sometimes the only, link between the churches of the West, now often in a declining condition, and the new centres of Christian life beyond the West. Two way traffic was now essential: could mission structures be decolonized without Western Christians losing interest and concern; avoiding dependency while cultivating mutual responsibility and the sense of interdependence. This issue has been at the heart of the last fifty years of the history of the missionary movement.[117]

The third Scottish characteristic identified by Cairns, a habit of strong theological thinking, deserves fuller consideration than can be given here. It must suffice to mention two instances where Scottish missions opened up new areas of thought and study.

The idea of missiology as an academic discipline was conceived in relation to Scottish missions, and first implemented in Scotland. Once again it was Alexander Duff who made the decisive move. In 1867 he persuaded the Free Church General Assembly to establish a chair of Evangelistic Theology at New College, Edinburgh.[118] The chair was to integrate the study of missions (and Duff held missions to be "the chief end of the Christian Church"[119]) with all the theological disciplines, and to introduce students to the cultures and religions of the world. It was the first chair of missiology anywhere.[120] Duff's plan was even more extensive: he conceived of an accompanying institute for research into Asian and African

---

[117] The history of this vital period of missionary history is still largely unwritten; for the Church of Scotland, some important parts of the story have been recorded by David H.S. Lyon, *In Pursuit of a Vision: the Story of the Church of Scotland's Developing Relationship with the Churches Emerging from the Missionary Movement in the Twenty-five years from 1947 to 1972* (Edinburgh: St Andrew Press, 1998).

[118] See Andrew F. Walls, "Missiological Education in Historical Perspective", in J. Dudley Woodberry, Charles Van Engen and E.J. Elliston ed., *Missiological Education for the 21st Century: the Book, the Circle and the Sandals. Essays in Honor of Paul E. Pierson* (Maryknoll NY: Orbis, 1996), 11-22.

[119] Alexander Duff, *Missions the Chief End of the Christian Church; also the qualifications, duties, and trials of an Indian missionary,* (Edinburgh: John Johnstone, 1839).

[120] See Olav Guttorm Myklebust, *The Study of Missions in Theological Education: an historical enquiry into the place of world evangelization in Western Protestant ministerial training, with particular reference to Alexander Duff's chair of Evangelistic Theology,* Vols. 1 and 2, (Oslo: Forlaget Land og Kirke, 1955 and 1957).

languages and cultures. He himself became the first incumbent of the chair; he had only one successor, and that only for a short time. The institute did not materialize – at least not until near the end of the next century.[121] Scotland may thus claim to have initiated the systematic study of mission and pioneered its place in theological thinking; but Scotland left to others the task of sustaining and developing that study and the thinking arising from it.

A second instance of "strong thinking in theology," allied with practical and strategic planning relates to medicine. We have noted several examples of the historical importance of the Edinburgh Medical Missionary Society, not only in assisting specifically Scottish missions, but in its provision of trained medical personnel for many missions, the training grounds being the medical faculty of the University of Edinburgh and the Cowgate Mission in the Edinburgh slums. One of the Society's trainees was Dugald Christie[122] of the United Presbyterian Mission in Manchuria,[123] who was an ordained minister as well as a medical doctor, and sought to present healing as part of Christian ministry, rooted in the teaching and practice of Christ. Over several decades Christie developed not only an impressive programme of medical services and medical training, but an outline theology of medical missions which deserves more attention than it seems to have received. Matters of medical policy are usually decided ad hoc, in relation to the conditions of a particular time and place; Christie was inviting contemporaries to wider consideration of the place of medicine in the whole ministry of the Church.[124] His views did not commend themselves to all – notably his insistence that healing should be as free as the Gospel. He put his theology into practice within a comprehensive programme for North-east China that comprehended local clinics, dispensaries, long-stay hospitals, and, in Mukden Medical College, a full medical training, based on based on the Edinburgh University curriculum, delivered in Chinese. The college was independent of the mission; it raised its own funding, as an investment for the Kingdom of God in China. Its

---

[121] The Centre for the Study of Christianity in the Non-Western World, now the Centre for the Study of World Christianity, established in the University of Edinburgh in 1986, may be seen as incorporating much of Duff's vision for the Institute, as well as of his vision for the chair.

[122] See Mrs Dugald Christie, *Dugald Christie of Manchuria, Pioneer and Medical Missionary: The Story of a Life with a Purpose* (London: J. Clarke, [1932]); Dugald Christie, *Thirty Years in Moukden: Being the Experience of Dugald Christie,* edited by his wife [Iza Christie] (London: Constable, 1912).

[123] Christie was actually a member of the Free Church, but took missionary service with the UP Church on account of its greater commitment to medical missions.

[124] A summary of this can be seen in Christie's paper at the Shanghai Missionary Conference of 1907. See Andrew F. Walls, "Christie, Dugald", in Gerald H. Anderson ed., *Biographical Dictionary of Christian Missions* (Grand Rapids: Eerdmans, 1999), 134, and A.F. Walls, "Christie, Dugald" in *Oxford Dictionary of National Biography*..

successor institution remains an important part of the medical services of "China beyond the wall."

After Three Centuries

The three hundred years of Scottish missions that have been the topic of this article roughly correspond with the period of Protestant overseas missionary effort. We noted at the beginning that this has to be seen as part of a wider story that began two centuries before 2009, and involved Catholic missions. The story that has concerned us here is very much a Protestant one; and the Scottish story is part of the wider story of the Protestant missionary movement from the West. It has not been possible here to consider even Scottish Catholic missionary activity, which belongs in the parallel story of the Catholic missionary movement. The missionary movement from the West, Catholic and Protestant, is a critical, if transitional event in Christian history; a period of activity in which the Christian faith, long acculturated to Europe, and embodied in European forms, languages and categories of thought, passed into minds and hearts and lives shaped by very different influences and categories. In the process the Christian Church was transformed.[125]

The missionary movement arose as a consequence of the movement of European peoples that began in the sixteenth century and ended in the middle of the twentieth. That migration created the modern world order that is now in flux, perhaps in process of dissolution. The Western maritime empires, and the hegemony of Europe of which they were the sign, have come and gone; and Christian accession in Africa and Asia, far from passing with them, has blossomed since their demise. Christians constitute a proportion of the world's population similar to that of a century ago; what has changed is the areas of the world where most Christians live.

The missionary period is now an episode in the story of major churches in all the continents. In the missionary record Scotland has its own part; any special emphases and distinctive features are of minor consequence in relation to the general direction of the story. The missionary movement from the West is now in its old age; in the mercy of God its old age can still be vigorous and useful within a worldwide Church. The reality of the Kingdom of God is that the heartlands of the Christian Church now lie in parts of the world once thought of as the mission field. There are centres of bubbling spiritual energy across the world from which, under the direction of the Holy Spirit, may be brought to bear on other parts of the world – including the cross-cultural re-evangelization of the post-Christian West.

---

[125] For a visual presentation of the shift in the Christian world, and commentary from several angles, see Todd M. Johnson and Kenneth R. Ross ed., *Atlas of Global Christianity 1910-2010* (Edinburgh: Edinburgh University Press, 2009).

THE WORLD MISSIONARY CONFERENCE 1910: ITS SCOTTISH PROVENANCE

Kenneth R. Ross

Introduction

For any student of world Christian history, "Edinburgh 1910" is a key reference point. The World Missionary Conference, held in the Scottish capital that year, is probably the best known ecclesiastical event to have taken place in Scotland and arguably the most influential. John R. Mott the Conference chairman called it: "the most notable gathering in the interest of the worldwide expansion of Christianity ever held, not only in missionary annals, but in all Christian annals."[1] Marking its golden jubilee in 1960, Hugh Martin observed that: "By the general consent of all competent judges the World Missionary Conference at Edinburgh in June, 1910, was one of the most creative events in the long history of the Christian Church. Its significance is all the more clear in the perspective of fifty years after. In many respects unique in itself, it was also unique in the impetus it gave to Christian activity in many directions. It opened a new era in the missionary enterprise but it was also the beginning of what we now call 'the ecumenical movement'. 'Edinburgh 1910' was in fact a fountain head of international and inter-Church co-operation on a depth and scale never before known."[2]

This assessment was given at what was perhaps the high water mark of the ecumenical cooperation which sprang from the Edinburgh 1910 Conference. Yet the passing of a further fifty years has not diminished its significance as a point of reference in regard to world Christianity. As Andrew Walls remarks: "The World Missionary Conference, Edinburgh 1910, has passed into Christian legend. It was a landmark in the history of mission; the starting point of the modern theology of mission; the high point of the modern Western missionary movement and the point from which it declined; the launch-pad of the modern ecumenical movement; the point at which Christians first began to glimpse something of what a world church would be like."[3]

---

[1] Cit. C. Howard Hopkins, *John R. Mott 1865-1955: A Biography* (Geneva and Grand Rapids: WCC and Eerdmans, 1979), 342.
[2] Hugh Martin, *Beginning at Edinburgh: A Jubilee Assessment of the World Missionary Conference 1910* (London: Edinburgh House Press, 1960), 3.
[3] Andrew F. Walls, *The Cross-Cultural Process in Christian History: Studies in the Transmission and Appropriation of Faith* (New York and Edinburgh: Orbis and T. & T. Clark, 2002), 53.

Why Scotland?

One question which has to be asked is why Edinburgh was chosen to be the location of the Conference? The simple answer is that the Scottish churches offered to host the event. Fairley Daly, the Secretary of the Livingstonia Mission Committee, wrote early in 1906 to Robert Speer, Secretary of the Presbyterian Board of Foreign Missions in New York, to raise the question of whether plans should be laid to hold a major Missionary Conference following the one which had been held in New York in 1900?[4] Speer and his American colleagues were positive about a Conference in Great Britain and Scottish foreign mission committees and missionary societies needed no further encouragement to offer to host the Conference in Edinburgh in 1910.[5]

What is more of a question is why the missionary leadership of a such a small nation had the temerity to offer to host a World Conference and why their counterparts elsewhere had confidence to accept the offer? It appears that this confidence was inspired by their understanding of Scotland's standing in the Western missionary movement which was then at its zenith: "Edinburgh was a fitting place of meeting. In the earlier missionary enterprise which evangelised Europe no country was more prominent than Scotland, and no country has in proportion to its size contributed to the evangelisation of the world during the last century so large a number of distinguished and devoted missionaries."[6] This latter point was emphasised by J.H. Oldham, the Conference Secretary, when he recalled at time of the Jubilee of the Conference that Scotland had been chosen because it was "the native land of David Livingstone, Alexander Duff and other famous missionaries."[7]

Statistics published by the Conference itself demonstrated that Scotland's involvement in the worldwide missionary enterprise was out of all proportion to its population or economic strength. The 788 societies engaged in missionary work worldwide had a combined income of £5,071,225. The combined income of the 35 Scottish societies was £335,630, 6.6% of the total.[8] Nearly two-thirds of this income belonged to the Foreign Mission Committee of the United Free Church which was, by any standards, a major player in worldwide mission. Furthermore, it has to

---

[4] World Missionary Conference, 1910, *The History and Records of the Conference* (Edinburgh & London: Oliphant, Anderson & Ferrier; New York, Chicago and Toronto: Fleming H. Revell, 1910), 5-6.
[5] World Missionary Conference, *History and Records,* 6. See further Brian Stanley, "Scotland and the World Missionary Conference, Edinburgh 1910", *Records of the Scottish Church History Society,* Vol. XLI (2012), 113-132.
[6] World Missionary Conference, *History and Records,* 18.
[7] J.H. Oldham, "Reflections on Edinburgh 1910", *Religion in Life,* Vol. XXIX (1959-60), 329-38 [329].
[8] World Missionary Conference, 1910, *Statistical Atlas of Christian Missions* (Edinburgh: World Missionary Conference, 1910), 58.

be recognised that these figures refer only to Scottish-based missionary societies. Scots and people of Scots descent were also prominent in the significant missionary work of Presbyterian Churches in England, Canada and the USA.

Nor was Scottish missionary engagement confined to Presbyterianism – far from it. The interdenominational London Missionary Society, which from its inception in 1795 was an important pioneer of the missionary enterprise, included among its staff such notable Scots as Robert Moffat,[9] John Philip,[10] David Livingstone,[11] James Legge,[12] John Mackenzie[13] and James Chalmers.[14] Besides the "big names", James Calder records that in the 1845-1995 period, "... the LMS appointed 548 missionaries. No less than 102 of them were Scots."[15] Scots were to be found within the ranks of the low-church Anglican Church Missionary Society while the Scottish Episcopal Church has an official link with the high-church Society for the Propagation of the Gospel.

As well as having a strong base within Scotland itself, Scottish influence was widely diffused within the wider missionary movement.[16] If this is apparent on a quantitative analysis, it is all the more so when considered qualitatively. Mission stations such as Lovedale[17] or Livingstonia[18] and

---

[9] See Bruce Ritchie, "The Missionary Theology of Robert Moffat of Kuruman", Ph.D. thesis, University of Malawi, 2006.

[10] See Andrew C. Ross, *John Philip: Missions, Race and Politics in South Africa* (Aberdeen: Aberdeen University Press, 1986).

[11] See Andrew C. Ross, *David Livingstone: Mission and Empire* (London & New York: Hambledon & London, 2002).

[12] See Norman J. Giradot, *The Victorian Translation of China: James Legge's Oriental Pilgrimage* (Berkeley: University of California Press, 2002); Lauren F. Pfister, *Striving for the "Whole Duty of Man": James Legge and the Scottish Protestant Encounter with China. Assessing Confluences in Scottish Nonconformism, Chinese Missionary Scholarship, Victorian Sinology, and Chinese Protestantism* (Frankfurt: Peter Lang, 2 vols, 2004).

[13] See Anthony Sillery, *John Mackenzie of Bechuanaland, 1835-1899: A Study in Humanitarian Imperialism* (Cape Town: A.A. Balkema, 1971).

[14] See J.M. Hitchen, "Training Tamate: Formation of the Nineteenth Century Missionary Worldview: the Case of James Chalmers", Ph.D. thesis, University of Aberdeen, 1984.

[15] James M. Calder, *Scotland's March Past: The Share of Scottish Churches in The London Missionary Society* (London: The Livingstone Press, 1945), 10.

[16] See A. F. Walls, "Missions", in Nigel M. de S. Cameron ed., *Dictionary of Scottish Church History and Theology* (Edinburgh: T. & T. Clark, 1993), 567-94 [573-74].

[17] See Graham A. Duncan, *Lovedale: Coercive Agency* (Pietermaritzburg: Cluster Publications, 2003).

[18] See John McCracken, *Politics and Christianity in Malawi, 1875-1940* (Cambridge: Cambridge University Press, 1977; 2nd ed. Blantyre: CLAIM, 2000).

educational institutions such as Wilson College in Bombay[19] or Madras Christian College[20] were highly regarded models of missionary engagement, as would be evident in the proceedings of the Conference. Hence there was little question, either in the minds of Scottish missionary leaders or in those of their counterparts elsewhere, that Scotland was an appropriate location for a major world missionary conference.

In the course of the 19th century, the missionary movement had established a degree of credibility in Scotland which enabled it to call on significant resources both from the Churches and from the wider society. Both the Moderator of the Church of Scotland, McAdam Muir, and the Moderator of the United Free Church of Scotland, John Young, were invited delegates at the Conference.[21] More significantly, several of the leading theological thinkers from both Churches were delegates: David Cairns,[22] James Denney,[23] H.A.A. Kennedy,[24] A.R. MacEwen,[25] W.P. Paterson[26] and Alexander Whyte.[27] This served to connect the missionary enterprise with mainstream thinking and concern in church life – a significant development for a movement which had earlier been regarded as peripheral and even eccentric.

This development was reinforced by the capacity of the organisers to call on the services of senior figures in the social and political establishment. President of the Conference was Lord Balfour of Burleigh who had recently served in the British Cabinet as Secretary of State for Scotland. Mover of the only formal resolution of the Conference was Sir Andrew Fraser who had recently retired as Lieutenant-Governor of Bengal. It may be a question whether the Conference was, in fact, too close to the establishment but it is clear that foreign mission had come to have a

---

[19] Elizabeth G.K. Hewat, *Vision and Achievement 1796-1956, A History of the Foreign Missions of the Churches United in the Church of Scotland* (London: Thomas Nelson, 1960), 43-53.

[20] Hewat, *Vision and Achievement*, 83-101.

[21] World Missionary Conference, *History and Records*, 39.

[22] See *David Cairns: An Autobiography, Some Recollections of a Long Life and Selected Letters*, edited by his Son and Daughter with a Memoir by D.M. Baillie (London: SCM, 1950).

[23] See John Randolph Taylor, *God Loves Like That! The Theology of James Denney* (London: SCM 1962); James M. Gordon, *James Denney (1856-1917): An Intellectual and Contextual Biography* (Milton Keynes: Paternoster, 2006).

[24] See John Baillie, "Kennedy, Harry Angus Alexander", *Dictionary of National Biography 1931-1940*, ed. L.G. Wickham Legg (London: Oxford University Press, 1949), 504-505.

[25] See David S. Cairns, *Life and Times of Alexander Robertson MacEwen.* (London: Hodder & Stoughton, 1925).

[26] See Clive L. Rawlins ed. *The Diaries of William Paterson Paterson* (Edinburgh: Faith and Life,1987).

[27] See G.F. Barbour, *The Life of Alexander Whyte* (London: Hodder & Stoughton, 1923).

standing in Scotland which allowed the conference organisers to involve senior statesmen in the leadership of the event.

There was also a movement of popular enthusiasm on which they could draw. Local committees to promote the work of the Conference were formed in all the important towns of Scotland. Public Meetings attracted attendances "varying from 350 to 3,500"[28] As the time for the Conference approached the Foreign Mission Committees of the Church of Scotland and the UF Church suggested that "each Presbytery might, at an early meeting, set aside half an hour for intercession on behalf of the Conference..."[29] The importance of prayer for the Conference was a constant emphasis and allied to this was the practical need for funds – a sum of £7,000 had to be raised to meet the costs of the conference.[30]

As Brian Stanley has recently demonstrated, the Conference did not achieve the upsurge in commitment to the cause of foreign mission for which its advocates had hoped.[31] It remained a minority pursuit, even within Scottish church life. Nonetheless it was cherished by a minority with sufficient energy and imagination to support and promote a relatively large scale of missionary engagement. Without a significant level of public support it would not have been possible to envisage hosting an event on such a world scale. It also provoked a generous response from Scotland's civic institutions. *The Scotsman* reported that "Edinburgh has received the World Missionary Conference in a manner which is worthy of the best traditions of the Scottish nation. The city, through the Lord Provost and Magistrates, has welcomed them; the Church, within the ancient walls of St Giles', has welcomed them; and the University has honoured them by conferring on representatives of their number its highest distinctions."[32] As Timothy Yates acknowledges: "Scotland had certain attributes and characteristics which made it peculiarly fitting for an epoch-making missionary conference to be held in its capital city."[33]

Vision, Diplomacy and Organisation

Scotland was a suggestive base for a World Missionary Conference but this is not to say that it would be successful in organising one. By universal consent, the fact that it did so is attributable, in no small measure, to the remarkable qualities of the Conference Secretary, Joseph Houldsworth

---

[28] World Missionary Conference 1910, *Monthly News Sheet*, March 1910, 123.
[29] World Missionary Conference 1910, *Monthly News Sheet*, April 1910, 144.
[30] World Missionary Conference, 1910, *Statement of Aims and Plans*, issued by authority of the Committee, no date., 5.
[31] Stanley, "Scotland and the World Missionary Conference".
[32] "World Missionary Conference" [by a Contributor], *The Scotsman*, 15 June 1910.
[33] Timothy Yates, *Christian Mission in the Twentieth Century* (Cambridge: Cambridge University Press), 1994, 21.

Oldham.[34] Invalided home at an early age from missionary service in India, Oldham had a mission studies remit from the UF Church when the unexpected call came for him to take up a full-time role as Secretary to the Committee organising the Conference.[35] Alarmed by the prospect of a world conference being organised by an exclusively Scottish committee "consisting of fossils",[36] Oldham set about establishing a fully international framework for the organisation of the Conference. Without this vision and the capacity to make it a reality, it is very doubtful if the Conference would have had the epoch-making significance which it did. Along with vision and organisational powers, Oldham demonstrated remarkable gifts of diplomacy. Missionary work generally attracts strong and domineering personalities and Scottish missionaries have not been an exception to this rule. In fact, Adrian Hastings has observed that: "The Church of Scotland missionary, whether of the Established or of the Free Church, had a strong tendency to be insensitively autocratic."[37] Oldham was of a different mould, quiet and unassuming. His strength lay in the warm relationships and careful diplomacy which enabled him to hold together a diverse coalition which was not without its jealousies and turf wars.

Perhaps his most notable achievement in this regard was to convince the Anglo-Catholic section of the Church of England to participate, which in turn made it possible for Randall Davidson, the Archbishop of Canterbury, to famously address the Conference.[38] Hitherto the Anglo-Catholics had kept their distance from conferences dominated by Evangelicals and Non-Conformists. Oldham had the vision to see that their participation would take the Conference to an entirely different level.[39] Despite initial favourable signs from the Society for the Propagation of the Gospel, it seemed that the Anglo-Catholics could not see their way to participate. An overnight stay with Bishop Gore of Birmingham enabled Oldham to turn the situation around. Looking back fifty years later, he commented: "This was the turning point of the ecumenical movement".[40] Oldham's years as an undergraduate at Trinity College, Oxford, had served well to give him a sympathetic understanding of Anglicanism and this enabled him to mediate between the assertive American approach and the sensitivities of the Church of England. (It is not without significance that Temple Gairdner, influential CMS missionary and the official chronicler of the Conference,

---

[34] See Keith Clements, *Faith on the Frontier: A Life of J.H. Oldham* (Edinburgh: T. & T. Clark; Geneva: WCC, 1999), 73-99.

[35] Clements, *Faith on the Frontier*, 74-78.

[36] Clements, *Faith on the Frontier*, 75.

[37] Adrian Hastings, *The Church in Africa 1450-1950* (Oxford: Clarendon Press, 1994), 557.

[38] George K. A. Bell, *Randall Davidson: Archbishop of Canterbury*, 3rd ed. (London: Oxford University Press, 1952), 572-75.

[39] Clements, *Faith at the Frontier*, 78-88.

[40] Oldham, "Reflections on Edinburgh 1910", 333.

had been Oldham's room-mate at Trinity; nor that Randall Davidson also was a Trinity man.)

By the end of 1909 Oldham had established the Conference offices on Princes Street in Edinburgh and had engaged a staff of 29.[41] They faced "... the sheer logistical nightmare of arranging the accommodation of over 1,200 visitors in hotels, boarding houses and private homes all over the city."[42] In the end the entire Conference organisation was a *tour de force*. In a passage oft-quoted in the annals of the Ecumenical Movement, Temple Gairdner in his account of the proceedings of the Conference wrote that:

> Just beneath [John R. Mott] at the Committee table, sat the General Secretary of the Conference, J.H. Oldham, a man strangely contrasted with the Chairman. Small of stature, and of unassuming face and mien, he slipped into or out of his place at the table, as one not merely unnoticed but not meriting notice. The Chairman, though he did not intervene in the discussions, at least gave the important closing address, and his voice was frequently and authoritatively heard, but the Secretary, from beginning to end, never opened his lips, save to give out formal notices. Why then was it that the first time he rose to give out a notice, the whole Conference applauded as though it would never cease? Some did so, perhaps, because they wanted to show their appreciation of a triumph of organisation. But those that knew were aware that, more than any other, the spirit that was in this very unobtrusive exterior had been at the back of that great Conference, not merely in respect of its organisation and its methods, but also of its ideals, its aspirations, and its hopes.[43]

The Work of the Commissions: Scottish Influence

A key role played by Oldham at this deeper level was that of guiding the work of the eight Commissions which would report to the Conference. This was one of the features which set Edinburgh 1910 apart from earlier conferences. Whereas they had concentrated on a demonstration of enthusiasm, Edinburgh aimed to be a working conference, its subtitle being "To consider Missionary Problems in relation to the Non-Christian World".[44] In order to do this, thorough preparatory work was carried out by eight Commissions on topics established by the Oxford meeting of the International Committee in June 1907.[45] It can be argued that it was the work of these Commissions which gave the Conference its depth and

---

[41] World Missionary Conference 1910, *Monthly News Sheet*, December 1909, 67.
[42] Clements, *Faith at the Frontier*, 88-89.
[43] W.H.T. Gairdner, *"Edinburgh 1910": An Account and Interpretation of the World Missionary Conference* (Edinburgh & London: Oliphant, Anderson & Ferrier; New York, Chicago and Toronto: Fleming H. Revell, 1910), 65.
[44] *History and Records*, iii.
[45] *Ibid*, 10-12.

enduring quality.[46] Time did not allow the Committee to settle the membership of the Commissions so considerable discretion was allowed to Mott and Oldham to finalise the selection. This they used to good effect, as will be seen shortly in regard to Commission IV. The Commissions used a questionnaire approach to gather the perspectives of a wide range of missionary correspondents in different parts of the world. A major responsibility of Oldham's staff was to type up the responses to the questionnaires and despatch them to the members of the Commissions. While responsibility for the writing of the Commission Reports lay with their Chairmen, Oldham played a coordinating role, sometimes advocating "quite drastic restructuring".[47] In this way, Oldham set his stamp upon the Conference at a much deeper level than simply ensuring that it ran smoothly. He also exploited to the full the Scottish provenance of the Conference to strengthen the work of the Commissions.

Commission IV: The Missionary Message in Relation to Non-Christian Religions

Scots participated in the work of all of the Commissions but on some they had a particularly formative influence; none more so than Commission IV. This was the most strikingly original of all the Commission Reports and the one which attracts the greatest interest today, described by Kenneth Cracknell as "... one of the great turning points in the Christian theology of religion."[48] It is remarkable for the degree to which it scotches the idea that Western missionaries were iconoclasts bent on the eradication of existing religions in order to impose their own understanding of Christianity. On the contrary, the Report concludes by noting "the practically universal testimony that the true attitude of the Christian missionary to the non-Christian religions should be one of true understanding and, as far as possible, of sympathy."[49] Scottish correspondents, notably Donald Fraser,[50] George Douglas, John Nicol Farquhar,[51] A.G. Hogg[52] and Nicol Macnicol,[53] played their full part in contributing to that testimony.

---

[46] See David A. Kerr and Kenneth R. Ross eds., *Edinburgh 2910: Mission Then and Now* (Oxford: Regnum, 2009).

[47] Clements, *Faith at the Frontier*, 89.

[48] Kenneth Cracknell, *Justice, Courtesy and Love: Theologians and Missionaries Encountering World Religions 1846-1914* (London: Epworth Press, 1995), xi.

[49] World Missionary Conference, 1910, *Report of Commission IV: The Missionary Message in Relation to Non-Christian Religions* (Edinburgh & London: Oliphant, Anderson & Ferrier; New York, Chicago and Toronto: Fleming H. Revell, 1910), 267.

[50] See T. Jack Thompson, *Christianity in Northern Malawi: Donald Fraser's Missionary Methods and Ngoni Culture* (Leiden: E.J. Brill, 1995).

[51] See Eric J. Sharpe, *J.N. Farquhar: A Memoir* (Calcutta: YMCA, 1963); Eric J. Sharpe, *"Not to Destroy but to Fulfil": The Contribution of J.N. Farquhar to*

Decisive, however, for the innovative and ground-breaking work of the Commission was the choice of the Chairman. Mott and Oldham opted not for a recognised missionary leader but for the Professor of Systematic Theology at the United Free Church College in Aberdeen, David Cairns. As Cracknell observes: "The choice of a theologian suggests already that Mott and Oldham were looking for something more than a competent survey of the world's religions."[54] If so, their choice was to be vindicated. Not only had they chosen a theologian but one who had wrestled with his own doubts and, in finding answers through re-thinking traditional theology, had been an important influence on the great Scottish missionary thinker in India, Alfred George Hogg.[55]

The key to the outcome of the Commission lay in the questions which Cairns prepared for the questionnaire. Question 5 read: "What attitude should the Christian preacher take toward the religion of the people among whom he labours?"[56] This allowed missionaries the world over to indicate the understanding, sympathy and respect which they believed should characterize the preacher's attitude, an outcome which Cracknell describes as "not less than stunning."[57] Question 6 read: "What are the elements in the said religion or religions which present points of contact with Christianity and may be regarded as a preparation for it?"[58] Again this was a leading question which allowed many missionary respondents to give expression to the fulfilment theology which turned out to be a strong feature of the Report.

Question 9 read: "To what extent do questions of 'higher criticism' and other developments of modern Western thought exert an influence in your part of the mission field, and what effect do they have on your missionary work?"[59] This recognised the intellectual ferment which had such a great impact on people like Cairns and Hogg around the turn of the century and

---

Protestant Missionary Thought in India before 1914 (Studia Missionalia Upsaliensia & Lund: C.W.K. Gleerup, 1965).
[52] See Eric J. Sharpe, *The Theology of A.G. Hogg* (Bangalore: CISRS and Madras: CLS, 1971); James L. Cox, "The Development of A.G. Hogg's Theology in Relation to Non-Christian Faith: Its Significance for the Tambaram Meeting of the International Missionary Council 1938", Ph.D. thesis, University of Aberdeen, 1977.
[53] See D.B.Forrester, "Macnicol, Nicol", in Cameron, *Dictionary of Scottish Church History and Theology,* 535.
[54] Cracknell, *Justice, Courtesy and Love,* 187.
[55] Eric J. Sharpe, "A.G. Hogg 1875-1954: The Christian Message to the Hindu", in Gerald H. Anderson, Robert T. Coote, Norman A. Horner & James M. Phillips, *Mission Legacies: Biographical Studies of Leaders of the Modern Missionary Movement* (New York: Orbis, 1994), 330-38 [331].
[56] *Report of Commission IV: The Missionary Message*, 2.
[57] Cracknell, *Justice, Courtesy and Love*, 202.
[58] *Report of Commission IV: The Missionary Message*, 2.
[59] *Report of Commission IV: The Missionary Message*, 2.

many respondents took the opportunity to reflect on their understanding of the presence and activity of God in the world's religious traditions. Question 10, addressed only to foreign missionaries, read: "Has your experience in missionary labour altered in either form or substance your impression as to what constitutes the most important and vital elements in the Christian Gospel?"[60] The distinction of form and substance in regard to the gospel was a portentous one, shocking to some of the correspondents but taken up eagerly by others as an opportunity to discuss how their understanding of the Christian gospel had changed through their encounter with people professing other religions.[61] For example, George Douglas, the UF missionary in Manchuria, acknowledged that "the old missionary appeal founded upon compassion for the millions hurrying to eternity was too limited in its outlook ... the individualist motive [must] give place to Christ's concentration on the idea of the Kingdom of God."[62]

A prominent contributor to the thinking of the Commission in the area of animistic religions was Donald Fraser of the Livingstonia Mission.[63] In response to Question 5 concerning the correct attitude to the religion among whom the missionary was working, Fraser wrote: "The Christian preacher should recognise that God has not left Himself without a witness among these people: that the God they ignorantly worship, we declare fully by the revelation of Christ that the immortality they believe in by their reverence of the spirits is a truth of God, but the condition of the spirits after death is revealed by the Bible: that their idea of the intercession of the spirits with God is the feeling after the one Intercessor, Jesus Christ through whom we have access to the Father. We should not declare the Gospel as antagonistic to their simple faith, but the clearer revelation of what they simply sought after."[64] Amongst the Livingstonia missionaries, Fraser was distinguished as one who was particularly sensitive to the religion and culture of the Ngoni people.[65] The direction his thought was taking was one which helped to make fulfilment theology the keynote of the Report.

The deeper roots of the Commission's thinking were found, however, not in Africa but in India. More than to any other single individual, the guiding theology of the Report is attributable to the work of John Nicol Farquhar, described by Andrew Walls as: "the most considerable Indologist produced by the missionary movement."[66] Anticipating his soon-to-be-

---

[60] *Report of Commission IV: The Missionary Message*, 2.

[61] See further Cracknell, *Justice, Courtesy and Love*, 197.

[62] Commission IV – Responses to Questionnaire, manuscripts held by the Centre for the Study of World Christianity, University of Edinburgh, George Douglas, No. 43.

[63] See J. Stanley Friesen, *Missionary Responses to Tribal Religions at Edinburgh, 1910* (New York et al: Peter Lang, 1996), 97-117.

[64] Commission IV – Responses to Questionnaire, Donald Fraser, No. 295.

[65] See Thompson, *Christianity in Northern Malawi*.

[66] A.F. Walls, "Farquhar, John Nicol", in Cameron, *Dictionary of Scottish Church History and Theology*, 315.

published and highly influential work, *The Crown of Hinduism*,[67] Farquhar's extensive response to the questionnaire developed the idea of fulfilment which saw Hinduism as India's Old Testament which prepared the way for the coming of Christ and found its fulfilment in him. This allowed him both to engage Hinduism with deep understanding and profound sympathy and to regard it as being fulfilled and therefore superceded by the coming of Christ.[68] As he would conclude his *magnum opus*: "In [Jesus Christ] is focused every ray of light that shines in Hinduism. He is the Crown of the faith in India."[69] As Eric Sharpe observes, though Farquhar was not present at Edinburgh 1910, "his influence is clearly seen in the Report of Commission IV."[70] The Report itself acknowledges that among those who saw Hindu theism and philosophy as "alike fulfilled and superseded by Christianity ... Mr Farquhar of Calcutta may be taken as a typical representative."[71]

The idea of fulfilment as a key to the interpretation of religion had its roots in the work of Max Muller[72] but it had no more articulate exponent in the missionary world than J.N. Farquhar and it was his approach which became the guiding light for David Cairns and his fellow Commissioners. It should be noted, however, that the fulfilment approach was not uncontested and Farquhar's "most rigorous critic"[73] was another Scottish missionary in India, Alfred George Hogg, who at this time was at an early stage in his distinguished teaching career at Madras Christian College. For Hogg the idea of fulfilment was an abstraction and a condescension. While eager to take a sympathetic approach and find points of affinity whenever possible, the essential point for Hogg was the contrast between Christianity and Hinduism on such crucial points as divine agency and the concept of merit.[74] For our purposes at this point it is sufficient to note that in the debate at the heart of this ground-breaking Commission there were no voices more influential than those of the three Scots: Farquhar, Hogg and Cairns.

---

[67] J.N. Farquhar, *The Crown of Hinduism* (London: Oxford University Press, 1913).
[68] See Eric J. Sharpe, "J.N. Farquhar 1861-1929", in Anderson et al., *Mission Legacies*, 290-96.
[69] Farquhar, *The Crown of Hinduism*, 458.
[70] Sharpe, *"J.N. Farquhar"*, 290.
[71] *Report of Commission IV: The Missionary Message*, 181.
[72] See Max F. Muller, *Essays on the Science of Religion* (New York: Charles Scribner's Sons, 1871); Max F. Muller, *Introduction to the Science of Religion* (London: Longmans, 1882 [1873]); also discussion in Friesen, *Missionary Responses*, 65-74.
[73] T.E. Yates, "Edinburgh Revisited: Edinburgh 1910 to Melbourne 1980", *The Churchman*, Vol. 94 No. 2 (1980), 152 [145-155].
[74] See further Eric Sharpe, *The Theology of Hogg* (Madras: Christian Literature Society, 1971), 47-59.

Commission III: Education and the Christianisation of National Life

Education was at the core of missionary work almost everywhere but it was something to which Scottish missionaries had given particular attention. As Andrew Walls remarks: "For many other missions, education was simply one branch of missionary activity, made necessary by the mission's other activities, or required as the price of its presence in the local setting. For the Scottish missions, at least for a substantial and determinative part of their existence, education *was* mission."[75] This was reflected in the work of Commission III on Education and the Christianisation of National Life. No surprise, then, that this Commission was chaired by John Campbell Gibson, a missionary of the English Presbyterian Church who had been born and educated in Scotland. Many Scots were also to be found among the influential correspondents: Dugald Mackichan,[76] William Miller,[77] Alexander Hetherwick[78] and Robert Laws.[79] Hetherwick's submission was typical of the Scottish perspective: "First and foremost among the most effective agencies in the spread of the Gospel I would put education. The School in Africa is the mother of the Church, and the Teacher is the first and the best Evangelist. We have always found the church to follow the school, and each village school becomes from the outset the centre of a Christian propagandum."[80]

Where Scottish influence was particularly felt, however, was in the circulation of a pamphlet by William Miller at the conference itself.[81] Having served as Principal of Madras Christian College from 1877 to 1907, Miller was, in the judgement of Duncan Forrester, "… the most influential educational missionary of his day in India."[82] Though Miller's concerns were not absent from the Commission's Report he believed that they were

---

[75] Andrew F. Walls, *The Cross-Cultural Process in Christian History* (New York: Orbis and Edinburgh: T. & T. Clark, 2002), 262.

[76] See Dugald Mackichan, *The Missionary Ideal in the Scottish Churches* (London: Hodder & Stoughton, 1927).

[77] See O. Chetty Kandaswamy, *Dr. William Miller* (Madras: Christian Literature Society, 1924).

[78] See Alexander Hetherwick, *The Romance of Blantyre: How Livingstone's Dream Came True* (London: James Clarke, no date [1931]).

[79] See Robert Laws, *Reminiscences of Livingstonia* (Edinburgh & London: Oliver & Boyd, 1934); also Hamish Macintosh, *Robert Laws: Servant of Africa* (Edinburgh: Handsel Press, 1993).

[80] Commission I – Responses to Questionnaire, Alexander Hetherwick, No. 408. Quoted by courtesy of The Burke Library at Union Theological Seminary in the City of New York, Columbia University Libraries.

[81] World Missionary Conference, 1910, *Education in Relation to the Christianization of National Life*, Report of Commission III (Edinburgh & London: Oliphant, Anderson & Ferrier; New York, Chicago and Toronto: Fleming H. Revell, 1910), 441-46.

[82] D.B. Forrester, "Miller, William", in Cameron, *Dictionary of Scottish Church History and Theology*, 564-65.

insufficiently emphasised. His pamphlet was devoted to expounding the philosophy of mission which had distinguished Scottish educational missionaries in India since the time of Alexander Duff. "It is a mistake," he argued, "to suppose that the making of individual converts was at any time the only, or even the main, aim of these schools and colleges."[83] Rather, "a long and gradual process of leavening or permeating the general community is absolutely necessary before the national life of India, that is, the life of the real people of the country, is Christianised."[84]

Taking a longer view and aiming to influence the entire community, rather than looking to the short term and focussing on individuals, were essential characteristics of the Scottish missionary approach. Miller stood at the heart of this tradition when he argued that the Indian context meant that missionaries were called upon "to take specially broad views and to work not only for immediate but also for distant ends."[85] While his views were accorded great respect by the conference, at the end of the day it was not convinced, being more inclined to place emphasis on the training of leaders for the emerging Indian church.[86] Nonetheless, his capacity to lobby the conference delegates with a distinctively Scottish perspective on missionary education in India, shows the extent to which the Scottish provenance of the conference influenced the course of its debates.

Commission V: The Preparation of Missionaries

The conference met at a time when the contribution of women to the missionary movement was becoming ever more substantial.[87] It was significant, therefore, that the secretary of Commission V, which examined the preparation of missionaries, was Miss Annie Small, Principal of the Women's Missionary College in Edinburgh.[88] The extent of her influence on the Commission is acknowledged in its Report: "This institution, which appears to be the only one exemplifying many of the methods which have commended themselves to the Commission, is necessarily used as an illustration here and elsewhere."[89] Not only was frequent reference made in

---

[83] World Missionary Conference, 1910, *Education in Relation to the Christianization of National Life*, 443.

[84] *Ibid*, 444.

[85] *Ibid*, 441-42.

[86] See Gairdner, *Edinburgh 1910*, 122.

[87] See Lesley Orr Macdonald, *A Unique and Glorious Mission: Women and Presbyterianism in Scotland, 1830-1930* (Edinburgh: John Donald, 2000), 104-166.

[88] See Isabel Lusk, *"A Throughly Furnished Woman": Annie Small and the Training of Women Missionaries* (Edinburgh: St Colm's, 1994), 18-19.

[89] World Missionary Conference, 1910, *The Preparation of Missionaries* (also titled *The Training of Teachers*), Report of Commission V (Edinburgh & London: Oliphant, Anderson & Ferrier; New York, Chicago and Toronto: Fleming H. Revell), 1910, 87.

the Report to the Edinburgh College but it included an appendix by Annie Small entitled: "The Women's Missionary College, Edinburgh"[90]

The College was distinguished by the extent to which it encouraged the students to think for themselves. No examinations were held and, Annie Small claimed: "The result of this method has been to help students past the domination of textbooks, to enable them to form and to appraise ideas, and to accustom them to commend these to other minds."[91] The ethos was one which fostered the freedom and independence of each student but encouraged them to have complete loyalty to one another.[92] These principles made a deep impression on the Commission and help to shape the recommendations which were pedagogically influential within the missionary movement in the years which followed. Chairing the Commission was Douglas Mackenzie of Hartford Theological Seminary in Connecticut, USA, who had been brought up by Scottish missionary parents in South Africa.

Commission VII: Missions and Governments

Commission VII was devoted to a topic which was regarded as "novel" and "unusual" at a missionary conference – the relation of missions and governments.[93] It was chaired by Lord Balfour of Burleigh, the leading Scottish politician and churchman who also served as President of the conference.[94] Lord Balfour was a former cabinet minister;[95] and it was because the Commission was able to recruit members of such stature that it had credibility in addressing a topic of political importance and sensitivity.[96] While Balfour brought weight to the Commission, it is apparent that much more influence on its content was wielded by its Secretary, Andrew Blair Wann of the Church of Scotland Foreign Mission Board who was responsible for drafting large sections of the Report.[97]

---

[90] World Missionary Conference, *The Preparation of Missionaries*, Appendix VII, 250-52. Appendix XIII, it may be noted, comprised the answers to the Commission's questions which has been provided by J.N. Farquhar who exercised great influence on Commission IV.

[91] World Missionary Conference, *The Preparation of Missionaries*, 251.

[92] World Missionary Conference, *The Preparation of Missionaries*, 251-2.

[93] Gairdner, *Edinburgh 1910*, 154-55.

[94] See World Missionary Conference, 1910, *Missions and Governments*, Report of Commission VII (Edinburgh & London: Oliphant, Anderson & Ferrier; New York, Chicago and Toronto: Fleming H. Revell, 1910).

[95] D.W. Bebbington, "Balfour of Burleigh, Lord", in Cameron, *Dictionary of Scottish Church History and Theology*, 53.

[96] See Gairdner, *Edinburgh 1910*, 156.

[97] See Brian Stanley, "Church, State, and the Hierarchy of 'Civilization': The Making of the 'Missions and Governments' Report at the World Missionary Conference, Edinburgh 1910", in Andrew Porter ed., *The Imperial Horizons of*

Wann was very cautious when it came to engaging overtly political questions and it appears that J.H. Oldham's intervention was decisive in ensuring that the Report did include sharply critical comment on such matters as opium, the liquor trade and forced labour.[98] He in turn was influenced by contributions from the mission field, such as the remark by James Henderson of Lovedale that: "I cannot help feeling that the Christian Church has a duty to the world in regard to the downtrodden races of Africa. The fatal exploitation of the Natives of the Congo, the slavery prevailing in Loanda and the extermination of the Natives of German South-West Africa demand to be brought home to the conscience of the world in the name of Christ."[99] The concern for social justice which marked Scottish missionary endeavour left an impression on the work of Commission Seven. While the Report represents the outworking of the tension between British and American perspectives, the influence of Scottish traditions of witnessing to social justice is not to be underestimated.

Commissions I, II, VI and VIII

The flagship Commission I on "Carrying the Gospel to all the non-Christian World", chaired by John R. Mott himself, had the redoubtable George Robson, editor of the United Free Church of Scotland Missionary Record, as its Vice-Chairman. It heard from numerous Scottish correspondents including Nicol Macnicol who offered a characteristically Scottish missionary perspective when he observed: "Of all the agencies that have been enumerated in the first part of this question there is one the importance of which I desire especially to emphasise, all the more because it is apt to be overlooked and because I am disappointed to find no indication that the World Missionary Conference is drawing attention to its value and its neglect as I hoped would be done. I refer to the production and dissemination of literature in the vernaculars and in English."[100]

Commission II – on "The Church on the Mission Field" – and Commission VI – on "The Home Base" – included such capable Scots as Rowland Ellis, Bishop of Aberdeen and Orkney, and Fairley Daly, Secretary of the Livingstonia Mission Committee. The influential Commission VIII, on Cooperation and the Promotion of Unity, was chaired

---

British Protestant Missions, 1880-1914 (Cambridge and Grand Rapids: Eerdmans, 2003), 60 [58-84].

[98] *Ibid*, 76-79.

[99] Commission I – Responses to Questionnaire, James Henderson, No. 416. Quoted by courtesy of The Burke Library at Union Theological Seminary in the City of New York, Columbia University Libraries.

[100] Commission I – Responses to Questionnaire, Nicol Macnicol, No. 244. Quoted by courtesy of The Burke Library at Union Theological Seminary in the City of New York, Columbia University Libraries.

by a Scot, the recently retired Lieutenant Governor of Bengal, Sir Andrew Fraser, J.H. Oldham's father-in-law.[101] To Fraser fell the task of formally moving the resolution to form a Continuation Committee,[102] the only formal decision of the Edinburgh conference and the action which gave rise to the International Missionary Council and the wider ecumenical movement.[103] Taken together there can be little question that Scots played a role in the Commissions out of all proportion to their numbers in the worldwide missionary movement.

Conclusion: How the World Missionary Conference was Shaped by its Scottish Provenance

To argue that the conduct and character of the Conference were greatly influenced by its venue is not necessarily to claim that this was altogether a good thing. Meeting in what Gairdner described as "the royal capital of a Christian king"[104] underlined the close complicity between mission and colonialism which would later expose the missionary movement to heavy criticism. Perhaps a different venue would have allowed for more critical distance. Or perhaps it would have made no difference since, in the judgement of Andrew Walls in regard to British missionaries: "almost without dissent they believed in the essential beneficence of empire."[105] The Assembly Hall setting and the involvement of the British Establishment underlined the close alliance of mission and empire. In this regard Edinburgh might later be regarded as a questionable choice of venue, not something which troubled the participants at the time. Nor one which will occupy us further here. For our analysis is concentrated on the degree to which its Scottish provenance influenced the conduct and outcomes of the Conference. This can be considered at two levels.

---

[101] See Katherine Prior, "Fraser, Sir Andrew Henderson Leith" in H.C.G. Matthew and Brian Harrison ed., *Oxford Dictionary of National Biography*, Vol. 20 (Oxford: Oxford University Press, 2004), 822-23.

[102] World Missionary Conference, 1910, *Cooperation and the Promotion of Unity*, Report of Commission VIII (Edinburgh & London: Oliphant, Anderson & Ferrier; New York, Chicago and Toronto: Fleming H. Revell, 1910), 202-04; cf Gairdner, *Edinburgh 1910*, 208-09.

[103] See Ruth Rouse and Stephen C. Neill, eds., *A History of the Ecumenical Movement, 1517-1948*, Vol. I (London: SPCK, 1967); Ans J. van der Bent, "Ecumenical Conferences", in Nicholas Lossky et al ed., *Dictionary of the Ecumenical Movement* (Geneva and Grand Rapids: WCC and Eerdmans, 1991), 325-336.

[104] Rouse and Neill, *A History of the Ecumenical Movement*, 38.

[105] Andrew F. Walls, "British Missions", in Torben Christensen & William R. Hutchison eds., *Missionary Ideologies in the Imperialist Era: 1880-1920* (Arhus, Denmark: Aros, 1982), 164; cit. Friesen, *Missionary Responses to Tribal Religions*, 98.

By all accounts, the delegates were deeply impressed by the organisation of the Conference and cheerfully accepted the Presbyterian flavour which permeated its proceedings. This can be illustrated by an apparently trivial point which arose at the most decisive moment of the Conference. Sir Andrew Fraser had moved the resolution to establish a Continuation Committee, the only formal decision which the Conference was to take. The delegates were fully ready to give their unanimous vote, "charged with the emotional intensity of expectation that has reached its climax."[106] Who but a Scottish Presbyterian would feel compelled at such a moment to make a procedural point? Wallace Williamson rose to ask: "... am I right in understanding that there is no provision under Section (4) for the continuance of the Continuation Committee? If so, I would therefore suggest the advantage of the words following upon Committee, 'which shall have power to fill up vacancies as they occur'."[107] Who but a Scottish Presbyterian, as Convener of the Business Committee, would have thought of this already? George Robson replied: "Might I say that that point was present to the minds of some of us, but it is in accordance with our Scottish custom at any rate that this provision for filling up vacancies is inserted in connection with the submission of the proposed members of the Committee."[108]

This is the kind of exchange in which the two men would have participated on many occasions in the courts of their respective Churches. It illustrates how the provenance of Scottish Presbyterianism influenced the conduct of the Conference. The very architecture of the Assembly Hall, specifically designed to accommodate the conciliar method of decision-making of a Presbyterian Church, left its mark upon the Conference.[109] Rather than being an exhibition on a platform as with earlier international missionary conferences, it was an occasion on which delegates listened to one another and sought to come to a collective mind. The character and conduct of the Conference cannot be adequately explained without reference to fact that the venue was constructed on Presbyterian principles and to the unmistakable evidence that guiding spirits of the Conference had been schooled in Scottish Presbyterian methods of debate and decision-making.[110]

---

[106] Gairdner, *Edinburgh 1910*, 209.

[107] *Report of Commission VIII: Cooperation and the Promotion of Unity*, 208.

[108] *Ibid*.

[109] A newspaper correspondent remarked: "One for a moment felt under the delusion that Lord Balfour was His Grace the Lord High Commissioner." *Scotsman*, 15 June 1910.

[110] When this chapter was first presented as a paper at the conference on "Roots and Fruits: Scottish Missionary Traditions" held in Edinburgh on 4 October 2008, the Conference Chair David Miller suggested that perhaps the Presbyterian flavour of the Conference was most clearly revealed in the fact that the only decision it took was to establish a committee!

The Scottish influence, however, went well beyond procedural matters. In 1911, the year following the Conference, David Cairns addressed a student conference on the question of which elements of Scottish religious history were of special significance for the missionary movement. One of them, he suggested was "strong theology, the tradition of strong thinking in religion".[111] Having served as Study Secretary of the United Free Church Foreign Mission Committee, Oldham was immersed in this tradition and it governed his approach to the Commissions and the Conference. He sought to connect the missionary movement with the intellectual and theological mainstream in a way which was unusual and innovative. Early in the preparations for the conference, for example, Oldham recruited James Denney, Professor of New Testament at the United Free Church College in Glasgow. Denney was not only one of the nation's most influential theologians but was also "becoming recognised as *the* ecclesiastical leader in Scotland".[112]

The second issue of the Monthly News Sheet featured an article by Denney entitled "Counting the Cost" in which he commented: "It can only help the cause to which it is devoted if we realise afresh in connection with it the incomparable good which we have in Christ and the gospel.... To realise the incomparable good which we have in Him we must realise what it cost to God to put it within our reach. We were bought with a price. It is only as a religion of redemption, and redemption through an infinite sacrifice, that Christianity has been and will remain a missionary religion. It is the sense of what we owe to God in Christ which contains in it the motives inspiring missionary work. It is the man who has the deepest sense of debt to Christ who feels most deeply that he is debtor to all men for Christ's sake."[113]

When it came to the conference itself prominent Scottish theologians were among the speakers who gave the influential evening addresses: W.P. Paterson, H.A.A. Kennedy, A.R. MacEwen and, of course, James Denney.[114] Their speeches demonstrated how much their thinking was informed by the missionary movement and how concerned they were to bring their theological learning into engagement with it. In an atmosphere that has often been characterised as triumphalist, Denney struck a sobering note: "Men [sic] are not coming forward as ministers, nor coming forward as missionaries, because they are not coming forward into the membership of the Christian Church at all. One is tempted to say that there is no use calling for reinforcements at the front while recruiting is stopped at home,

---

[111] Walls, *The Cross-Cultural Process*, 261.

[112] K.R. Ross, "Denney, James", in Cameron, *Dictionary of Scottish Church History and Theology*, 240.

[113] World Missionary Conference 1910, *Monthly News Sheet*, November 1909, 27-28.

[114] World Missionary Conference 1910, *History and Records*, 156-63, 173-85, 195-205, 322-29.

and that is to a large extent the grave situation with which we are confronted. Something must happen to the Church at home if it is going even to look at the work which has been put upon it by this Conference."[115] "His address", remarked Temple Gairdner, "was one of power. It impressed because it hurt."[116] The presence of a theologian of Denney's stature brought to the conference a perspective which could look wider than the immediate demands of the foreign missionary movement to the challenges which lay ahead for the church in the so-called "Christian world".

The character and influence of the Scottish intellectual tradition has recently been the subject of renewed consideration.[117] So far as the modern Western missionary movement is concerned, Edinburgh 1910 brought it into engagement with greater depth of theological analysis and more sophisticated intellectual discourse than anything which had gone before. In its 19th century history it had been, in the main, an activist movement, if not anti-intellectual then simply so occupied with the immediate demands of its activity that it had no scope for extensive reflection. Perhaps Oldham's most distinctive contribution was his determination to recruit Scotland's most capable and creative theologians to bring their scholarly acumen to the work of the Conference. The Reports of the eight Commissions marked a new maturity in the missionary movement and set the bar by which subsequent ecumenical conferences would be measured. As we have seen, the role of Scots in the creation of the Commission Reports was entirely disproportionate to their numbers either as a nation or as participants in the missionary movement. The Scottish provenance of the 1910 World Missionary Conference therefore lent it a depth of intellectual grounding and a sophistication of theological analysis which marked it out as a distinctive and ground-breaking event.

---

[115] *Ibid*, 323.

[116] Gairdner, *Edinburgh 1910*, 261.

[117] See Arthur Herman, *How the Scots Invented the Modern World: The True Story of How Western Europe's Poorest Nation Created Our World and Everything in It* (New York: Crown Publishers, 2001); James Buchan, *Capital of the Mind: How Edinburgh Changed the World* (London: John Murray, 2003).

THE INFLUENCE OF THE MISSIONARY MOVEMENT IN SCOTLAND

Esther Breitenbach

Introduction

There are a number of ways in which one can approach the theme of the "influence" of the Scottish Presbyterian missionary movement, for example, its influence as foreign missions in other countries in terms of Christianisation and institution building, or as a form of cultural imperialism, or, indeed, in terms of unintended consequences of mission interventions. There is also a question about the relationship between impact abroad and influence at home, though this is by no means a straightforward one to answer. The focus here, however, is on the home base, since it has been argued that the degree of support at home is likely to have been a factor in the choice of Edinburgh as the location for the World Missionary Conference of 1910.

By the time of the World Missionary Conference, the Scottish foreign mission movement had achieved a high public profile in Scotland. This chapter aims to give an account of how this came about, and an assessment of the nature of the influence of the foreign mission movement. The World Missionary Conference attracted widespread coverage in the press, as evidenced by the numerous reports in *The Scotsman*. The Conference was attended by 1200 delegates, "representing 160 Churches and Evangelical Societies all over the world", with *The Scotsman* declaring it "a signal honour for Scotland that Edinburgh should have been chosen" as the site for the meeting place for "the greatest Missionary Conference which has ever been held".[1] The newspaper provided extensive coverage of the conference and its proceedings over a period of approximately three weeks, and of the various public events which accompanied it. This included a civic reception, the conferring of fourteen honorary degrees by Edinburgh University, breakfast meetings, exhibitions, women's meetings, and also parallel meetings in Glasgow. The civic reception was hosted by the Lord Provost, magistrates and the Town Council at the Royal Scottish Museum. It was attended by 5000 people, a "wonderfully cosmopolitan" gathering.[2] As *The Scotsman* also noted, guests at the reception were able to enjoy the ethnographical collection in the museum, to which many missionaries, including David Livingstone, had contributed.

---

[1] *The Scotsman,* 14 June 1910.
[2] *The Scotsman,* 14 June 1910.

It was commented that the enthusiasm for the conference indicated how much public support for foreign missions had grown. The Convenor of the United Free Church Foreign Mission Committee was quoted as having declared that: "the missionary temperature was rising at home. People were now receiving missionaries with a measure of intelligent welcome and friendly confidence, and with a desire to help".[3] At the same time, press coverage of the conference claimed a foremost place for the Scottish movement. According to *The Scotsman* the choice of Edinburgh as the location for the 1910 World Missionary Conference might reflect the fact that "in that great enterprise Scotland has always led the way". Indeed:

> It was Scotland in the persons of Mungo Park and Livingstone that opened up the way into the recesses of the erstwhile dark continent of Africa; it was Scotland in the person of Mackay, of Uganda, that established a native Christian state under the protectorate of Britain; it was Scotland that led the way in Lovedale and Blantyre, proving what Christianity could do for the natives by teaching them through industrial missions; it was Scotland in the person of Paton that spread most potently the power of Christianity in the south seas, and in the person of Chalmers so greatly impressed Robert Louis Stevenson that he wrote: 'Those who deblatterate against missions have only one thing to do, to come and see them on the spot'. It was Scotland also that led the way in India by establishing colleges for the higher education of Hindus – colleges which exercised a great influence on the policy of national education in India. In proportion to its population Scotland has done more for missions than any country in the world. It has sent some of the best of its manhood to establish and to man the outposts of Christianity.[4]

The evidence from press coverage, and of the public recognition given to the missionary movement by civic leaders and other prominent public figures, suggests that by 1910 foreign missions aroused wide interest among the Scottish public and that the missionaries and missions had, at least from time to time, a high public profile. The subsequent celebrations of the Livingstone Centenary in 1913 are further evidence of the continuing interest in foreign missions in this period. However, foreign missions had not always enjoyed widespread support. This was alluded to in the *Scotsman's* coverage of the conference, with its reference to Sydney Smith's famous attack on missionaries, published in the *Edinburgh Review* in 1806: "The day is past when men deemed it the right thing to sneer at missions, and designated missionaries in the words of Sydney Smith, as 'little detachments of maniacs'".[5] Such a long journalistic memory is perhaps remarkable, though it serves as a useful pointer to the timescale of the movement's evolution from a small group of dedicated supporters in the late eighteenth century to a well-known presence in Scottish life, which also had an international reputation by the early twentieth century.

---

[3] *The Scotsman*, 3 June 1910.
[4] *The Scotsman*, 14 June 1910.
[5] *The Scotsman*, 14 June 1910.

The Development of the Foreign Mission Movement in Scotland

Missionary societies were first formed in Scotland in 1796, inspired by the example of the Baptist Missionary Society founded in 1792 and the London Missionary Society founded in 1795. These were the Glasgow Missionary Society and Edinburgh Missionary Society, the latter of which became almost immediately the Scottish Missionary Society. Both societies were non-denominational and tended to be supported by evangelicals, many of whom had links to the Scottish anti-slavery movement of the 1880s.[6] The Church of Scotland General Assembly was asked in 1796 to support the missionary societies, but declined to do so. The view that "heathens" needed to be "civilised" before they could be Christianised prevailed, while at the same time leading Moderates were nervous of the potential radicalism of the new type of voluntary societies, such as abolitionist and missionary societies, which were viewed with suspicion in the atmosphere of reaction which arose in Britain in response to the revolution in France. This context of anxiety provoked by political and social unrest at least partly explains Sydney Smith's attack on Methodist and Anabaptist missionaries, whom he blamed for provoking the 1806 mutiny in Vellore in South India.[7]

In 1824, the Church of Scotland was prevailed upon to endorse foreign missions, and in 1830 the first Church of Scotland missionary, Alexander Duff, commenced work in Calcutta in India. Meanwhile the non-denominational societies had supported agents in various places in India, Africa and the West Indies, with some reorganisation of affiliations between the societies and the Church of Scotland occurring prior to the Disruption of 1843. It is a notable feature of support for foreign missions that women were actively involved from an early stage. For example, by the 1820s there were a number of Ladies and Female Missionary Societies, such as the Lanark Ladies' Scottish Missionary Society and Dunfermline Ladies Association.[8] Women's organisations were put on a more permanent footing with the formation of the Edinburgh Ladies' Association for the Advancement of Female Education in India in 1837, and the Glasgow Ladies' Association for promoting Female Education in Kaffraria [South Africa] in 1839, with the first female missionary agent being employed by the Edinburgh Association in 1838.[9] In 1841 the non-denominational Edinburgh Medical Missionary Society was established.

The Disruption of 1843, the major event within church history in nineteenth century Scotland, as might be expected, had a considerable

---

[6] Iain Whyte, *Scotland and the Abolition of Black Slavery, 1756-1838* (Edinburgh: Edinburgh University Press, 2006).
[7] Sydney Smith, "Indian Missions" in *Edinburgh Review*, No. 12 (1806), 151-81.
[8] *Scottish Missionary and Philanthropic Register*, 1826.
[9] See Lesley Orr Macdonald, *A Unique and Glorious Mission: Women and Presbyterianism in Scotland* (Edinburgh: John Donald, 2000).

impact on the developing foreign mission movement. At the Disruption, all but one of the Church of Scotland missionaries went over to the Free Church, and the Church of Scotland had to effectively start again to build up its missionary work-force. While this did recover in time, it never caught up with the Free Church in terms of numerical strength of the missionary workforce, nor with the United Presbyterian Church, formed in 1847 by the union of the Secession and Relief Churches, and also active in promoting foreign missions. The remaining Scottish Missionary Society and Glasgow Missionary Society missionaries were transferred to the Free Church and United Presbyterian Church. The Ladies' Associations also split on denominational lines in the aftermath of the Disruption. Thus from 1843 onwards Scottish foreign missions were mostly organised on denominational lines, with the three main Presbyterian churches being dominant in this field. The non-denominational Edinburgh Medical Missionary Society was an exception to this. It supported directly few of the missionaries it trained, but rather tended to place them with Church of Scotland, Free Church or London Missionary Society missions. The London Missionary Society, also non-denominational, though effectively becoming the province of Congregationalists continued to derive active support from Scotland, both in the form of missionary recruits and in the work of locally based auxiliaries, such as that in Edinburgh. Later in the century, the Scottish Episcopalian church also established its own missions, around 1870, while prior to this period it had channelled support to its sister Anglican church. The Catholic Church in Scotland did not send missionaries from Scotland until the 1930s. Thus Scottish supported foreign missions in the nineteenth and early twentieth centuries were a Protestant phenomenon, and one that was dominated by the main Presbyterian churches, notwithstanding the fact that it was from the dissenting churches that some of the most famous of Scottish missionaries emerged, such as Robert Moffat, David Livingstone, and James Chalmers, who all served with the London Missionary Society.

By the 1840s, then, foreign missions had become an established part of Presbyterian life, even if the actual numbers of missionaries were still relatively small. The splits in the church had the effect of energising religious life, and the foreign mission movement subsequently expanded at the same time as church extension programmes were carried out at home. Such expansion did not necessarily follow a smooth path, and there were frequent appeals both for money and missionary recruits, and occasional crises in the financial maintenance of missions. Various episodes and events did, however, serve to stimulate further interest in foreign missions from time to time. For example, the Indian uprising of 1857 and 1858 provoked widespread debate on the role of missionaries in India. On the one hand critics held missionary activities responsible for the provocation of Hindu and Muslim hostility. On the other hand missionary supporters denied that missionaries had been the object of attack as missionaries, rather than as Europeans, and argued that it was Indians who had been Christianised who remained loyal to the British state. Evangelicals were widely of the opinion that the "Mutiny" was a sign of God's wrath for Britain's failure to adequately carry out the task of Christianisation of India accorded them by divine Providence. They therefore lobbied strenuously for greater access for missionary ventures, and were rewarded with an increase in support for missions in the period immediately following the uprising.

Livingstone's explorations in Africa and his plea for people in Britain to follow his path in bringing "Christianity and Commerce" aroused further interest in missions in various parts of Britain, though it was not until after his death in 1873 that the Scottish Presbyterian churches acted on this appeal. The expedition to Nyasaland [Malawi], launched in 1875, was to result in the establishment of missions there by both the Church of Scotland and the Free Church, with the United Presbyterian Church also contributing in the person of Dr Robert Laws. Despite the occasional troubles of missions in Nyasaland and resulting negative publicity, defence of the interests of the Scottish missions was to become the subject of a popular campaign in the late 1880s, with the British government being urged to secure the territory from encroachments by the Portuguese.[10] Developments in Nyasaland continued to be of interest to the Scottish "mission public",[11] as did missionary activities in South Africa and West Africa. Missionary figures such as Robert Laws in Nyasaland, James Stewart in South Africa, and Mary Slessor in Nigeria became well known to the Scottish public.

If foreign missions in Africa came to have a higher public profile in the late nineteenth and early twentieth centuries, the continuing work in India was not neglected. Indeed, India continued to be the destination for the majority of missionaries. The low numbers of conversions in India were sometimes a matter for soul searching among the committees and supporters at home, with the emphasis on educational work in missions in India being questioned. Nonetheless, figures such as Alexander Duff and John Wilson were revered as missionary and educational pioneers, and educationists such as William Miller and Dugald MacKichan were also prominent figures. Despite the questioning of emphasis on teaching, pride was taken in the achievements of Scots in establishing educational institutions in India and in their work with women.

---

[10] See John McCracken, *Politics and Christianity in Malawi 1875-1940: the Impact of the Livingstonia Mission in the Northern Province* (Cambridge: Cambridge University Press, 1977), and Andrew Ross, "Scotland and Malawi, 1859-1964" in Stewart J Brown and George Newlands, Eds. *Scottish Christianity in the Modern World* (Edinburgh: T & T Clark, 2000), 283-309.
[11] See Catherine Hall for a definition of "missionary public". Catherine Hall, *Civilising Subjects: Metropole and Colony in the English Imagination 1830-1867* (Cambridge: Polity Press, 2002), 293-94.

New missions and new approaches were able to stimulate new waves of interest. Developments at home also had the capacity to feed missionary enthusiasm, such as the Moody and Sankey revival of the 1870s and the growth of the Student Volunteer Movement in the 1880s. Arguably, imperialist expansion in the late nineteenth century also fuelled interest in the foreign mission movement, since this best exemplified the "civilising mission" which British rule claimed to embody. Women's role in missions, and the extension of this as they gained access to higher education was another factor in stimulating interest, complemented by a parallel reorganisation of women's participation in church life. Thus support for the foreign mission movement in Scotland continued to grow throughout the nineteenth and into the twentieth centuries. This was not necessarily a steady growth, and it witnessed periods of stasis and occasional crises, but the general trend was one of expansion. At the same time the movement enjoyed a wider audience for its publicity in church circles, and a heightened public profile, as evidenced by public celebrations and press coverage.

Financing and Resourcing Foreign Missions

Notwithstanding the growing public profile of foreign missions in the latter decades of the nineteenth century, there has been some debate about how well supported financially the movement was by the Scottish church-going public. Andrew Ross challenged the notion that the period following Livingstone's death saw "the golden era of Scottish missionary enthusiasm".[12] As he demonstrated with respect to the Blantyre mission in Nyasaland, it was undoubtedly the case that from time to time there were financial problems, when possible closures of missions were considered, or curtailment of activity occurred through lack of resources in terms of both money and personnel. Ross argued that missions could be dependent on substantial donations from a relatively small number of wealthy supporters, and that church members generally did not give generously, and that this undercuts the pride taken subsequently by the Church of Scotland in the "essential unity of church and mission".[13] Lesley Orr has also indicated that the Ladies' Associations generally struggled to raise enough money, and that it was not until the reorganisation of women's support for missions and closer links with church organisation in the 1880s that such support began to increase significantly.[14]

Supporters of missions frequently complained that the funds given were inadequate and that not enough people came forward to offer themselves as

[12] Andrew Ross, "Scottish Missionary Concern 1874-1914: A Golden Era?" in *Scottish Historical Review,* 1972, 52-72.
[13] Ross, "Scottish Missionary Concern", 68.
[14] Orr Macdonald, *Unique and Glorious Mission.*

missionaries. Even where income for foreign missions was increasing congregations could be castigated for lack of generosity. George Smith, for example, quoted figures in the *Free Church Monthly* in June 1885, which indicated a steady increase in income for foreign missions – which had risen from an annual total of £6,403 in 1843-44 to £61,437 in 1884-85.[15] However, the purely congregational element of this had declined from 68% to 26% of the total income. Smith argued that congregational giving could rise much further – to double the level it was then at. Without further research into the financing of Scottish foreign missions, it is not possible to say what the overall patterns were in terms of growth or decline, or the distribution of support. What we do know is that from time to time significant efforts were made to put in place organisational structures throughout Scotland in order to ensure regular financial support was forthcoming for foreign missions, and these appeared to meet with success at least in the short term. Alexander Duff campaigned actively throughout Scotland for the Church of Scotland in 1836 for locally based associations to take on the task of providing regular financial support for foreign missions, and subsequently undertook a similar campaigning tour for the Free Church in the 1850s. Ross noted that the Church of Scotland also reorganised its fundraising structures in both the 1880s and 1890s, and as indicated women's organisations increased their capacity to raise funds in the latter decades of the nineteenth century. And, as noted, particular events also stimulated a rise in missionary enthusiasm – for example, the Disruption itself did so, as did the Indian "Mutiny", Livingstone's death and the inauguration of the Livingstonia expedition.

It is difficult to know how justified complaints of lack of support were. As noted, there were clearly occasional funding crises. On the other hand, however, such was the magnitude of the task of missionary work that support was always bound to be insufficient. And if Foreign Mission committees and women's organisations encountered financial difficulties, it is apparent that the movement did successfully continue to grow, as the increase in numbers of missionaries indicates. Estimated figures suggest that the numbers of missionaries supported by Scots from the earliest days until the early 1830s totalled around twenty, and that the cumulative total had grown to around 100 by 1850.[16] Lists of missionaries of the Church of Scotland and Free Church of Scotland published in 1900 indicated that since 1829 the churches had respectively employed cumulative totals of 252 and 335 missionaries (these figures involve some double counting as the Free Church figures included those missionaries who came over from the Church of Scotland at the Disruption, but the number was relatively small).[17] By the early 1870s the three main Presbyterian churches were

---

[15] George Smith, *Free Church Monthly,* June, 1885.

[16] Figures compiled from *New Edinburgh Almanac.*

[17] Rev. R. W. Weir, *Foreign Missions of the Church of Scotland* (Edinburgh: R & R Clark, 1900); "Roll of Missionaries from Scotland, 1829-1900." *Proceedings and*

fielding around 120 missionaries between them; by 1890 this had risen to 327; and by 1910 had reached a total of 509. By 1930 the reunified Church of Scotland was supporting 702 missionaries (this figure includes 193 missionaries' wives, who would have been working without pay).[18] In 1904 the majority of Scots missionaries were in India and Africa – 82 per cent of those supported by the two main Presbyterian churches – and this reflected a consistent pattern over time, with India retaining the bigger share.[19]

Missionary Literature

If, on the issue of financial support as such, there is some reason to doubt that there was universal enthusiasm for foreign missions, and therefore to question the influence the movement had in motivating practical support, there are however other aspects of the phenomenon which support the argument that the movement was influential across Scotland. This includes the capacity of the foreign mission movement to disseminate information and to shape the ways in which people understood the nature of empire and colonial peoples, and the way in which the movement came itself to be represented as a specifically Scottish contribution to empire.

Active missionary supporters at home may have been a minority of church-goers, and may have been critical at lack of enthusiasm from the public at large. Nonetheless, through a range of activities they succeeded in bringing the missionary movement to the attention of the wider Scottish population. In addition to fund-raising, public meetings, and exhibitions, the production and dissemination of literature was central to their activities.

Debates of the General Assembly of the Free Church of Scotland, Held at Edinburgh, May 1900 (Edinburgh: Lorimer and Gillies; London: James Nisbet, 1900).

[18] Figures for the early 1870s compiled from the *New Edinburgh Almanac*, 1873. Figures for 1890 compiled from "Report on Foreign Missions for 1890", *The Proceedings of the Synod of the United Presbyterian Church, May 1891* (Edinburgh, United Presbyterian Church, 1891); Report of the Foreign Mission Committee. *Reports on the Schemes of the Church of Scotland, 1890* (Edinburgh: William Blackwood and Sons, 1890); and *Proceedings and Debates of the General Assembly of the Free Church of Scotland, 1890* (Edinburgh: Lorimer and Gillies; London: James Nisbet, 1890). Figures for 1910 compiled from Report of the Foreign Mission Committee. *Reports on the Schemes of the Church of Scotland, 1910* (Edinburgh: William Blackwood and Sons, 1910); and Tenth Report on Foreign Mission (for 1909). *Reports to the General Assembly of the United Free Church of Scotland*, 1910 (Edinburgh: United Free Church of Scotland, 1910). Figures for 1930 quoted in Macdonald, *Unique and Glorious Mission*, 116. Following the way in which these figures were reported at the time, figures for 1890 include the working wives of missionaries for the Church of Scotland and Free Church of Scotland, while figures for 1910 include the working wives of missionaries for the Church of Scotland only.

[19] Figures derived from the *New Edinburgh Almanac*, 1904.

The provision of "missionary intelligence" was part of a missionary's contract, and this arrangement supplied much of the material for missionary periodicals, though there were also contributors at home and they were edited at home. Missionary magazines were published from the earliest days of the missionary societies' existence, also often accompanied by the copying and circulating of letters from missionaries. Following the Disruption periodicals were produced on denominational lines, with separate periodicals being published for women on women's work. The Free Church also published a children's missionary magazine. By the late nineteenth century the three main Presbyterian denominations between them were circulating around 250,000 copies of missionary periodicals, and by the early twentieth century, around a third of members of the Free Church of Scotland and of the United Presbyterian Church were subscribers.[20] There is also evidence of the active encouragement of church members by ministers to read and subscribe to periodicals, including free distribution of these to all members of the congregation. Ministers also read extracts from such literature in the pulpit, and meetings of women missionary supporters, for example, also entailed the study of missionary literature. In addition to the regularly published periodicals, there was an abundant literature of sermons, public addresses, pamphlets of various kinds, histories of missions, and the occasional memoir or autobiography.

Missionary biographies of Scottish missionaries emerged as a popular genre around the late 1870s, with the period of most prolific production spanning the 1890s to around 1920, though memoirs and biographies of missionaries were produced both before and after this period. The earliest such publication on the life of a Scottish missionary was John Wilson's memoir of his wife Margaret, published in 1838, and largely based on letters written by Margaret Wilson to her family and friends.[21] Between 1838 and the late 1870s works by or about the following missionaries were published: Robert Moffat, John Philip, Robert Nesbit and Hope Waddell. After the late 1870s, with the publication of works on Robert Moffat and Alexander Duff, there was a steady flow of biographies. Some of these were published in popular editions and special editions for children might also be produced, for example *The White Queen of Okoyong*, on Mary Slessor.[22] Biographies might go through several editions and some missionaries were the subject of multiple biographies, with Robert Moffat,

---

[20] Derek Alexander Dow, "Domestic Response and Reaction to the Foreign Missionary Enterprises of the Principal Scottish Presbyterian Churches, 1873-1929", PhD thesis, Edinburgh University, 1977.

[21] John Wilson, *Memoir of Margaret Wilson* (Edinburgh: John Johnstone, and London: Whittaker and Co and J Nisbet and Co, 1838).

[22] W.P. Livingstone, *The White Queen of Okoyong* (London: Hodder and Stoughton, c. 1919).

Mary Slessor and Alexander Duff coming into this category.[23] Livingstone is in a league of his own, with over 100 books written about him between the 1870s and the 1950s.[24] Some missionary biographies continued to be reprinted until at least the 1960s and they remained popular as Sunday School prizes with Livingstone and Slessor being the most likely to feature here.

Of the three main Presbyterian denominations, the Free Church was by far the ablest publicist and benefited from the services of professional writers such as George Smith and William Pringle Livingstone as authors of biographies and histories. The United Presbyterian Church too was active as a publicist of missionary lives, while the Church of Scotland produced very little in this genre. It is notable of course that Livingstone and Moffat were London Missionary Society missionaries, and not agents of any of the main Presbyterian churches. However, their biographies, and indeed their own accounts, stressed their Scottish origins and character. Taken together these forms of missionary literature, and in particular missionary biographies, created over time a Scottish missionary tradition, in which Scottish missionaries were represented as the heirs of the Reformation.

Coverage in the Secular Press

As noted, by the late nineteenth century missionary periodicals had achieved a fairly high level of circulation amongst church members. Readership of missionary biographies was also extensive. Furthermore, the activities of missionaries were given coverage in the secular press. Indeed, the work of foreign missions had been routinely reported in newspapers such as *The Scotsman* from its early days (it was founded in 1817), for example, as part of the reporting of the General Assemblies, with public meetings of societies such as the Scottish Missionary Society and London Missionary Society also being reported.[25] Influential in heightening the public profile of missionaries was the Edinburgh *Witness* (1840-1861), founded by Hugh Miller, and which was instrumental in generating support for the secession of 1843 and remaining close to the Free Church thereafter.

---

[23] Robert Moffat was the subject of at least fifteen biographies between 1884 and 1961, with five of these being in the period examined here and a number being reprinted. At least ten biographies of Mary Slessor were published between 1915 and 2001. Alexander Duff was the subject of at least six biographies between 1879 and 1992.

[24] John MacKenzie "David Livingstone: the Construction of the Myth" in Graham Walker and Tom Gallagher Eds., *Sermons and Battle Hymns: Protestant Culture in Modern Scotland* (Edinburgh: Edinburgh University Press, 1990).

[25] See, for example, *The Scotsman*, 23 July 1823, 3 September 1823, 31 May 1826, 27 June 1827.

In addition to such routine reporting, as noted previously various episodes gave missionary work a high profile, and often led to surges of support, though this was not consistently maintained. The Indian "Mutiny" of 1857, the publication of Livingstone's *Travels* in the same year, Livingstone's death in 1873, the launch of the Livingstonia expedition in 1875, and subsequent developments in Nyasaland all attracted extensive press coverage. Publicity was not always positive, with occasional episodes of malpractice or scandal in missions being widely publicised, such as the "Blantyre atrocities" of 1879 (where missionaries were deemed to have exceeded their authority in meting out to Africans punishments of extreme severity) and the Calcutta mission "scandal" of 1883 (this involved a libel action taken by Mary Pigot against Church of Scotland missionary William Hastie, to which he responded with allegations of sexual impropriety and mismanagement against Pigot).[26] In addition debates about lack of conversions and criticisms of missionary emphasis on teaching to the detriment of preaching sometimes surfaced in *The Scotsman*. By and large, however, the higher profile of the foreign mission movement in the secular press towards the end of the nineteenth century was positive. This is in contrast to the lukewarm attitude towards missionaries expressed by Margaret Oliphant in *Blackwoods Magazine* in the late 1850s: "the missionary is not an interesting nor an attractive personage to the general eye of the world. He is the hero of a limited religious circle, who chronicle his doings and his sayings in a missionary magazine".[27] Ironically, this view found its expression in a review of Livingstone's *Travels*. No doubt there were some groups within Scottish society that maintained a sceptical attitude towards the value of missionary endeavours, but press coverage of later decades suggests a general shift in attitudes.

As well as newspaper coverage, the achievements of missionaries in exploration and science were given space in the *Scottish Geographical Magazine* (the Royal Scottish Geographical Society was founded in 1884), and the intense interest in Africa as the "scramble" between European powers developed kept Scottish missionaries in the public eye. Coverage in newspapers and secular periodicals indicates the degree to which the foreign mission movement was supported by the middle-class Scottish public, in the sense at least of popular acclaim and admiration of missionary "heroes", though levels and patterns of financial support may not have directly related to the popularity of iconic imagery and its representation of the role Scots played in "civilising" colonised peoples. By

---

[26] For a detailed account of this episode, see Orr Macdonald, *Unique and Glorious Mission*.

[27] Margaret Oliphant, "The Missionary Explorer" in *Blackwood"s Magazine*, Vol. 83, April 1858. The article was published anonymously. Attribution to Oliphant is given in Walter E. Houghton (ed.), *The Wellesley Index to Victorian Periodicals, 1824-1900*, Vol. I (Toronto: University of Toronto Press, and London: Routledge and Kegan Paul, 1966), 106.

the late nineteenth century the foreign mission movement had come to be widely represented as a Scottish contribution to the "civilising mission" of empire. This movement was not only that supported by the main Presbyterian churches but also included Scottish leading lights of the London Missionary Society, especially David Livingstone. As John MacKenzie has argued, it was possible for Livingstone to be appropriated as an icon by the divided Scottish churches as he did not belong to any of them, and it is also evident that his Scottishness came to be increasingly emphasised in Scotland into the early decades of the twentieth century.[28] In this sense then the movement was indeed influential, emblematic of Scotland's national reputation, and attracting recognition from elsewhere. As a representation of Scotland's contribution to the empire it came to be representative of pride both in Scottish identity and the British empire. Furthermore, it was also influential in shaping how people at home understood empire and how they regarded colonial peoples, a legacy that was ambiguous in that a racialised world view competed with and often overpowered egalitarian and humanitarian discourses.

Conclusion

By the late nineteenth century the Scottish Presbyterian foreign mission movement had achieved both a high public profile in Scotland and an international reputation. Eugene Stock's *Handbook of Missions*, published in 1904, applauded the pioneering efforts of a number of Scottish missionaries, and praised the "Scotch Presbyterians" for their "foremost" role in the development of educational missions and for also having led the way in medical missions.[29] His figures for missionaries of the principal British societies in 1900 indicated that Scots made up 9.7 per cent of the total, at a time (1901) when the Scottish population was around 11.6 per cent of the total UK population.[30] This rather undercuts *The Scotsman's* claim of a disproportionate contribution by Scots. What Stock's book does, however, is emphasise the tendency for Scottish missionaries to be well-educated and professionally qualified. In many ways education was central to the success of the Scottish foreign mission movement. The relative openness to higher education for men, the level of education provided for girls, and access for women to higher education towards the end of the century, all contributed to a well educated missionary workforce, which in turn promoted the value of education for others. This was crucial not just to the calibre of recruits for Scottish missions, but also to the missionary practice which they instituted. It also made Scots attractive recruits to

---

[28] John MacKenzie, "David Livingstone: the construction of the myth".
[29] Eugene Stock, *A Short Handbook of Missions* (London: Longmans, 1904).
[30] Stock, *Handbook of Missions*; population figure quoted in *Twentieth Century Facts,* Research Paper 99/111, Office for National Statistics.

societies such as the London Missionary Society. Furthermore, missionaries emerged as a professional middle-class group, notwithstanding iconic working-class figures such as Livingstone and Slessor, and thus attained a social and class position which provided links to powerful players both in Scottish society and abroad.

Within Scottish society in this period there were many overlaps between the religious and secular spheres, which facilitated the publicising of foreign mission work. For example, the leading members of elites had many interconnections, with civic leaders being active in churches and their views being shaped by religious convictions.[31] Typically coalitions of church leaders, university professors and civic leaders such as the Lord Provost, town council and local MPs came together in promotion of various public causes, including the anti-slavery movement, public meetings and exhibitions on missions, particularly from the Livingstone era onwards. Key missionary figures were also celebrated for secular achievements, for example, exploration, scientific contributions, applications of modern technology, and as educationists, as well as being celebrated as models of Christian virtue and benevolence. Such overlaps also contributed to the publicity given to missionaries in the secular press.

For all these reasons, it can be argued that the foreign mission movement had become an influential force in Scottish life by the late nineteenth century. Ross argued that the "folk-memory" of a golden age of missionary support did not reflect the reality of a period of financial difficulty, but recognised that the perceived success of missionaries in the field, especially in Africa, the high profile of missions in both the church and secular press, and the public interest demonstrated by large attendances at missionary meetings, may well have provided the basis for this view.[32] He also recognised that interest in British imperial expansion, the role of missionaries in communicating news and information about empire, and the social function of church meetings, may all have contributed to the idea that there was wide popular interest in the foreign mission movement in the late nineteenth and early twentieth centuries. The evidence considered here suggests that these factors did indeed combine to produce a high public profile for the foreign mission movement in Scotland, and also indicates that the foreign mission movement was widely regarded as a Scottish contribution to empire and as a source of national pride. Its influence in generating practical support may have fallen short of the churches' aspirations, but its influence on the popular imagination was nonetheless significant, as emblematic of Presbyterian values and of the part played by Scots in the "civilising mission" of empire.

---

[31] See Stewart J. Brown, *Providence and Empire: Religion, Politics and Society in the United Kingdom, 1815-1914* (Harlow: Pearson/Longman, 2008).
[32] Ross, "Scottish Missionary Concern".

'THE EVANGELISATION OF THE WORLD IN THIS GENERATION': VIGNETTES FROM SCOTTISH EVANGELICALS' RESPONSE 1890-2009

Rose Dowsett

In 1892, John R. Mott, who was later to play a decisive role in inspiring and chairing Edinburgh 1910, wrote a short pamphlet entitled "The Purpose of the Student Volunteer Movement". The SVM, birthed in 1888, and with Mott as its first chairman, had from the beginning adopted the motto "the evangelisation of the world in this generation". In his pamphlet, four years later, Mott wrote this explanation:

> ...the ultimate and fundamental object of the Student Volunteer Movement [is] the evangelisation of the world in this generation.... What does it mean? It does not mean the conversion, or the Christianisation, or the civilisation of the world, no matter how much the volunteers may believe in each of these. It does mean that the Christians of this generation are to give every person of this age an opportunity to accept Jesus Christ. The volunteers believe that this is an awful necessity, because without it millions will perish. They believe that it is a solemn duty because Christ has commanded it....[1]

Mott was disassociating himself from the concept of mission as western colonisation or Christianisation through power.

Eighteen years later, Mott began the Report of the Commission on "Carrying the Gospel to all the Non-Christian World" (a commission which he had chaired) with these words:

> It is a startling and solemnising fact that even as late as the twentieth century the Great Command of Jesus Christ to carry the Gospel to all mankind is still so largely unfulfilled.... Therefore, the first duty of a World Missionary Conference meeting at such an auspicious time is to consider the present world situation from the point of view of making the Gospel known to all men, and to determine what should be done to accomplish this Christ-given purpose.[2]

It is important to recognise that this was the key motivation for calling the Edinburgh 1910 conference, and indeed probably for the majority of the participants in both the event and the study process leading up to it, and that Mott's passionate vision sprang directly out of his evangelical heritage and

---

[1] Excerpt from one of the first pamphlets written by J.R. Mott (in 1892), cited in Robert C. Mackie, *Layman Extraordinary* (London: Hodder & Stoughton, 1965).
[2] W.H.T. Gairdner, *Edinburgh 1910: An Account and Interpretation of the World Missionary Conference* (Edinburgh & London: Oliphant, Anderson & Ferrier; New York, Chicago and Toronto: Fleming H. Revell, 1910).

convictions. These same convictions and the same motivation lay behind evangelical mission in the century before Edinburgh 1910, and have informed evangelical mission in the century since. And, whatever the shortcomings of the evangelical movement may be deemed to be, there are today, in the grace of God, countless Christian communities whose roots humanly speaking can be traced to evangelical pioneers who gave their lives in service to the previously non-Christian world. In many cases, no other part of the world church was engaged in pioneering in those places, and without their commitment to and understanding of Christian mission there would be no church there today.

Scottish evangelicals have played a life-bringing role in this history. As promised in our title, we can only select a few vignettes rather than tell the whole story, and almost all of them share the common thread of the Bible Training Institute, now the International Christian College. This of course is only one very small part of the Scottish evangelical story, and there are many strands which we must leave for another occasion.

D.L. Moody, and the Glasgow United Evangelistic Association

The famous American evangelist, D.L. Moody, visited Glasgow several times, the first time from February to May in 1874. At the time, Glasgow was suffering from all the consequences of accelerated expansion: in 1801, the population numbered approximately 84,000, but by 1874 that had mushroomed to nearly 900,000. The churches, on their own admission, were overwhelmed, the numbers of totally unchurched grew steadily, and every kind of vice and deprivation flourished. The Glasgow City Mission had been formed by David Naismith in 1826, the first of the great City Missions, and was doing a valiant job, warmly commended by church leaders such as Thomas Chalmers.[3] But there was much more needed, and following Moody's 1874 visit the group that had co-ordinated it formed themselves into the Glasgow United Evangelistic Association. Under the Presidency of John Campbell White, later to become Lord Overtoun, the GUEA brought together, or initiated, an astonishing range of ministries, many of them soon to be housed in a complex of purpose-built new buildings in Bothwell Street in central Glasgow.

By the time Moody made his visit in 1892, he had already set up the Bible Training Institute in Chicago, to equip laymen and women for effective ministry alongside ordained ministers, and with a particular focus on work among the poor. At its 1892 AGM, Moody challenged the GUEA committee to establish a similar institution in Glasgow. As it happened, this had already been under discussion, and almost at once the BTI came into being. By 1894, it had moved into new buildings built alongside the others

---

[3] *A Short History of Glasgow City Mission,* Centenary Report , 1926, 16.

in Bothwell Street, much of the cost covered by a legacy of £30,000 from Lord Overtoun's sister's estate.

BTI's Early Years

In 1893, at its first annual business meeting, Lord Overtoun could describe the purpose of the BTI as to reach those unreached by ministers trained in the universities. Then as now, there were large numbers of people in the city, especially among the poor, with whom the established churches were ill-equipped to connect, and who were themselves largely antagonistic to the churches. The focus for the BTI was on training men and women to be evangelists, giving thorough Bible training, and equipping them with practical ministry skills. "In the Institute," went on Lord Overtoun, "theology is taught in its biblical, spiritual and practical side, not so much in the view of controversy as of soul-winning". In 1895, he was to say the BTI aims "to provide systematic practical training in the knowledge and use of Holy Scripture, and in methods of Christian service for young men and young women who intend to occupy themselves, either wholly or in part, in labouring for the extension of the Redeemer's Kingdom, at home or abroad".[4]

By 1915, a thousand full-time students had passed through. Over half came from Scotland, about a third from England and Wales, 41 from Ireland, 17 from Germany, and 95 from 25 other countries around the world. Among the Scots, initially the largest numbers came from the Free/United Free churches, from the Mission Halls, and from the Baptists, but the college was thoroughly interdenominational. Study was not a soft option: by 1908, the curriculum included Greek, Latin, Maths, elocution, music and medicine, as well as biblical and theological studies. From the beginning, many students went overseas. For example, there were at least eight Scots among the China Inland Mission missionaries martyred in the Boxer Rebellion in 1900, and among them was John Young of Strathaven, who had studied at the BTI from 1894-6.[5] In the BTI archives is a photo taken in 1900 of 14 former BTI students in Shanghai.

The student body rapidly became international. Among the early overseas students who studied at BTI, was Canadian Jessie McDonald. She was a remarkable woman in that she was an early woman surgeon, who went from the BTI to serve from 1913 to 1939 at the CIM hospital at Kaifeng in Honan, where Scottish doctors Dr T. Murray and Dr and Mrs R.N. Walker also served. In 1939, when political upheavals made evacuation from Kaifeng necessary, Jessie McDonald transferred to Tali, now Dali, in Yunnan, where she stayed till the Revolution led to the

---

[4] From the minutes of the Annual Business Meetings of the BTI, 1893 and 1895.
[5] *China's Millions*, November 1900, 192-3 of annual bound volume. CIM's first martyr was also a Scot, William Fleming of Broughty Ferry, who died in 1898.

withdrawal of all missionaries in 1952, 39 years after her arrival in China. Still active, in 1954 she then joined the faculty of Biola School of Missionary Medicine. She died in 1980.[6] At Dali, she worked alongside other Scots, among them twins Drs John and William Toop, and William's wife, Dr Dorothy, all of whom had joined the CIM via the Edinburgh Medical Missionary Society. The Dali hospital survives to this day, now as an AIDS care hospital, whose leaders still recall with gratitude the skill and commitment of those missionary doctors.

One of the most intriguing examples of early overseas students is Che'eng Ching-yi, not least because he was one of only three Chinese national delegates to Edinburgh 1910. His seven minute speech in which he said that the Chinese mind was not interested in denominationalism made a powerful impact on the whole assembly. Ch'eng's father, brought to faith through London Missionary Society missionaries, became an LMS pastor. Through that connection, Ch'eng was invited to assist LMS missionary George Owen working on a revised translation of the New Testament into Chinese, and when Owen had to return to England for health reasons in 1903 he asked Ch'eng to accompany him. The project completed, Ch'eng then came north to study at the BTI from 1906-1908, before returning to Peking (Beijing). At the conclusion of the Edinburgh conference, Ch'eng was elected to the Continuation Committee, which later became the International Missionary Council, and while still young in a culture where age was important served as a leader of the National Christian Council. He died in 1939 while still in his fifties.[7]

The BTI had a very strong connection with the China Inland Mission, and many of its graduates went on to serve there, right up to the expulsion of missionaries in 1951-2. As early as 1909, 83 BTI graduates had gone to China, along with 45 to India and 49 to Africa.[8] That pattern continued right through the difficult years of the 1920s to 1940s, despite all the upheavals – political, economic and theological – that convulsed much of the world, Scotland included. Doctors, nurses, evangelists and church planters, Bible translators, teachers, farmers, shop staff, people with every skill imaginable, all made their way through BTI to China. But China was not the only place on the map, and we turn our attention now to Australia and New Zealand.

---

[6] www.wheaton.edu/bgc/archives/GUIDES/246.htm
[7] Howard L. Boorman ed., *Biographical Dictionary of Republican China* (New York: Columbia University Press, 1964).
[8] *Bible Training Institute Annual Report for 1908-9*, 7.

Australia and New Zealand

At a time when Scottish emigration was high,[9] and settlers were being sought for the colonies, it was natural for Scottish evangelicals to join their ranks. The Queensland Presbyterian Church had been formed by a small group of concerned Scots settlers who met at Kangaroo Point in 1849.[10] For fifty years, despite some funding from churches back in Scotland, the fledgling network in Queensland struggled to find both money and ministers. In 1899, a lay evangelist from Edinburgh by the name of Andrew Stewart arrived in Brisbane. Converted during one of D.L. Moody's visits to Scotland, Andrew Stewart was part of a well-to-do family engaged in the tweed and woollen industry, and had already gone briefly to China (where he contracted hepatitis and was soon invalided home), and then in 1897-8 had accompanied the Rev Pat Mackay, chaplain to the Cameron Highlanders, to military bases in Gibraltar, Egypt, the Holy Land, and India.

Stewart was a passionate and gifted evangelist, and as he itinerated widely around Queensland, both in the growing towns and in the outback, he became convinced of the urgent need for missionaries. He went back to Scotland, and then returned to Brisbane in 1901 with six evangelists, all of whom had trained at the BTI. Stewart paid their passage, and also their stipend. The men were contracted to stay for at least three years (after which their passage home would be paid, or they could choose to remain), must remain single until given permission to marry in order to be able to travel widely (some of them in due course married women who had trained at BTI, and who travelled out to join them), and must commit to an ongoing seven year study programme preparing them for ordained ministry, mostly within the Queensland Presbyterian Church. Over the next fifty years, until his death in 1952, Stewart personally interviewed, funded and sent about a hundred men, most of them from the BTI. The retiring Home Missions Director, the Rev William Radcliffe, wrote in 1934 to Stewart: "Thanks to you, we began to move and when the history of the Church in the first half of this century is written, I hope the historians will have the vision to perceive that you, under God, have been its moving spirit". Many of the Home Mission Charges in time became fully fledged parishes, and many of the BTI men went on to become ordained ministers. By 1928, at least eleven parishes in Brisbane alone had ministers trained initially through BTI.

One Scot who went to Queensland was Jock Sloan. Stewart was to write of him:

---

[9] Scottish emigration was at its highest shortly before the First World War.

[10] Much of the information for this section relating to Queensland in particular comes from unpublished records of the Presbyterian Church of Queensland, held in Brisbane, and from ongoing private correspondence between myself and the Rev David and Mrs Dianne Parker, Brisbane.

The greatest pioneering work was accomplished by Jock Sloan, who evangelised in Queensland for fifty years. In the first thirty years of work, he covered over a million miles, and wore out five motor cycles and nine motor cars! He travelled through trackless bushland, was caught in cloudbursts, "bogged" in black mud, lost in sandstorms, was within an ace of death again and again, and brought thousands of men and women to the knowledge of Christ's redeeming love who might never have heard but for his courage, endurance and love. Once, when preaching outside a public house, the men told him to shut up. He continued, so they tried to throw him in the Creek, but he got away (he had been a boxer), and was back the next night preaching in the same place, and this time they let him alone. He was like a bulldog for determination and loyalty.

In 1911, several ship-loads of Scottish men arrived to build the railways. Several of the BTI men held season passes, and would travel along the new lines, getting on and off the train along the route, conducting services and ministering to the labourers and the communities growing around them.

It was not only the Presbyterians in Queensland who benefited from the BTI trained men and women. At least a dozen became Baptist pastors. Among them was W.G. Reekie, who went out from Renwick United Free Church in 1920, but later moved to the Baptists. Reekie's wife also studied at BTI. The Queensland Baptist magazine of December 1923 says: ' It is also of interest that in Mrs Reekie the pastor has an excellent helpmeet, who has filled the pulpit on many an occasion with great acceptance. She was trained in the Bible Training Institute, Glasgow, and holds the diploma for the curriculum of study in that college".[11] Mrs Reekie is highly commended again in the following month's issue of the *Queensland Baptist*, with special reference to her fine preaching, and clearly made a great impression! Then as now, evangelical women missionaries often (though not always) had freedom for a wider range of ministries than would have been the case in some of the churches back home.

Sometimes the send-off for missionaries was a memorable affair for those remaining, and perhaps reflected the respect felt by the Christian community for those going overseas. In 1926, an unknown observer wrote to Andrew Stewart as follows:

Dear Mr Stewart

You will be interested to learn that Messrs Blacklock and Kerr had a great "send off" from the Waverley last night. The station was very crowded and a great testimony was borne by an enthusiastic company. The Market Hall Leith with their Gospel Waggon were up, and a large company with them, being representatives from the Christian Endeavour meetings at Market Hall, had met Mr Kerr as House Leader at Ardeneden (Tignabruich) where he acted in that capacity during August and they were present in force. Carrubbers Close came in a mass after the evening meeting. They had a march down from Byth Street, singing all the way, Mr R. Miller, Jock

---

[11] *Queensland Baptist,* December 1923, p 18.

Troup[12] and John Blacklock leading, followed by a large company of City Missionaries and C Close workers and others actively engaged in Christian work in the city. Needless to say the people in Waverley Station knew they were there and they had a rally before the train went and a further rally after the train had gone.

I have seen many companies gathered for a send off to the foreign field, but I never saw a larger more enthusiastic send off than that of that night. It must live in their memories for ever and be an inspiration and incentive to them for many a day.

While that was good, and great, we would also remember that there are two mothers with heavy hearts because their boys have gone from them.

May the Lord uphold them.

Kindest regards[13]

One further spin-off of all these BTI graduates migrating to Australia and New Zealand was that they became instrumental in the formation of numerous Bible Colleges in those countries, most of which are still alive and well and still training women and men for Christian service at home and abroad. Among them were Bible Colleges in Melbourne, Sydney, Adelaide and Auckland. Worldwide, the Bible Colleges trained more than half of all Protestant missionaries in the twentieth century, and consequently played a significant role in shaping the theology and spirituality of many Christian communities in today's Global South.

Fewer BTI graduates went to New Zealand, but the Presbyterian Church of New Zealand archives record the ministry of Daniel MacIntyre, born in Leith in 1880, and Charles Jardine Mackay, born in Glasgow in 1894. Both studied at BTI, as did MacIntyre's wife Elizabeth, and all initially went overseas as Home Missionaries, the MacIntyres directly to New Zealand, Mackay initially to New South Wales. MacIntyre, after the pattern of many of the Queensland men, was ordained in 1923 to the Presbytery of Dunedin, and continued in parish ministry till his death in 1962. Mackay went from New South Wales to San Francisco, then to Canada, and in 1933 went to New Zealand, his wife's homeland, continuing to serve as a Home Missionary till ill-health forced his retirement in 1944.[14]

Joseph William Kemp studied at BTI in its very early days from 1893 to 1895. After Baptist pastorates in Kelso, Hawick, and at Charlotte Chapel, Edinburgh (the latter from 1902-1915), he was called successively to Calvary Baptist, New York, the Metropolitan Tabernacle, London, and then in 1920 to Auckland Baptist Tabernacle. While in Edinburgh, Kemp had been instrumental in extraordinary revival, with prayer meetings every

---

[12] Jock Troup was a well-known Brethren evangelist, initially working among fishing communities and then more widely, from 1921 onwards in Scotland.
[13] Letter reproduced in *New Directions,* Presbyterian Church of Queensland magazine, 12/5 (Oct/Nov 2008).
[14] pcanz.org.nz/archives/Page 179.htm (accessed November 2009).

night for two years, and some eighteen hundred men and women professing faith: this from an initial congregation of only thirty-five.[15] In his early ministry he was passionate about prophecy, and fundamentalist in theology and spirituality, as were many of his evangelical contemporaries, but after a visit to the US in 1926 and seeing some of the worst results of fundamentalism there, his own position softened considerably. He had by then already established a small college in Auckland to train laymen and women for ministry to a scattered and largely unchurched developing population, but after his return the college adopted a more open evangelical ethos. Today this is Laidlaw College, until recently known as the Bible College of New Zealand, where many New Zealanders have been trained for ministry at home and overseas.

A Snapshot from the 1920s and 30s

The obscene tragedy of World War I and the long period of economic hardship that followed, coupled with the emasculating impact of much theological liberalism on one hand and the polarising rise of aggressive fundamentalism on the other, the latter largely driven from North America, severely damaged the nerve of Scottish churches, along with churches throughout Europe. Where at the turn of the century most Scottish churches would at least have given lip service to the need to engage in world mission, and would have agreed with Mott's famous slogan, during the 20s and 30s much of that conviction and confidence evaporated, and increasing numbers of former churchgoers concluded that Christianity had been discredited.

But at the BTI students continued to arrive, and while the older evangelical mission agencies, many of them interdenominational and some of them so-called "faith missions", tended to be growing, many new agencies were also springing up. The sense of imminent catastrophic global disaster, a far cry from the confident optimism that had informed Edinburgh 1910, led some evangelicals, especially in North America, to stress urgent evangelism as the sole rightful calling of mission, whereas Mott's use of the word "evangelisation", a term widely used in the missionary community, had been from the far rounder context of wholistic mission, which was the dominant pattern of 19th century evangelical mission.

Nonetheless, BTI continued to see its graduates going on to every kind of care and compassion ministry, education and practical service, alongside evangelism and church planting. The polarisation between evangelism and social action was far more pronounced in North America than in Britain, and the criticisms levelled at evangelicals on this score are often not borne

---

[15] Eye witness accounts can be found in J. Oswald Sanders, *Prayer Power Unlimited* (Grand Rapids: Discovery House Publishers, 1979), 163-7.

out by the practice on the ground. At the same time it would be true that evangelicals were slower than others to address political issues where those touched on aspirations for self-determination, especially within countries forming part of the British Empire, and also increasingly withdrew from some of the debates convulsing wider Protestantism. It would also be true to say that evangelicals put more emphasis on conversion and the authority of the Bible than missionaries and denominations who were retreating from both, considerable emphasis on personal pietistic spirituality, and less emphasis than some others on denominational distinctives. Nor were they especially interested in structural unification of churches. That doesn't mean that they had no recognisable ecclesiology, simply that it was different from many traditional ones, especially those that centred around a high sacramentalism and/or ministry being the exclusive preserve of ordained men.

One of the issues which had been contentious at the time of Edinburgh 1910 was the legitimacy or otherwise of Protestant missions in traditionally Orthodox or Roman Catholic countries, with so-called proselytism regarded by some as utterly outrageous. Evangelicals argued that just as there were many people in traditionally Protestant countries who were either completely unchurched or entirely nominal in their Christian "profession", and who needed to be confronted with the Gospel and urged to embark on active personal discipleship, so it was in the Orthodox and Roman Catholic contexts. The primary concern was not to make them Protestant but to bring them to lively faith in Christ. Consequently, evangelicals were engaged in mission in both contexts.

BTI graduates went to both Orthodox and Roman Catholic settings, and nationals from those contexts came to study at BTI. Amongst them was Emmanuel Gebre Selassie of Ethiopia, who studied at BTI from 1932 to 1934, and who died as recently as 1997. It is estimated that in 1936, not more than 200 Ethiopian nationals in Addis Ababa would have publicly admitted to being evangelical, but by 1932 Gebre Selassie had already been teaching at a mission school for boys. He returned there after BTI, and became a fearless evangelist. The Italian authorities planned to execute him, but after some confusion he was taken to a concentration camp in 1937 where he spent the next three years. From 1941, under a British regime, Gebre Selassie served as an interpreter for the British Legation till 1961. From 1963 he worked with the Lutheran radio station, "Voice of the Gospel", until that was shut down by the Derg regime in 1977. He served on the Board of the Ethiopian Bible Society and was one of the founding members of the YMCA in Ethiopia, claiming that his experience at BTI had convinced him that interdenominational evangelical co-operation in the cause of the Gospel was both possible and essential.[16] He is still remembered with affection and honour in Addis Ababa.

After World War II

Following the Second World War, there was a huge surge of evangelical missionaries, including men and women from Scotland. Some of them returned to places where they had served in the armed forces during the war, for instance Japan and Malaysia, wishing to contribute not only the Gospel but also some measure of reconstruction and healing instead of the destruction and violence of wartime. Some went to Africa and India, where Britain's ambiguous role as colonial power increasingly troubled many Christian consciences but also sometimes made it easier to gain access. Some went to China, or after 1950 when further entry became impossible, went elsewhere in Asia instead. Some went to Latin America, which had not been a very strong destination for British evangelicals up till then, other than some Anglicans and some Brethren. Many of this generation were a little older when they embarked on their missionary careers, and had lived through tough experiences during the war years. This reflected both in the age of incoming students to BTI and also in the life experiences that they brought with them.

BTI remained in the thick of things, steadily doing what it did best, training people in evangelism and ministry skills, in a deep love of the Scriptures, in theology, and in the vital place of faith and prayer. In the midst of an increasingly dark and pessimistic world, and with many of the older northern churches losing their nerve and any confidence in Scripture or the Gospel, evangelicals were frequently more and more distinct in their understanding and practice of mission. Contrary to charges often laid against them, British evangelicals remained deeply committed to a wide range of compassion ministries, to education, and to development, but were unwilling to separate this from evangelism, and remained convinced of the need of those of other faiths to hear the Gospel and of the uniqueness of Christ and of Christian revelation.

So it was that David Ellis, an engineer, and then a student at BTI from 1959 to 1961 could write as follows:

> The prevailing ethos was that of a warm family/community with a very strong emphasis on Bible content and a devotional prayer life.... I don't think we ever heard the term "missiology" or ever thought of it as some science yet the fact that Mr MacBeath [the Principal at the time] had served with the BMS in Congo meant that he breathed missions through all that he said so that the whole ethos of his teaching and indeed that of BTI was saturated with

---

[16] See Johannes Launhardt, *Evangelicals in Addis Ababa (1919-1991): with special reference to the Ethiopian Church Mekane Yesus and the Addis Ababa Synod* (Berlin, Hamburg and Munster: LIT Verlag, 2005).

missions.... And I think we learned a great deal from him about serving the emerging churches and being willing to work under national leadership.[17]

David Ellis married the Principal's daughter, Adele, and together they went to Indonesia to work under a national church, followed later by mission leadership in Indonesia, Singapore and the UK. Others studying at BTI in the same period also highlight the emphasis on prayer and grasp of the Scriptures, along with practical ministry experience locally, and also regular opportunities to meet missionaries on home leave, coupled with many prayer groups.

Rowland and Kathie Bell studied at BTI in the early 1950s. Bell, like so many of the much earlier BTI students, came from a humble village background and had had very limited formal education. BTI helped establish in him a joyous habit of lifelong learning. This fed a passionate desire to enable new Christian believers in rural Thailand, with similarly limited formal education, to study the Bible for themselves and along with it material that would equip them for effective ministry. Bell's hair-raising adventures as he travelled by motorbike to scattered young believers became legendary. In time this led to the development of a Home Bible Seminary, for which Bell wrote and painstakingly roneo-ed all the study materials for years, and which continues to be a vital tool in helping establish local churches throughout central Thailand. By 2009, several hundred Thai have either completed the course or are currently studying on it, and many have become pastors or church leaders.

The Bells were only one couple from among many Scots who went to Thailand from the early 1950s onwards. There were very few churches in Thailand at the time, and such as there were, were almost only to be found in the cities and largest of towns: this at a time when well over 70% of Asians were rural or tribal. There is nothing glamorous about living in a community where nobody has met a Christian before, and patiently seeking to establish a witness there, nor is it something that can be done without long-term commitment, long years of language and culture learning, and prayerful dependence on God. BTI graduates, and other Scottish evangelicals, have played a significant role under God in a growing Thai church, both among Thai and the tribal minorities, with national pastors and leadership, Bible schools and seminaries, and the beginnings of a missionary movement to other parts of the world. Many expatriates, of course, now work under the direction of national leaders, or in partnership with them, but national leaders still also ask for expatriate pioneers. Whatever may be the situation in some other parts of the world, for instance Latin America or sub-Saharan Africa, it is a mistake to claim that the need for expatriate missionaries is past in Asia. That is emphatically not the case, though today's missionaries may come from many different parts of the world.

---

[17] Personal correspondence, 9 July 2009.

But in the past 50 years, many Scots, from BTI and elsewhere, have gone on missionary service in Africa. Scottish missionary links with Africa trace back long before Edinburgh 1910, for example through Robert Moffatt and David Livingstone, and at the time of the conference Mary Slessor was still active in Nigeria, though drawing to a close after (then) nearly forty years of extraordinary ministry. Since World War II, Scottish evangelicals have been deeply involved in medical work, helped establish colleges and universities, worked in many roles with the churches under national leadership, initiated sustainable water and sanitation projects, championed the cause of the vulnerable and brought hope to the hopeless.

BTI has played its part in this. One person who would have thrilled D.L. Moody's heart was Bill Gilvear. Gilvear arrived at BTI having evaded almost all education during a deeply dysfunctional, violent and poverty-stricken Glasgow childhood and gangland teens. He came to faith through the Tent Hall Mission, one of the many ministries associated with the Glasgow United Evangelistic Association with which our story began, and some years later became convinced that God was calling him into missionary service in Africa. BTI took this "rough diamond"[18] and gently nurtured him, so that in due time he was able to go with the Unevangelised Fields Mission to Congo. He served as a missionary nurse through the troubled early 1960s but was back in Scotland when the Simba rebellion exploded. Many of his colleagues and national friends were killed, but Bill returned to Congo to help with relief to the suffering churches. Two years later, with violence erupting again, Bill was evacuated once more, but the love and commitment he had shown by returning to such a volatile and dangerous situation had brought joy and encouragement to many Congolese believers. He returned yet again, this time married to Margaret, who had been working with Sunday Schools. Together, despite many setbacks, they were able to spend a further couple of years serving the church before being invalided home, where they continued to encourage prayer for a troubled country and a hurting church.

Katie MacKinnon was another BTI graduate who brought the compassion of the Lord Jesus to Africa, this time to Kenya. With a fierce, obstinate love for very sick babies, many of them premature or twins in a culture that deemed them cursed, Katie set about rescuing them. Initially caring for them in her own small home, along with her regular work as a hospital nurse, she was gradually able to train and employ Kenyans to work with them in several different locations. Eventually, numerous centres were established, and purpose-built and equipped Homes set up, in teamwork with the Africa Inland Churches.

Sometimes men or women, themselves discipled by BTI graduates, have come from their distant homelands to study in Scotland. One such was a

---

[18] Sheana Brown, *Rough Diamond: the Life Story of Bill Gilvear* (Fearn: Christian Focus, 1996).

West African bishop, whose vibrant faith was a blessing to the whole college community. After his first term, unfamiliar with the treachery of icy Glasgow pavements, he slipped and fell and broke his hip, and spent the next few months in an orthopaedic ward. Joyously he set about sharing the gospel with all his fellow patients, most of them like himself there for a long time, and led one after another to faith in Christ.

The Tradition Continues

In 1990, the BTI was formally separated from the GUEA, and became the Glasgow Bible College. In turn, joining forces with Northumbria Bible College in 1998, the combined college became the International Christian College. From this combined heritage, at the present time alumni/graduates are serving in around sixty different countries. In addition, many more who formerly served overseas are still actively engaged in Christian ministry back in the UK or other home country, helping their congregations think and pray globally as well as locally. At present, as down through the years, Scottish evangelicals, and evangelicals trained in Scotland, are evangelists and church planters, Bible translators and radio workers, pastors and youth workers, agriculturalists, professionals of every hue. Some work with street children, abused women, children caught up in the sex trade, orphans, or victims of AIDS. Some serve through development projects. Some encourage believers in places very hostile to the gospel, or are still a bridgehead of witness where there is no believing community as yet. Some are leaders in well established national churches, some are scholars, missiologists or apologists. Some have returned to the acute mission field of Scotland, where their cross-cultural experience could be very valuable as Scottish churches face up to reaching a population increasingly alienated from them.

During the past century many things have changed, and some are exactly the same. Much of Scottish Protestantism, and some other traditions, too, have lost confidence in the gospel, in the Word of God, and the uniqueness of Christ, and their concept of mission would be unrecognisable to our forebears of 1910. While gladly conceding that a hundred years ago, world mission from the north and west was too often skewed by political and economic power, by simplistic assumptions about cultural superiority, and all those other things that we are wearily accustomed to being condemned for, we should not lose sight of those elements that under God birthed churches where there were none, many of them now vibrant and numerous and growing. Authentic mission now as then requires a combination of word, deed and character, reflecting the grace and being and activity of the Triune God.

During the 20th century, the academy has shifted its focus from the mission of the church, to the Missio Dei, to the mission of the Spirit, with plenty of other dominant themes along the way: reconciliation, justice, liberation.... The thoughtful practitioner meanwhile knows, and has always known, that mission is all of these, not one or another. Evangelicalism has been labelled activist, and so it is, if that means actually doing something, though evangelicals have sometimes been simplistic or too wedded to strategies. But genuine evangelicalism has always also known that alongside obeying the command of Christ to make disciples as one goes, must be fervent prayer because God alone can create life out of death and light out of darkness. Part of the Scottish evangelical missionary story has been the tradition of many prayer groups, of encouraging prayer through letters and visits, magazines and books. Unashamedly, and against the forces of political correctness and theological liberalism, evangelicals continue to believe that men and women, boys and girls, not only need to hear the gospel, see it at work transformingly, experience its compassion, they also need to respond and convert to become disciples of Christ, and that all three persons of the Trinity, and the Lord's people, have a part in that.

At the same time, there is no room for triumphalism. If the gospel calls for conversion, then whichever part of the church family we come from, there needs to be painful recognition that much of the way we live out our Christian profession in Scotland, and from Scotland, is a denial of the gospel. Evangelicals have not always engaged in the kind of critical reflection that rightly needs to go on, or have wrongly brushed aside some of the legitimate challenges raised by other theologies, by other faiths, by secularism, and by scholarship. For these things we need to repent. But we also affirm that Mott's passionate plea for "the evangelisation of the world in this generation" is as urgent and as pertinent now as then. We pray that in the grace of God, Scottish Christians will continue to play their part in that.

ANDREW ROSS AND THE RADICAL STRAND IN SCOTLAND'S MISSIONARY TRADITION

John McCracken

Andrew Ross, who died in July 2008, was a distinguished missionary historian; he was also a long-term friend of Malawi and a staunch advocate of human justice. In this chapter I seek to explore the relationship between Ross's personal beliefs and experiences and his academic concerns. A respected member for more than 30 years of Edinburgh University's Faculty of Divinity, Ross was a thoroughly professional academic who set high standards of scholarship. But, to a degree that set him apart from many of his academic colleagues, he was also a committed activist convinced that the aim of scholarship should be not just to understand the world but to make it a better place. Much of his writing, in consequence, focused on the activist strand in the Scottish missionary tradition, a strand exemplified in Ross's analysis by three remarkable individuals, John Philip, David Livingstone and David Clement Scott. All three, like Andrew Ross himself, spoke out against the racism of the societies in which they lived. All were committed to the creation of more just, more humane societies. All, even Livingstone so Ross demonstrates, were prepared to confront secular governments with their shortcomings should the occasion require. And each one of them, Ross suggests, combined a sensitivity to global events and intellectual influences with a profound sense of Scottishness. Indeed, in the paper which he was planning to write for this collection, Ross aimed to advance the argument that Scottish campaigning groups played a crucial role both in the shaping of modern Malawi and also, through their campaigning, in articulating a renewed sense of Scottish identity.[1]

The Missionary Activist

In March 1959, as a young Scottish clergyman, Andrew Ross entered the pulpit at the Presbyterian Church in Zomba, the then capital of Nyasaland (present-day Malawi). Only a matter of days earlier, the colonial government had declared a state of emergency in the territory leading to the killing of nearly 60 Malawians by government forces and the detention without trial of 1,300 of their compatriots. Ross at that time had spent only a few months in Nyasaland but as a firm socialist, with first-hand

---

[1] For useful accounts of Ross's career see Kenneth R. Ross, "Andrew Ross: CCAP Minister, Church Historian and Social Activist", *Religion in Malawi* 15 (2008-09), 43-45; and Stewart J. Brown and David Fergusson, "The Rev Andrew Ross: Missionary and Church Historian", *The Independent*, 3 September 2008.

experience in 1957-58 of racial injustice in New York's East Harlem, there was no question as to what his stance must be. In an uncompromising sermon, delivered to a shocked European congregation composed largely of colonial officials and their families, he spelt out the message that "God has built into history such a law that any nation or group of people who set themselves against God's demands of love, justice and mercy will surely destroy themselves." God had been mocked by Hitler's Nazi state and that had been destroyed. God was being mocked in South Africa's apartheid state and it would be swept away. God was also being mocked in the Central African Federation, of which Nyasaland was a part: "where men talk glibly of multi-racism and partnership and all the while mean white supremacy". Without a change in attitude that state would also fall.[2]

Writing a few days later to George Macleod, the founder of the Iona Community, Ross made his convictions clear. Church of Scotland missionaries, he believed, had the duty of speaking out against colonial oppression on behalf of their African parishioners even if that meant breaking the emergency regulations.[3] In the course of the subsequent year, he took on the role of chaplain at Kanjedza Camp, where most of the detainees were held and established close relations with a number of the leading nationalists. To the concern of senior church officials in Scotland, he became one of the first two Europeans to join the Malawi Congress Party and later stood, unsuccessfully, as an MCP candidate for parliament. In a move of equal importance, Ross became a highly successful parish minister in Balaka and Ntcheu, identifying himself closely with the local communities and speaking Chinyanja with fluency. It was a matter of great personal regret to him and his family that he was forced to leave Malawi in 1965 following the split between the Prime Minister Kamuzu Banda and his younger ministers, some of whom had become close personal friends of Ross. Not until the fall of the Banda regime in the 1990s was he able to return.

Ross's subsequent career as missionary historian in Edinburgh has been admirably sketched elsewhere but three features require amplification. First, and from the time that he set about his PhD thesis, later published as *Blantyre Mission and the Making of Modern Malawi,* Ross was able to bring to his scholarship the insights gained not simply as a missionary but as an active rural parish minister.[4] This meant, at one level, that he could draw on his personal experiences of dealing with everyday Malawian moral problems in writing about such issues as witchcraft and initiation ceremonies. It also meant that could empathise with individuals like David Clement Scott, whose personal frustrations with what he saw as a

[2] Notes of sermon in Andrew Ross to George Macleod, 17 March 1959, Macleod of Fuinary Papers, National Library of Scotland Acc. 9084/68.
[3] Ross to Macleod, 17 March 1959, *ibid.*
[4] Andrew C. Ross, *Blantyre Mission and the Making of Modern Malawi* (Blantyre, Malawi: CLAIM, 1996).

conservative-minded home board were mirrored by Ross's own experiences. Secondly, Ross stressed the importance of Scottish culture and identity in shaping the attitudes of figures like Philip and Livingstone in a manner that that was at odds with much historical writing in the 1970s and 80s, though not with the work of his Edinburgh PhD supervisor, George Shepperson, a pioneer in this field.[5] Finally, and perhaps most importantly, he wrote as a committed activist, anxious to demonstrate in the lives of those he discussed qualities of relevance to the battle for a better life today. Many academic historians see publication primarily as a means of enhancing their careers. Ross, by contrast, looked to the past to uncover examples of individual Scots whose struggles against racism and injustice could inspire those committed to similar campaigns in the present. The life stories of John Philip, for 30 years the highly controversial champion of African rights in South Africa, of David Livingstone, the great explorer and of David Clement Scott the visionary leader of the Blantyre Mission, differed in many respects. But in his three major African-focused monographs Ross demonstrates the common commitment of his subjects to the creation of non-racist, just societies

The Historian

In the introduction to his biography of John Philip, published in 1986, Andrew Ross points to the paradox that the best known, in some circles most hated, missionary in South Africa was almost completely unknown in his homeland.[6] In previous generations the prevailing tendency among Scottish missionary biographers had been to focus on individuals such as Robert Moffat or Mary Slessor who could be portrayed as selfless pioneers working beyond the confines of the imperial state. Philip, the archetypical "political missionary", who spent most of his life in Cape Town deeply embroiled in a series of political and ecclesiastical disputes, did not fit the mould. Yet, as Ross demonstrates, Philip's role in the Cape Colony between 1819 and the late 1840s in championing the cause of the exploited Khoi people was of great importance. Ross's initial contribution to our understanding of Philip is to situate him in his Scottish context, as a Lowlander who had witnessed at first-hand the collapse and then, as he saw it, regeneration of Highland society and who looked for a similar transformation among the African peoples of South Africa. As Ross notes, Philip combined this essentially optimistic belief in the stimulating impact of education and free trade with his commitment to a fiercely egalitarian strain of evangelicalism which emphasised the equality of all souls before

---

[5] See for example George Shepperson, "David Livingstone the Scot", *Scottish Historical Review*, 39 (1969), 113-21.

[6] Andrew Ross, *John Philip (1775-1851): Missions, Race and Politics in South Africa* (Aberdeen: Aberdeen University Press, 1986), 1-2.

Christ and was militantly opposed to slavery. In consequence, as resident director of the London Missionary Society at the Cape, he took the lead in the ultimately successful campaign to extend civil rights in the Colony to the Khoi while at the same time clashing with Robert Moffat and other missionaries who were critical of his political activities.

Ross ends his study with the provocative suggestion that the one man who could successfully have taken up Philip's mantle as the defender of African interests, had he remained in South Africa, was David Livingstone. This is a view that the great majority of Livingstone's biographers would reject on the grounds that the explorer's South African years were merely a prelude to his travels in Central Africa. However, Ross goes out to substantiate his assertion in some detail in his biography, *David Livingstone: Mission and Empire* (2006).[7] As in *John Philip*, Ross emphasises the importance of the Scottishness of his subject, even in circumstances that do not cast a favourable light upon him. Hence, "Livingstone's readiness to take offence and maintain a feud-like antagonism towards those who, in his eyes, had betrayed him can be explained by some consideration of the culture that helped shape him." Oliver Ransford, an earlier biographer, "who saw these things in Livingstone as signs of a clinical case of manic-depressive personality, clearly had never been in a pub in Coatbridge or Sauchiehall Street."[8] On a slightly different note, Ross stresses the extent to which Livingstone's Scottish Calvinist faith was modified by the belief, drawn from the American Awakening, that Jesus died for all not just for the "elect". This in turn led him to the conviction, previously articulated by Philip, of the need to transform the world as well as to save souls. In particular, he held that there was a moral requirement to condemn slavery and slave-trading outright rather than to compromise with those involved as many early missionaries had done.

Ross's Livingstone is thus a fiercer, more controversial, more political figure than the one depicted by many earlier biographers. As Ross rightly emphasises, one of Livingstone's central characteristics was his passionate commitment to the essential equality of human beings of all races at a time when in Britain such views were being routinely derided by the proponents of Social Darwinism and "Scientific Racism". In a direct repudiation of those scholars who have depicted Livingstone as a missionary imperialist, committed by 1857 to the creation of colonies in Central Africa, Ross points to the explorer's spirited support of Xhosa attempts to defend their land during the War of Mlanjeni in 1850. Indeed in 1852, so Ross demonstrates quoting from a hitherto unpublished draft article, Livingstone condemned Britain for applauding Kossuth's struggle for freedom in

---

[7] Andrew Ross, *David Livingstone: Mission and Empire* (London, Hambledon: Continuum, 2006).

[8] Ross, *Livingstone,* 52.

Hungary while at the same time seeking to crush the Xhosa people, who were "fighting as bravely for nationality as ever Magyar did". In Livingstone's view, based, in part it would seem, on his interpretation of Scottish history: "No nation ever secured its freedom without fighting for it. And every nation on earth worthy of freedom is ready to shed blood in its defence."[9] Livingstone, prior to and during his famous Zambesi Expedition from 1858 to 1864, did propose schemes for the establishment of small Christian settlements in the Malawi region. In that sense, the Blantyre and Livingstonia Missions founded following his death drew upon Livingstone's legacy for inspiration. But, as Ross makes clear, he had no time for large-scale colonies of white settlement such as Cecil Rhodes was to establish south of the Zambesi.

Ross's ambition to write a biography of David Clement Scott was thwarted by the destruction of Scott's family papers. But in his PhD thesis, subsequently published under the title *Blantyre Mission and the Making of Modern Malawi*, Ross goes a considerable distance to demonstrate the significance of the man.[10] It is a tribute to his research that, in the late 1950s when Ross began work in Nyasaland, little or nothing was known about Scott, even in missionary circles. In publications of the day admiring tributes were made to the two great missionary barons, Robert Laws of Livingstonia and Alexander Hetherwick, Scott's successor at Blantyre. Their pioneering contribution as mission-builders, happy to work in close alliance with the colonial state, was contrasted favourably with the activities of the new generation of Scottish missionaries, Ross among them, who were depicted as left-wing anti-colonial meddlers, all too keen "to project themselves into the political field".[11] It must have been deeply satisfying to Ross that, as his researches deepened, David Scott emerged as a spiritual forebear, sharing many of his own concerns. The son of a middle-class lawyer, educated at Edinburgh University, Scott came from a very different social sphere to that of Philip and Livingstone. But like them he brought to Africa a deep commitment to racial equality that permeated much that he attempted at Blantyre between 1881 and 1898. Through his prompting, a genuinely African church began to emerge, one in which Malawians held positions of considerable responsibility. What is more, with the development of the church went clashes with the Home Committee which was concerned both by Scott's cavalier way with his budget and also by his introduction of non-Presbyterian elements into Church services.

---

[9] Quoted in Ross, *Livingstone*, 71.

[10] Ross, *Blantyre Mission*.

[11] Frank Debenham, *Nyasaland: Land of the Lake* (London: HMSO, 1955), 143-44. Much harsher assessments can be found in a confidential pamphlet circulated by the Nyasaland Government to selected journalists and used in the pamphlet, *The Kirk's New Face in Africa*, published by the pro-Federation Rhodesia and Nyasaland Committee.

It was with the new colonial government, however, that Scott had his greatest difficulties. Like Philip he was not opposed to the extension of imperial power as such and indeed played an active part in the Scottish-based campaign that led to the British annexation of much of the Malawi region in 1891. However, while Scott envisaged the creation of a system of loose overrule in which the rights of local chiefs would be protected, Harry Johnston, the first Commissioner and Consul-General, committed himself to a series of military expeditions during which British paramountcy was established by force. In the conflict that followed, as Ross vividly demonstrated, Scott and his lieutenant Hetherwick repeatedly clashed with Johnston over the legitimacy of his campaigns and also over the high rate of tax he imposed. They also robustly opposed the threatened takeover of Nyasaland by Cecil Rhodes's British South Africa Company in the first round of a protracted campaign aimed at bringing Nyasaland under the control of settler-dominated Southern Rhodesia.[12] Here, therefore, was another activist missionary, insistent, in the great tradition exemplified by Philip and Scott, in confronting injustice even when that meant criticising the colonial government outright.

It will not escape the reader that this essay sketches the activities of four activist missionaries, not just three. When Andrew Ross and his family arrived in Nyasaland late in 1958 his knowledge of David Scott was confined to the limited comments made about him in George Shepperson and Thomas Price's *Independent African*, a magnificent study of the 1915 Nyasaland Rising, published that year.[13] However, if he could not look for inspiration to Scott's anti-colonial activities, he could refer to the popular Livingstone tradition which emphasised the role of the explorer in making Nyasaland a land of particular interest to Scots. And he could also draw on the experiences of a select group of liberal-minded Scottish missionaries already working in the country, among them Tom Colvin, Albert McAdam and Hamish and Anne Hepburn. Scholars elsewhere have frequently been inspired by historical figures. But in the case of Ross it looks as if he acted first and found inspiration afterwards through researches covering more than 40 years. Thus, when he began as a young missionary to travel in the countryside, stopping off in Malawian homes and eating local food, he did so with the ambition of getting as close as possible to his parishioners. Yet he quickly discovered from these same parishioners that in acting in this way he was mirroring the behaviour of David Clement Scott and of Robert

---

[12] See particularly Andrew C, Ross, "The African – A Child or a Man" in Eric Stokes and Richard Brown Eds., *The Zambesian Past: Studies in Central African History* (Manchester: Manchester University Press, 1966).

[13] It is worth noting that Roland Oliver's *Sir Harry Johnston and the Scramble for Africa* (London: Chatto & Windus), was published in 1959. This contained a highly critical account of the Blantyre Mission's relations with Johnston, an account which Ross went out of his way to refute in his pioneering 1966 article, "The African – A Child or a Man."

Napier, an exceptionally able young missionary who was killed in 1918 and who was still warmly remembered in southern Malawi four decades later. It was only subsequently, through his researches on Philip and Livingstone, that Ross was able to demonstrate that, far from being an aberration, as the Nyasaland Government claimed, he and his fellow-missionaries were following a proud tradition of Scottish missionary activism extending back 140 years in their opposition to the Central African Federation. It his singular achievement both to have both chronicled this story and to have participated actively within it.

EDINBURGH 1910 AND SCOTTISH EXPERIENCE OF SERVING IN MISSION 1950-2000

Kenneth R. Ross and James L. Wilkie

Scots and the Missionary Experience

Edinburgh 1910 has often been discussed in terms of the effect which it has had on mission theology and policy.[1] This chapter, by contrast, seeks to examine the lived experience of people who were influenced by the movement which emerged from the famous 1910 conference. In so doing, it aims to shed light on the significance of the conference as well as unearthing an aspect of Scotland's story that has not always been adequately recognised. A wealth of raw material was generated by a day conference on "Roots and Fruits: Retrieving Scotland's Missionary Story" which was held at the International Christian College in Glasgow on 25 April 2009. Participants were invited to write a 1,000 word reflection on their experience. Thirty-three chose to do so. These were people who had gone overseas from Scotland in the service of God's mission. Their experience extended to Argentina, Bhutan, Belgium, France, the Netherlands, Ghana, Hong Kong, India, Israel/Palestine, Jamaica, Kenya, Madagascar, Malawi, Nigeria, Pakistan, South Africa, and Zambia.

They were asked not to offer a narrative of what transpired through missionary work in the countries where they served, but rather, to try to reveal the inner spirit and guiding philosophy that inspired the effort. What was the aim of Scottish missionary work? What were its core values? What were its main spiritual and intellectual dimensions? Lest this seem too abstract an approach for some, an alternative approach suggested was that they might use the project to review their own personal involvement overseas, reflecting on the expectations, the reality and the outcomes of their missionary service. E. Stanley Jones starts his famous book *The Christ of the Indian Road* with these words: "When the early evangelists of the Good News were sent out on their own, they returned and told Jesus 'what they had done and what they had taught'. This evangelist must add a third to what he had done and what he has taught – *what he has learned*."[2] This would be true of many, if not all, of those whose reflections inform this

---

[1] See, e.g., Brian Stanley, *The World Missionary Conference, Edinburgh 1910* (Grand Rapids and Cambridge: Eerdmans, 2009); David A. Kerr & Kenneth R. Ross eds., *Edinburgh 2010: Mission Then and Now* (Oxford: Regnum, 2009).
[2] E. Stanley Jones, *The Christ of the Indian Road* (London; Hodder & Stoughton, 1925), 15, our italics.

chapter. Without exception, they are deeply grateful for the experience they had and what stands out is how much they learned through it.

Five themes recurred in the papers which were presented:
1. How the legacy of 1910 worked out in the implementation of mission policy.
2. How individual people obeyed and developed God's call to be a missionary.
3. Mission amidst social and political change.
4. Was there a distinctively Scottish dimension to missionary involvement?
5. Seeking to serve God's mission today.

The Legacy of Edinburgh 1910
in the Implementation of Mission Policy

Where there is abundant evidence of the legacy of the Edinburgh 1910 World Missionary Conference is in regard to what was then described as "The Church on the Mission Field".[3] As the 20th century progressed the "younger churches", established through missionary initiatives, matured in strength. The role of the missionary was to "decrease" in order that local leaders might "increase". As Tony Ashcroft looks back on his years in Madagascar from 1958 he reflects: "Since leaving the Tanala [forest people] in the hands of a very capable local pastor I am convinced that my decision to hand over my missionary responsibility to the Malagasy church was the right one. Over the years my oversight of the churches in the Betsileo area was taken over by local leaders and the pastoral college where I had become director was given to someone more capable than I was. To me this was success."[4]

In terms of authority and governance, this meant that the missionary-controlled Mission Councils gave way to government by the appropriate bodies of the local church. Anne Hepburn recalls that in Blantyre, Malawi, during the 1950s, "the policy of integration was agreed and implemented gradually. For a short time there was a joint council of elected missionaries and African representatives of the Church. When this joint council was dissolved all authority passed to the Blantyre Synod of the CCAP by which time Church of Scotland ministers were fully recognised ministers of the CCAP."[5] In a parallel movement at Livingstonia, in the north of Malawi, the Mission Council was dissolved and, as Eric Jeffrey recalls: "There was

---

[3] See World Missionary Conference, 1910, *The Church in the Mission Field,* Report of Commission II (Edinburgh & London: Oliphant, Anderson & Ferrier; New York, Chicago, and Toronto: Fleming H. Revell, 1910).

[4] Tony Ashcroft, "Roots and Fruits – Madagascar", paper presented to "Roots and Fruits" conference, Glasgow, 25 April 2009, 3.

[5] Anne Hepburn, "Roots and Fruits – Malawi 1950-1966", paper presented to "Roots and Fruits" conference, Glasgow, 25 April 2009, 1.

a very moving service in Livingstonia church where all ministers and elders formally left the Church of Scotland and were welcomed into the CCAP [Church of Central Africa Presbyterian]. For probably the first time in all of Central and Southern Africa, Africans had authority over Europeans. The trust was in the belief that they would use this new power responsibly. We were not disappointed."[6]

Janet Brown provides a good example of the understanding of missionary vocation which had come to prevail by the 1960s: "I was to be a living expression of the partnership between the Church of Scotland and the Church of Pakistan, a link between those partners, sharing in the life and work of the Church in Pakistan and having a part in equipping its members to be 'the people of God in Pakistan' and in serving the wider community through its educational work."[7] The experience of becoming fully accepted as part of the local church was a deeply moving one for many missionaries during the middle years of the 20th century. Dorothy Wallace, who served at Darjeeling in north India, recalls; "The Synod Executive decided to appoint six delegates to visit all parts of Rajasthan and report to Synod. My name was suggested as one of the delegates but someone said, 'she's a foreign missionary'. The Moderator replied, 'She's here as an elected member, not as a foreign missionary, so she has every right to represent the Synod.' I was appointed one of the delegates to visit Rajasthan which was a wonderful experience, and I really felt I had accomplished what God wanted me to be – a part of his church in North India."[8] Likewise Margaret MacGregor recalls that: "The Bengal Church Council (United Church of Northern India) was the first to have Integration ... and those of us who had come from abroad, sent by the Church of Scotland or the London Missionary Society, felt that we were treated as people, not as a race apart, and were expected to play a full part in the life of the church."[9]

Somewhat against its original intention, Edinburgh 1910 cast a vision of growing ecumenical convergence leading to organic unity of the churches.[10] It was a vision which found remarkable fulfilment in mid-century in such countries as China and India. Yet it is a vision which has receded in more recent decades. As Murdoch Mackenzie comments sadly: "As we approach the centenary of Edinburgh 1910 I suppose our biggest

---

[6] Eric W.S. Jeffrey, "Roots and Fruits – Northern Malawi", paper presented to "Roots and Fruits" conference, Glasgow, 25 April 2009, 3.

[7] Janet Brown, "Reflections on Time Spent in Pakistan", paper presented to "Roots and Fruits" conference, Glasgow, 25 April 2009, 1.

[8] Dorothy Wallace, "Darjeeling, Eastern Himalaya Diocese, Church of North India", paper presented to "Roots and Fruits" conference, Glasgow, 25 April 2009, 1-2.

[9] Margaret S. MacGregor, "Roots and Fruits: Bengal", paper presented to "Roots and Fruits" conference, Glasgow, 25 April 2009, 1.

[10] See Stanley, *The World Missionary Conference,* 277-302.

disappointment in life is the lack of seriousness with which most churches and most Christians entertain the possibility of full organic unity."[11]

What did happen was that a stream of missionary co-operation flowed through Edinburgh 1910. In the mission "fields", comity agreements among missionary organisations (mentioned by Norman Macrae as already existing in Nigeria), developed in almost all the areas where the Church of Scotland's missionaries operated and led to individual countries being "divided up" among those seeking to do mission there: "You go to the left hand and I will go to the right". This in turn reduced rivalry and led in time, first to cooperation through Missionary Associations and Christian Councils, and later, as trust developed, to united national churches. The United Church of Zambia, founded in 1965, was one of these. The mission board of the Church of Scotland wholeheartedly embraced this tradition. It was led in this by James Dougall who was massively influential in the formative post-War years,[12] and later Lesslie Newbigin was its inspiration.[13]

The Missionary Call

"You touch the heart of the modern missionary movement when you enter this sphere [of the missionary call]. For while it is a movement which has many dimensions and is capable of being considered from many different angles, it was with this sense of call that every missionary career began and it was this inner momentum which lent a distinctive quality to missionary service."[14] This distinctive sense of being called to missionary service clearly marked the experience of the pioneering missionaries of the 19th century and it remained sharp and definitive in the later years of the 20th century. This can be illustrated by a number of examples which also show the variety of forms in which the missionary call could be received.

Elspeth Kerr recalls how her journey to service at Tabeetha School in Jaffa began on a winter's evening in 1969 at Jordanhill Church in Glasgow: "My minister, the Revd Dr Michael Orr preached from St Luke chapter 12 and took his text from verse 4: "Everyone to whom much is given, of him will much be required.' What had this to do with me? I had a wonderful teaching job, which I so enjoyed, and a busy social life. Why should I give

---

[11] Murdoch and Anne Mackenzie, "Roots and Fruits: Madras, India, 1966-1978", paper presented to "Roots and Fruits" conference, Glasgow, 25 April 2009, 2.
[12] See further Kenneth R. Ross, "James Dougall 1896-1980: Architect of Scottish Post-War Foreign Mission Policy", *Records of the Scottish Church History Society*, XXXVII (2007), 183-206.
[13] See further Geoffrey Wainwright, *Lesslie Newbigin: A Theological Life*, Oxford: Oxford University Press, 2000.
[14] Kenneth Ross, "Serving by Going: The Missionary Call Then and Now", in David Wright and David Stay ed., *Serving the Word of God* (Edinburgh: Rutherford House, 2002), 121.

it all up? The call of God was so insistent that I could do no other and so it was to Jaffa that I came."[15]

The missionary movement often acted as its own recruiting agent with missionary vocation being nurtured through family life and circles of friends. Alasdair Morton recalls that, "An aunt had been a missionary in Manchuria.... She and other missionaries I met on furlough further whetted my appetite for following in the footsteps of some. Africa particularly interested and challenged me and I read widely in that area. In second year at secondary school I made my commitment not only to Christ as his follower but to aim at missionary service in Africa."[16]

John and Muriel Berkeley were experienced medical doctors and in the midst of bringing up their family when, at the 1963 Keswick Convention, they sensed a call to "full-time" service. It took much persistence, faith and determination to see them reach the point five years later when they began their leprosy work in Bhutan. Their work helped to bring leprosy under control in Bhutan and offered a practical Christian witness in a context where proselytizing was strictly forbidden.[17]

After a lifetime in nursing, Molly Paton took the opportunity afforded by early retirement to offer for missionary service, an offer which took her to Ghana where she worked from 1992 to 1997. She is clear on the motivating factors: "The main aim was certainly to show the people of Ghana in practical ways the love of Christ. However, I feel strongly that there was an element of trying to atone for the previous involvement of the British in the slave trade."[18]

Few mission stations afforded less encouragement than the Keith Falconer Mission at Sheikh Othman in Aden, now part of Yemen. James Ritchie reflects on his experience there in the 1950s and 1960s: "A place where no one except a handful of exceptional people ever showed an interest in becoming a Christian, or if they did, they kept it to themselves, had been my place of residence and work for the best part of nine years. I was walking to my house over arid ground in the intense heat of the sun and thinking to myself, Why am I here at all? What is the value of the Mission's presence among these people? The answer was another question, prompted, I believe, by the Holy Spirit: 'Are you not here because God has called you to be here?' My heart and mind responded immediately:

---

[15] Elspeth Kerr, "Roots and Fruits – Israel/Palestine", paper presented to "Roots and Fruits" conference, Glasgow, 25 April 2009, 1.

[16] Alasdair Morton, "Zambia", Roots and Fruits", paper presented to "Roots and Fruits" conference, Glasgow, 25 April 2009, 1.

[17] John and Muriel Berkeley, " Roots and Fruits", paper presented to "Roots and Fruits" conference, Glasgow, 25 April 2009, 1-5.

[18] Molly Paton, "My Ghanaian Experience", paper presented to "Roots and Fruits" conference, Glasgow, 25 April 2009, 1.

'Yes.'"[19] This inner sense of the call of God sustained missionary efforts amidst what could sometimes be very discouraging situations.

Those who embraced a missionary vocation, by and large, express a high degree of fulfilment. Vernon Stone, for example, recalls in regard to his years in Malawi in the 1950s that: "... not only was I preaching the Gospel constantly, I was also using all my previous education and training to keep a whole enterprise going – administering affairs, keeping accounts, even sometimes, God help them and me, supervising buildings. I was fully stretched and happy."[20]

As Clarence Musgrave reflects on his call he remarks: "It was a question of being prepared to 'be', rather than to 'do', and in the 'being' to find out what required to be done – or perhaps more pertinently, what I might be able to do, given my total lack of experience of work in any part of Africa. My recollection of the conversations with the Secretaries of the Overseas Council reinforces this rather non-specific approach. I was encouraged to look, listen and keep quiet, until I had got some experience under my belt which might equip me to make a contribution to discussions within the Church."[21]

Carol Jeffrey looks back on her years of teaching in Ghana during the 1950s and reports that; "I had the great privilege of going back in 2006 and meeting up with about 15 of my former pupils and campers and also some of the men who had been at boys' camps in the 1950s. Many had found that following Christ was often difficult, but all those I met still rejoice in his love and care. Many are still actively involved as elders and teachers in their churches and in voluntary Christian work.... How marvellous to have played a small part in this."[22]

The reflections of retired missionaries, again and again, strike this note of marvelling at how much they *received* through the exercise of their calling. Reflecting on his experience in Kenya, Laurie Campbell comments that: "'mission' is two-way traffic and ... [the missionaries'] contribution to the World Church was hugely enhanced by what they received from the people of God in Kenya, as much as by what they were able to give. Unless we see it that way then, ... our Church mission theology is still marked by its own in-built colonialism."[23]

---

[19] James McI. Ritchie, "South Arabia Mission in Sheikh Othman, a Township in Aden Colony", paper presented to "Roots and Fruits" conference, Glasgow, 25 April 2009, 1.
[20] Vernon Stone, "Reflections on Malawi 1949-56 and Zambia 1956-67", paper presented to "Roots and Fruits" conference, Glasgow, 25 April 2009, 1.
[21] Joan and Clarence Musgrave, "Roots and Fruits – Zambia", paper presented to "Roots and Fruits" conference, Glasgow, 25 April 2009, 2.
[22] Carol Jeffrey, "Gold Coast / Ghana: A Reflection", paper presented to "Roots and Fruits" conference, Glasgow, 25 April 2009, 1-2.
[23] Laurie Campbell, "Roots and Fruits – Kenya", paper presented to "Roots and Fruits" conference, Glasgow, 25 April 2009, 1-2.

People responded to God's Spirit in different ways. Some took personal responsibility for their training, and personally negotiated their placements overseas. Some were guided by a personal 'guru', e.g. Lesslie Newbigin. Most turned to their Church: "Here am I, I believe God is calling me to mission, please test my call, train me and work out with me where you believe God wants me to go." For most of the 20th century this last approach worked very well. Initial training was given partly in Scotland at St. Colm's Missionary College, and training – especially in the local language – continued "on the field" under the supervision of senior missionaries. Thus the sense of call ripened into a steady process of formation and ultimately to a period of service which proved to be very fulfilling. Though often isolated from compatriots, sometimes exposed to a significant level of danger, and always living very modestly, those who accepted and fulfilled the missionary call have no regrets that they did so.

Mission amidst Social and Political Change

The missionary engagement which resulted from acceptance of the call by both the individual and the Church was not conducted in a vacuum. Nor was its influence restricted to a private spiritual sphere. On the contrary, it has been marked by profound interaction, at every level, with its social and political context. This is well illustrated in Scotland's "special relationship" with Malawi which has ensured that missionary service has been inextricably interwoven with the political destiny of the nation, particularly at moments of crisis.[24] Anne Hepburn recalls the imposition of the State of Emergency in Nyasaland (as Malawi was then known) in 1959. The underlying cause of this crisis was the near-unanimous opposition of the African population to the racist Federation of Rhodesia and Nyasaland. Being close to the people, the Scottish missionaries were sensitive to this strong feeling and relayed the criticisms being made of the racist political arrangements to the Foreign Mission Committee of the Church of Scotland which in turn could, and did, influence British Government policy in the direction of full independence for Malawi.[25] Important in this was the fact that the Church not only spoke but acted. The passing of authority in church life from European to African hands, suggests Eric Jeffrey, "... made real impact not only in church circles but throughout Malawi and beyond as the implications of what occurred sank in. The Church was demonstrating the wind of change not only to the authorities in Malawi but also to the British Government in Westminster. It made the movement

---

[24] See further Kenneth R. Ross, "Crisis and Identity: Presbyterian Ecclesiology in Southern Malawi 1891-1993", *Missionalia*, Vol. 25 No. 3 (1997), 375-91.
[25] Anne Hepburn, "Roots and Fruits – Malawi 1950-1966", paper presented to "Roots and Fruits" conference, Glasgow, 25 April 2009, 2; see further Andrew C. Ross, *Colonialism to Cabinet Crisis: A Political History of Malawi* (Zomba: Kachere Series, 2009), 179-205.

towards independence and self-rule much smoother than it might have been."[26]

In neighbouring Northern Rhodesia (now Zambia) Bill Mackenzie found himself amidst a parallel struggle for political independence: "... our district, Chinsali, became the main stage for a Cha-Cha-Cha, a merry dance around the security forces. To show their frustration over the issue of independence UNIP closed roads, burnt bridges and schools – having removed the Bibles from them. Many went into hiding in the bush and ministry took me there among them. After his release from prison in 1961, Kenneth Kaunda, son of our first minister, came to his home near Lubwa where we planned a private church meeting. This turned into a very public meeting which led to my falling foul of the provincial government, but I believe it was a turning point in the political agenda. In spite of the nickname 'Mr UNIP' I took no active part in the political scene."[27]

Ian Moir began his work in South Africa as Superintendent for Pholela Training and High School in Natal a few years after the Bantu Education Act of 1955 had led to mission schools being integrated into the system of African Education which was developed under apartheid. Moir soon discovered that the students were "no longer the grateful recipients of paternalistic goodwill, but people who had been radicalised by the black consciousness movement and were now angry young activists demanding social and political change."[28] This led to the development of pastoral practice based on the realisation articulated by Albert Nolan, South African Dominican priest, when he stated that you do not "incarnate good news into a situation; good news arises out of a situation".[29] Amidst these troubled times, each year Moir saw 40-50 students become members of the church.

Nowhere has mission been conditioned by its political environment more than in the Middle East where, as Colin Morton writes, "conflicting histories clash, and religion and politics are inextricably intertwined."[30] Particularly the situation in Israel and Palestine has called for a re-shaping of mission strategy. Morton's years as minister of the war memorial church St Andrew's Jerusalem from 1988 to 1997 saw a shift in emphasis from historic commitment to Jewish mission and unquestioning support for the state of Israel to the development of close relations with the Arab Christian

---

[26] Eric W.S. Jeffrey, "Roots and Fruits – Northern Malawi", paper presented to "Roots and Fruits" conference, Glasgow, 25 April 2009, 3.

[27] Bill Mackenzie, "Lubwa, Northern Rhodesia/Zambia", paper presented to "Roots and Fruits" conference, Glasgow, 25 April 2009, 2.

[28] Ian Moir, "Roots and Fruits: South Africa", paper presented to "Roots and Fruits" conference, Glasgow, 25 April 2009, 2.

[29] Albert Nolan, *God in South Africa: Challenge of the Gospel* (London: Catholic Institute for International Relations, 1988); cit. Moir, "Roots and Fruits: South Africa", 2,

[30] Colin Morton, "Roots and Fruits: Israel/Palestine", paper presented to "Roots and Fruits" conference, Glasgow, 25 April 2009, 1.

community and commitment to working for justice, peace and reconciliation within the region. Morton recalls: "St Andrew's became a place where Palestinians and Israelis, Muslims and Jews could meet, and much was done to encourage pilgrims and tourists not only to visit the dead stones, but also to meet the living stones of the land."[31] Christians, under the pressure of the situation, are emigrating from the Middle East in unprecedented numbers, raising questions as to the future of Christian faith in the region of its origin. Offering meaningful solidarity has become a gospel imperative and this has motivated people like Colin Morton to commit their lives to this calling. Another Church-run institution which has attracted the committed service of numerous Scots is Tabeetha School in Jaffa. Elspeth Kerr comments: "Today's children are living in a world where we still have to learn 'to do justice and to love kindness and to walk humbly with your God'. This they are learning in a wee, old school in downtown Jaffa."[32]

Political developments could sometimes apparently cause great harm to missionary work, yet apparent set-backs sometimes created positive results. Norman Macrae remarks that: "One of the unforeseen consequences [of the Nigerian civil war] was the end of the direct Scottish mission connection with the Church. Our mission area had been almost exclusively within the Biafran enclave... which had tried to secede from the Federation of Nigeria, and those of our mission staff who were there at the time had inevitably become closely involved with refugee and famine relief in the Biafran area. After the defeat of the Biafran cause, they were no longer acceptable to the Nigerian authorities or allowed to remain.... As has happened in other countries the departure of missionary partners was followed by the growth and further expansion of the local church."[33]

For the most part, Scottish missionaries operated in areas where the British Raj provided access and some security. (Chaplains to expatriates of course were in a different situation). The break-up of the British Empire affected the politics of almost every area. However the insistence by mission boards that missionaries should learn local languages meant that they were well placed to understand and identify with the aspirations of the local people. This enabled them to make the somewhat bumpy ride to independent nationhood in warm supportive company.

---

[31] Ibid, 2.

[32] Elspeth Kerr, "Roots and Fruits – Israel/Palestine", paper presented to "Roots and Fruits" conference, Glasgow, 25 April 2009, 2.

[33] Norman C. Macrae, "But Why Edinburgh?", paper presented to "Roots and Fruits" conference, Glasgow, 25 April 2009, 3-4.

Was There a Distinctively Scottish Dimension to Missionary Involvement?

One function of the Edinburgh 1910 World Missionary Conference was to demonstrate the wide commonality which characterised the Western missionary movement as a whole. In terms of attitudes and programmes there is much that was essentially the same, regardless of the national character of the missionary effort. It is therefore not always easy to identify distinctive features in Scottish missionary endeavour. Nonetheless, David Cairns, who played a notable role at Edinburgh 1910 as the Chairman of Commission Four on the relation of Christianity to other religions,[34] the following year pointed out that, in his view, there are three elements of Scottish religious history which have a bearing on Scotland's contribution to the missionary movement. These are, as summarised by Andrew Walls:

> The first of these elements is the kingdom of God – the central stream of Scottish religious life is theocratic. The aim of the preaching of the gospel ... was not simply saving souls or enlarging the church, but a Christian world society in which the legislative and economic order were brought into accordance with the mind of Christ. The second significant element Cairns identifies in Scottish religious life is the vital importance of the church.... The third element is strong theology, the tradition of strong thinking in religion, an element he saw as much needed in the contemporary flabby intellectual climate.[35]

These distinctive features do appear to have run through to the later 20th century. Many of the reflections offered by missionaries of this period are marked by the "strong thinking in religion" which Cairns identified as distinctively Scottish. They also demonstrate the holistic approach of the Calvinist tradition which sought to embrace life in its totality. Howard Taylor observes that: "The Church of Scotland mission in Malawi had some characteristics which were not characteristics that all other missions had. In contrast to some other missions, it believed the salvation of Christ, as well as the creation of God, embraced body and mind as well as spirit. Therefore at most mission stations there were a church for the spiritual, a school for the mind and a hospital for the body. Other missions may have had schools and hospitals too, but some of them saw schools and hospitals as a way in for the spiritual gospel rather than aspects of the gospel itself."[36]

---

[34] See World Missionary Conference, 1910, *The Missionary Message in Relation to Non-Christian Religions*, Report of Commission IV (Edinburgh & London: Oliphant, Anderson & Ferrier; New York, Chicago and Toronto: Fleming H. Revell, 1910); also Kenneth Cracknell, *Justice, Courtesy and Love: Theologians and Missionaries Encountering World Religions, 1846-1914* (London: Epworth Press, 1995).

[35] Andrew F. Walls, *The Cross-Cultural Process in Christian History* (Maryknoll NY: Orbis & Edinburgh T. & T. Clark, 2002), 260-61.

[36] Howard Taylor, "Malawi 1965-81", paper presented to "Roots and Fruits" conference, Glasgow, 25 April 2009, 1.

In the Scottish Presbyterian tradition, particular emphasis has been placed on the conviction that responsibility for mission lies with the church. Rather than delegating responsibility to para-church agencies or societies, the church itself should take responsibility for missionary endeavour. This found expression in such practical matters as remuneration. Church of Scotland missionaries, regardless of professional qualifications or seniority, were paid on a standard scale from central funds. This contrasts with the "faith mission" approach where each individual missionary is responsible for raising their own support. Anne Hepburn remarks; "The Church of Scotland policy seemed to us to be more in line with the Gospel than that."[37]

At a slightly later time, Howard Taylor saw how the Scottish emphasis on the church took effect in Malawi: "The Church of Scotland saw the church as an organisation and body of believers and this was important for the nature of the gospel. Some other missions tended to see the church as relatively unimportant. The Church of Scotland's emphasis meant that Africans of the CCAP [Church of Central Africa Presbyterian] strongly guarded their view of what the church was all about. They didn't really understand such organisations as Scripture Union and the new Student Christian Organisation which considered themselves para-church organisations over which the Church had no formal control."[38]

5. Seeking to Serve God's Mission Today

A glance at the history of Christian mission shows that it is never static. Even an event as definitive as the Edinburgh 1910 World Missionary Conference is soon out of date.[39] Whereas in 1910 the Western missionary movement assumed that it would hold the initiative for many years to come, the ensuing years have witnessed, on the one hand, a recession of Christian faith in the Western world more severe than any in history while, on the other hand, the churches which emerged on the "mission field" of the non-Western world have gone from strength to strength. This provokes sharp questions about the relation between the two and about what partnership will mean in today's context. As Roy and Jane Dodman ask: "What happens when we stretch the metaphor of roots and fruits and imagine that the fruit has dropped to the ground and the seed has sprouted and there is now a vigorous young tree growing beside the old tree? ... What happens when the young tree has become strong and vibrant and the old tree shows alarming signs of being in a state of possibly terminal decay? How do the two trees relate and how can both trees survive and

---

[37] Hepburn, "Roots and Fruits", 1.
[38] Taylor, "Malawi 1965-81", 1.
[39] See further Kenneth R. Ross and David A. Kerr, "The Commissions After a Century", in Kerr & Ross, *Edinburgh 2010*, 307-317.

produce good fruit? ... Truly Scotland in the twenty-first century is a mission field."[40] If Scotland, like other nations which in 1910 regarded themselves as part of "the Christian world" is now categorised as a mission field, how is it going to be reached with the gospel of Christ? One factor to be considered is patterns of migration.

Migration and mission ran together in the 19th and 20th centuries but, though overlapping, they could be distinguished from one another. This is becoming ever less the case. The people who take the faith from one place to another are more often migrants or refugees than missionaries in the traditional Western sense. Dynamic witness to Jesus Christ is borne by a criss-crossing pattern of diasporic communities spread across the face of the earth. Despite widespread resentment against immigrants from the South and the barriers put in their path, it seems safe to predict that South-to-North migration will continue to occur on a massive scale for the foreseeable future. So long as many of the migrants are people of profound and adventurous Christian faith, the potential of this vast movement to contribute to worldwide missionary engagement is enormous.

The Scots International Church in Rotterdam has been alert to these new dynamics. As its minister Robert Calvert explains: "As an old migrant church we decided to stand alongside vulnerable immigrant Christians..."[41] The Scots Church traces its history back to 1643 when it began as a chaplaincy to the Scottish community in Rotterdam. It continued this service for many years and it was only at the turn of the 21st century that the congregational life took on a new character and composition. As Calvert writes: "I found myself on a steep learning curve about the 'universal' Jesus. The church now had people from more than forty nations and the team of elders was drawn from four continents. African traditions were 'blended' with our liturgy and an African rhythm group had been started by our first West African elder. A Korean Methodist church was renting space in our church and we extended the same offer to Dutch, Portuguese and French-speaking churches. Opening the hall as a place of hospitality eventually led to a weekly reception for refugees and a safe house."[42] Currents of mission flowing across the world and bringing fresh life to a long-established Church of Scotland congregation – here is a ministry which encapsulates the reality of the close integration of mission and migration in today's world.

As Christian mission stands at the new frontier presented by the post-Christian West, its protagonists are challenged by the question of whether the lessons learnt across 200 years of the modern missionary movement can

---

[40] Roy and Jane Dodman, "Roots and Fruits: The Jamaican Experience", paper presented to "Roots and Fruits" conference, Glasgow, 25 April 2009, 1-2.
[41] Robert Calvert, "Scots International Church, Rotterdam", paper presented to "Roots and Fruits" conference, Glasgow, 25 April 2009, 2.
[42] Ibid.

be applied to this new situation.[43] Can they bring all this wealth of experience home to Scotland and to God's call to mission here in the secular West? Chris Wigglesworth recalls working with people from a variety of religious traditions in India in the 1960s and 1970s in the face of serious droughts, hunger, soil erosion, deforestation, inter-communal riots etc. "Instead of seeking first the ecclesiastical joinery and politics, working with these friends day-to-day was both practically satisfying and theologically taxing."[44] This leads him today to conclude that: "the Church has no monopoly of God's Truth (or the Life or the Way). Certainly seen more clearly in Christ's earthly life, today the fruits of the Spirit, the 'first-fruits of the New Creation', are sometimes found inside, but more often outside the institutional churches."[45] Such perspectives have profound implications for inter-faith relations and for the practice of mission. Another fresh perspective is offered by Alastair Hulbert who drew inspiration from Lesslie Newbigin's distinction of mission to individuals, mission to structures and mission to ideologies.[46] He finds his own vocation described in a 1991 World Council of Churches document: "There is an urgent need today for a new type of mission, not into foreign lands but into 'foreign' structures. By this term we mean economic, social and political structures which do not at all conform to Christian moral standards."[47] Here is the impetus of the missionary movement being carried to new frontiers and translated into new forms.

Conclusion

Three stages can be discerned in the missionary experience under review: preparation, participation in one's context of service, and reintegration into the home situation. While appreciation was expressed for preparatory training, there is wide agreement that the real formation took place through experience of active missionary involvement. An initial understanding of mission as a matter of giving (with its assumptions of superiority and power) tended to give way to an understanding of mission as sharing, learning, receiving and dialogue. Immersion in local language and culture enabled missionaries to identify with their host communities as they travelled through the tumultuous era of decolonisation. Though not without

---

[43] See further David Smith, "Junction or Terminus? Christianity in the West at the Dawn of the Third Millennium", in Timothy Yates ed., *Mission – An Invitation to God's Future* (Calver: Cliff College, 2000), 90-92.

[44] Chris Wigglesworth, "Western India, the Church and I", paper presented to "Roots and Fruits" conference, Glasgow, 25 April 2009, 2.

[45] Ibid.

[46] Alastair Hulbert, "Mission to Structures and Ideologies", paper presented to "Roots and Fruits" conference, Glasgow, 25 April 2009, 1.

[47] *Signs of the Spirit* (Geneva: World Council of Churches, 1991), 66, cit. Hulbert, "Mission to Structures and Ideologies", 1.

their own blind-spots, missionaries of this period were able to develop a model of mission which was more humble and reciprocal, helping to realise the hopes of Edinburgh 1910 for "the church on the mission field". Their experience of mission also led them to value the yearning for unity which was such a strong feature of Edinburgh 1910. Meeting crises together and making common cause with Christians of all denominations was an experience which forged a practical unity. This inspiring experience powered the ecumenical movement with its ambition to achieve visible church unity. Return to Scotland meant an encounter with the new missionary frontier presented by the post-Christian West and the more creative returned missionaries have sought to work out how their experience of mission in the non-Western world can become a resource to help engage this new challenge facing the church.

Notwithstanding the fact that these missionaries were part of a movement which was highly international in character, their reflections reveal the influence of their roots in the Scottish missionary tradition. Those who embraced God's call to go out from Scotland took "the world" seriously – the people among whom they went to live, and the social and political contexts in which they became immersed. And they took the church seriously, both the Church which sent them and, where they found one, that into which they became integrated. Invariably this journey involved encounter with cultural realities which were strange and unfamiliar and participation in a church life which was formed by continuous dialogue with its distinctive context. Culture shapes the human voice which answers the voice of God. The Scottish ecclesiological tradition seems to have imparted a confidence that the life of the church may properly evolve through continuous dialogue with the local context. The tradition of strong thinking in religion, identified by David Cairns as a distinctive feature of Scottish missionary engagement, is needed to hold together two vital insights which make sense of mission. On the one hand, there is God's mission in God's world today ushering in God's kingdom. On the other hand, there is the church of Jesus Christ – his single, broken, flawed, yet beloved body – bearing and interpreting for that world God's purpose revealed in the tradition of the Christian Bible and finding its fulfilment in an infinite variety of particular contexts. God's missionary dialogue continues today – with individuals, with structures, with ideologies – and with churches!

SHARING GIFTS: EXPLORING SOME EXPERIENCES OF RECEPTIVE ECUMENISM IN SCOTLAND

Stephen Smyth

Introduction

The invitation to contribute and present a paper to the Towards 2010 "Roots and Fruits" conference series provided me with the opportunity to explore some ideas and impressions gained from my ecumenical work here in Scotland, especially as General Secretary of ACTS (Action of Churches Together in Scotland).

The process of focussing, researching and writing down the results has been immensely enjoyable and encouraging. It was particularly beneficial to interview some senior church figures who have a much longer and richer experience of ecumenism in the Scottish context than I have. Through their sharing, and from across our traditions, I heard an honest acknowledgement of our particular history; much recognition of change – for the better; and, a clear message of faith and hope for the future of ecumenical work in Scotland.

In 2010, the world celebrated the centenary of the Edinburgh 1910 World Missionary Conference: an event that helped inspire and shape missionary action and ecumenical cooperation throughout the 20th century. There is a lot of hope that the centenary, and initiatives like Towards 2010, will help stimulate new initiatives for the 21st century.

It is worth reminding ourselves that the aim of ecumenical cooperation is to work towards the "Full Visible Unity of the One Church of Jesus Christ". This may seem like an impossible task, but it remains the commitment of many churches worldwide and in Scotland. In 2006, the 9th Assembly of the World Council of Churches re-affirmed this commitment by saying: "the primary purpose of the fellowship of churches in the World Council of Churches is to call one another to visible unity in one faith and in one eucharistic fellowship expressed in worship and in common life in Christ, through witness and service to the world, and to advance towards that unity in order that the world may believe". Our continuing divisions are real wounds to the body of Christ, and God's mission in the world suffers.[1] Similarly, in 1995, in the encyclical *Ut Unum Sint* (On commitment to Ecumenism), Pope John Paul II reminded us: "The ultimate

---

[1] World Council of Churches, "Called to Be One", Document of Ninth Assembly of WCC, Porto Allegre, Brazil, 2006.

goal of the ecumenical movement is to re-establish full visible unity among all the baptized."[2]

In Scotland, ACTS expresses this commitment in its "Charitable Purposes" as: "to further the mission and realise the unity of the Church Universal by providing a national focus of interchurch counsel, education and action, specifically to promote, participate in, implement and manage actions, projects, programmes and initiatives."[3]

Full Visible Unity of the One Church of Jesus Christ. This is the invitation and challenge offered to us by our ecumenical engagement. I hope that sharing the ideas and experience reflected in these pages might offer some little gift or insight from our Scottish experience that can encourage us for the ecumenical pilgrimage ahead.

Receptive Ecumenism and Founding Charism

Two main ideas served as starting points for this paper. They are: "Receptive Ecumenism" and "Founding Charism".

"Receptive Ecumenism" is an insight that is just beginning to gain ground in ecumenical circles. Receptive Ecumenism encourages churches to recognise the gifts that are more present, or more evident, in other traditions and to "receive" these gifts into the belief and practice of their own tradition. The aim is to move away from the mindset of "What do they have to learn from us?" towards "What might we have to learn from them?" The aim and hope are that, in the experience of sharing one another's gifts, our churches may grow closer together – and the whole body of the church may be more complete. [4]

In recent years I have participated in two major international conferences on Receptive Ecumenism, held in Ushaw College, Durham.[5] The first of these (2006) focussed more on relationships among the Roman Catholic, Anglican, Methodist and Orthodox churches; the second (2009) had broader scope and participation. Both conferences recognised the current,

---

[2] *Ut Unum Sint – On Commitment to Ecumenism,* Papal Encyclical, Rome, May 1995, art 77.

[3] ACTS (Action of Churches Together in Scotland), *Memorandum and Articles of Association,* 8 Sept 2008.

[4] Paul Murray "Receptive Ecumenism and Catholic Learning – Establishing the Agenda", in Paul Murray ed., *Receptive Ecumenism and the Call to Catholic Learning – Exploring a Way for Contemporary Ecumenism* (Oxford: Oxford University Press, 2008), 12.

[5] The first, "Receptive Ecumenism and the Call to Catholic Learning – Exploring a Way for Contemporary Ecumenism", 12-17 Jan 06. The second, "Receptive Ecumenism and Ecclesial Learning: Learning to Be Church Together", 11-15 Jan 09. Both were organised and hosted by The Centre for Catholic Studies, Department of Theology and Religion, Durham University and St Cuthbert's Seminary, Ushaw College, Durham.

somewhat sluggish, state of ecumenical matters among the traditional churches; noted the areas of real progress and of disappointment; and explored Receptive Ecumenism as a possible way forwards – a way that is perhaps more relational and less structural than some previous parts of our pilgrimage as churches together. This approach is promoted through the development of "spiritual ecumenism" or "ecumenism of life". In very practical and everyday ways, institutions and individuals are encouraged to share in prayer and witness together.[6]

In most countries, the main partners in ecumenical dialogue tend to be from churches that are episcopally ordered: Roman Catholic, Anglican, Lutheran and Orthodox. These traditions have many ecclesial features in common. In Scotland, however, the main partners in the dialogue represent two very different ecclesiologies: Presbyterian and Episcopal. Differences in understanding, tradition, perspective and language can pose special problems for churches in Scotland trying to engage in dialogue. Receptive Ecumenism, provides an opportunity for us to consider what gifts there might be within each others' churches. We might further consider what our particular ecumenical experience might have to say to the wider church and ecumenical movement.

"Founding Charism" is a concept which is familiar to Roman Catholic religious orders. A charism is understood as a grace given for the sake not only of the recipient but also and primarily for the upbuilding of the Church.[7] After the Second Vatican Council (1962-65), the Catholic church issued a challenge to its religious orders to re-visit the origins and inspirations of their own group, along with church tradition and the Scriptures, in order to help discern how best to live their vocations today.[8] The orders were encouraged to identify what particular gift their group expresses for the church; and, what their special contribution is for the benefit of the whole community.

For example, I am a member of the Marist Brothers, an international community of Brothers, vowed laymen, who traditionally have worked in education. In the Catholic Church, there are many orders of Brothers who live in community and work in education.[9] So, what is "special" or "distinct" about the Marist Brothers? Our research and reflection brought

---

[6] In *A Handbook of Spiritual Ecumenism*, Walter Kasper provides a user-friendly resource for individuals and groups who wish to develop greater understanding and practice of spiritual ecumenism. Walter Kasper, *A Handbook of Spiritual Ecumenism* (New York: New City Press, 2007).

[7] Sandra Schneiders, *Finding the Treasure – Locating Catholic Religious Life in a New Ecclesial and Cultural Context* (Mahwah, NJ: Paulist Press, 2000).

[8] *Perfectae Caritatis* (Decree on the Up-to-Date Renewal of Religious Life), para 2. Austin Flannery ed., *Vatican Council II – The Conciliar and Post Conciliar Documents* (Leominster: Fowler Wright, 1980).

[9] For example: Brothers of the Sacred Heart, Christian Brothers, De la Mennais Brothers, De la Salle Brothers, Presentation Brothers – and the Marist Brothers.

us a fresh appreciation of our founder, St Marcellin Champagnat, his work in rural post-revolutionary France, and his initial band of followers. In particular, we regained a sense of Marcellin's character and his sensitivity to the religious and social needs of his time. This involved some demythologising of community lore. Today, Marcellin's vision continues to inspire many followers around the world. We like to think that you can recognise some of his very practical character traits, sensitivity and social concern within our Brothers, their communities and their work today.

In my experience of working with Glasgow Churches Together and ACTS, I have observed that, while churches hold many things in common, each tradition manifests some characteristics, perspectives and concerns which are special to its own community. I found myself wondering if the concept of "founding charism" might have a parallel in the origins of our denominations.

We recognise that the history of setting up new church communities includes more than enough examples of quarrels, hurts, divisions, anathemas, politics, persecutions and even wars. The scars of these can still impede ecumenical understanding and respect. What, though, might we learn from one another if we decide to focus more on the inspiration, principles and vision that led an individual or group to decide to express their church identity in a particular way? What founding insight or gift might we find for the whole church in the life and experience of any one community of our sisters and brothers in the faith?

The Interview Process

With "Receptive Ecumenism" and "Founding Charism" in mind, I set out on this brief exploration of the experience of the ecumenical journey in Scotland. I sought to identify, first, what gifts our member churches saw in themselves and in one another; and, second, what gifts might there be in our particular Scottish experience of ecumenism that we can share with the wider church.

I approached senior figures in four of our ACTS member churches and asked to interview them. They represented both the Presbyterian and Episcopal traditions: the Church of Scotland and United Free Church of Scotland; and the Roman Catholic Church and Scottish Episcopal Church. Other members of the ACTS networks knew of the initiative. One of these challenged me saying: "See, Stephen, you are doing it again, what people always do: asking the big boys. What about the rest of us? Don't you think the smaller churches, the non-conformist churches, also have something to say about the ecumenical story in Scotland?" He was, of course, right. So, I organised a fifth interview with someone from the Salvation Army.

The five interviews involved six people:[10] Most Rev Archbishop Mario Conti, Roman Catholic Archbishop of Glasgow; Rt Rev Idris Jones, retiring Primus of the Scottish Episcopal Church and Bishop of Glasgow and Galloway; Very Rev Sheilagh Kesting, Church of Scotland Ecumenical Officer and former Moderator of the General Assembly; Lt Col Robert McIntyre, Scotland Secretary of the Salvation Army; and from the United Free Church of Scotland Rev Douglas Scrimgeour, Clerk of the Presbytery of the West, and Rev Andrew McMillan, Convener of the Ecumenical Relations Committee, who were interviewed together.

At the time of writing, this group have together given 249 years of ordained ministry to their churches. For each one, their ecumenical story began early on in their ministry, even before ordination, engaging with clergy of other denominations at the local level. Formal or structural roles within their denominations came later. They form an inspiring group of people.

Each interviewee was given the same set of questions to help prepare for the interview:

1. What would you see as the "founding charism" of your church? (e.g. its vision / inspiration / what makes it so special to its members)
2. What particular gift, do you think, does your church bring to the wider church today?
3. What examples would you see of gifts your church has gained from its engagement with other churches?
4. What would you see, particularly in Scotland, as the main obstacles that we face on the road towards the "Full Visible Unity of the One Church of Jesus Christ"?
5. Again, particularly in Scotland, what would you see as the main opportunities available to our churches in reaching towards this goal?
6. Reflecting on our experience as churches here in Scotland, what ecumenical insights / lessons might we have to share with the world church?
7. Might there be a special gift from our experience? If so, what might it be?

Interviews took place in the denominational offices and lasted between 45-60 minutes. Extensive notes were taken and the interviews taped, as backup. Regrettably the first two interview tapes were spoiled. It was agreed that interviewees would see a draft of this paper and would be able to make clarifications or necessary amendments.

---

[10] Interviews: Archbishop Mario Conti, Roman Catholic Church (16 June 2009), Rev Douglas Scrimgeour & Rev Andrew McMillan, United Free Church (18 June 2009), Most Rev Idris Jones, Scottish Episcopal Church (19 June 2009), Rt Rev Sheilagh Kesting (26 June 2009), Lt Col Robert McIntyre (8 July 2009).

Feedback from the Interviews

In reporting the feedback from the interviews I have kept the responses to Questions 1-3 identifiable by contributor; and, for Questions 4-7, I have merged comments thematically.

i) Founding Charism

Question: *What would you see as the "founding charism" of your church?*

Mario Conti sees the Roman Catholic Church as grounded firmly in the earliest tradition of the apostolic faith. There is a clear and continuous line of history from the earliest apostolic foundations to the Roman Catholic Church today.

He considers the founding charism and particular gift as being the inspiration of the Holy Spirit, promised and handed down in the church over the years. Even the structures of the church, which sometimes need reworking, bear testimony to the initial gift of the Holy Spirit. Doctrine, for example, can develop over the years. But it develops from within and is preserved from error, including in moral questions. The Roman Catholic Church understands itself as a universal teaching church and its faithfulness to that role is expressed by the bishops as a whole and the Pope when he speaks infallibly for the whole church.

Sheilagh Kesting understands the Church of Scotland to be part of an ever-changing church, an ever-reforming church, which traces its roots back to the New Testament and early church community, through the missionary work of Ninian (4th century) and Columba (6th century) in what was to become Scotland, and through the Reformation (16-17th centuries)[11] to today.

One particular gift is the church's central focus on the Word of God, the Bible. The authority to interpret the Word of God is given to the whole church and the interpretation of Scripture is fundamental. This year, as we celebrate the 500th anniversary of the birth of John Calvin, we are reminded of Calvin's concern that it is not just about repeating the Scripture, but wrestling with the text, seeking its truth for today.

Another gift is the Church of Scotland's refusal to split the church between clergy and lay people. All are members of the *laos*, the People of God. All partake in the "priesthood of all believers". For Calvin, community is important. We are all bonded together in Baptism; Holy Communion is central; and, we live our faith in the context of the Communion of Saints. Baptism, Holy Communion and the Communion of Saints: this is also a very good basis for ecumenism.

Idris Jones shares the understanding that the Scottish Episcopal Church has its origins back in the early church community. The SEC is deeply

---

[11] The Reformed Church in Scotland came into being in 1560 and was established in 1567.

rooted in Scottish church history. Initially, after the Reformation in Scotland, there was only the one reformed church in the nation. In the main this church was Presbyterian, but one party sought to maintain the historic episcopal tradition. The two wings of the church coexisted for 130 years and finally split in 1690 when the Scottish Episcopal Church was formed. Idris noted that the foundation of the church also involved some very human struggles over political power.

The Scottish Episcopal Church's particular gifts lie in being part of the reformed church while maintaining the Catholic tradition as expressed in the threefold order of ministry: bishop, priest and deacon. This tradition includes the importance of liturgical form and the use of the common prayer book.

Robert McIntyre recounted the founding of the Salvation Army by William Booth in 1865. Booth was concerned for the welfare of people who were not churched, especially in the poorest areas of the East End of London. The Salvation Army reached out to the homeless and prostitutes and those who had to work in risky industrial conditions.

The Salvation Army still considers its gift as being a church for the marginalised and poor. Salvation Army churches are situated in mainly poor areas. Many people there, who are not members of ordinary churches, will use the Salvation Army for their rites of passage. The 2009 Salvation Army Report "Seeds of Exclusion" expresses the Army's distinctiveness and expertise. It identifies those who fall through the social support networks and how to reach them. It seeks to identify and address the causes of exclusion as well as the symptoms. "Engagement in social justice for the poor – is part of our DNA." said Robert.

Another gift is the strong musical tradition: the bands and choirs. Many Salvation Army services will include congregational singing in parts. One other major charism has been, from the very beginning, the equality of female leadership in ministry. This includes having had two women Generals, the leaders of The Salvation Army worldwide.

Douglas Scrimgeour and Andrew McMillan described the founding of the present United Free Church of Scotland in 1929.[12] Around 1900, there

---

[12] The United Free Church of Scotland was formed in a reunion of some Presbyterian churches in 1900. See A.D. Scrimgeour, "Historical Paper from the United Free Church: 1929 – As the Continuers Saw It" in Report of Committee on Ecumenical Relations, Appendix 1X. *Reports to the 2005 General Assembly of the Church of Scotland* (Edinburgh: Church of Scotland, 2005), 26/52-26/54. From 1908, that United Free Church and the then Church of Scotland were in conversation regarding union. A Memorandum, which prefigured the Church of Scotland Act 1921, was successfully presented to both General Assemblies in 1912. The act took effect in 1926 and union took place in 1929. Some members of the United Free Church chose not to join the union, but to continue as the United Free Church we know today. See Marjory Maclean, "Historical Paper from the Church of Scotland: The 1921 Settlement and the 1929 Union" in Report of Committee on

was a move for reunion among many Presbyterian churches, including the formation of the earlier United Free Church. In 1929 most of the existing United Free Church united with the then Church of Scotland. A group chose not to unite and formed the United Free Church as we know it today.

The United Free Church is a Presbyterian church and is aware of being a small denomination today. Its founding vision identified three key principles all regarding the relationship between church and state: Autonomy, Equality and Voluntaryism.[13] Autonomy opposes "the state establishment of religion", and the danger of state interference in religious matters; Equality regards the special recognition by the state of any one particular denomination as "not in the interests of the best Inter-Church relations"; Voluntaryism promotes that churches should be funded from the freewill offerings of their members, and not from the state with the danger of added strings.

These founding principles were very meaningful to the church community at the time. However, some of the issues have been overtaken by history and changes in church-state relations. While the principles are there in the background, they may not be so familiar to people today. Current members would be more familiar with the church's evangelical spirit and its sense of community and fellowship.

One gift of the church is the significant status and role given to church elders and to women. For example: elders take part in the laying on of hands in the ordination of new ministers. There have been women elders in the church since its foundation and women ministers since 1931. Women have played an equal role at all levels of church service, including Moderator of the General Assembly. In 1929, these initiatives were in the vanguard of developments in Presbyterian church life and practice. The church willingly recognises how much has changed since 1929 and how far the churches have journeyed together. The church to which to the United Free Church is most close is the Church of Scotland.

ii) Gift of your own church

Question: *What particular gift, do you think, does your church bring to the wider church today?*

The Church of Scotland, United Free Church and the Scottish Episcopal Church are all effectively one-nation churches.[14] They each have partnership or covenant relationships with churches in other parts of the world. The Salvation Army and the Roman Catholic Church are

---

Ecumenical Relations, Appendix 1X. *Reports to the 2005 General Assembly of the Church of Scotland* (Edinburgh: Church of Scotland, 2005), 26/46-26/51.

[13] United Free Church of Scotland: Statement of Principles.

[14] The Church of Scotland has some congregations in England, Europe and a few ex-British colonies.

international churches. Interviewees shared further reflections on the gifts of their own denominations.

The Church of Scotland is deeply embedded in Scottish culture and recognises "the way people express their Christian faith comes out of the specificity of their cultural context."[15] The church has always emphasised its role in education, health provision and, especially, making the Scriptures available to the people.

This was significantly expressed in the Scottish contribution to the Missionary Movement: providing schools, hospitals and the translation of the Scriptures into local languages and sensitive to local cultures. The work was undertaken for the benefit of the recipients, not the benefit of the missioning church. Partners from many former mission countries, including Desmond Tutu, Kenneth Kaunda and Nelson Mandela, have spoken at the General Assembly of the Church of Scotland of the great legacy this approach and generosity has handed on to Christians in their nations. The church shows this same generosity in its commitment to ecumenism: not just for what "we get out of it", but in solidarity with others for the good of all.

Traditionally, the church has also enjoyed a particular relationship with and access to civic society and government. It is widely respected for this. Of particular note is the contribution of reports on social issues from the Church and Society Council. The church has a sense of responsibility for the territorial spread of Scotland and the provision of clergy for every parish, with a special emphasis on rural and priority areas. This is more difficult today and may provide an opportunity for new ecumenical partnerships.

From its earliest days, the United Free Church has brought an openness to ecumenical engagement and has enjoyed good relationships with neighbouring denominations across the country. There has been close cooperation with the Congregational Church in the training of ministers. The United Free Church has played an active role in the World Council of Churches and in the former Scottish Churches Council and British Council of Churches. It continues to do so today in ACTS and CTBI (Churches Together in Britain and Ireland). This has not always been without some internal resistance or difficulty in resourcing, but it remains a strong commitment. At their ordination, ministers and elders promise "to cherish the spirit of brotherhood to all the faithful followers of Christ" – not just their own denomination.[16] This gift of engagement and participation is important for the United Free Church which recognises that it is a small church. It is difficult to know how much the other, larger denominations are aware of this contribution.

---

[15] Interview: Sheilagh Kesting, 26 June 2009.
[16] Interview: Douglas Scrimgeour & Andrew McMillan, 18 June 2009.

The particular gift of the Scottish Episcopal Church is in its openness to diversity and its ability to live with diversity. This includes holding "the two elements of reformed and catholic in a creative tension".[17] Liturgy is an important gift of the tradition. The SEC is not a "confessional" church, but its liturgy expresses its doctrine: 'lex orandi, lex credendi'.[18]

While the origins of the SEC are specifically within the Reformation in Scotland, it is a member of the world-wide Anglican Communion. A core question for the communion today is about how much diversity can it tolerate and still live in union. You can only achieve this by permitting diversity in doctrine, in liturgical practice and in discipline. This is also a key question for the ecumenical movement.

The Catholic Church considers its most important gift to be that of unity. It is not holier than anyone else and not without examples of damage or corruption. But, it has maintained a remarkable cohesion as a church over time and space, and in different cultures and histories. There is a "real sense of its members as belonging to one body".[19]

The Salvation Army have a gift for "rolling their sleeves up and providing a service that is practical" to people in need, e.g. the homeless or old folk; we "have a heart for people".[20] This is not to say that other churches are not practical in their Christianity, but the very practical character of the Salvation Army is widely recognised by their brothers and sisters in other Christian denominations. Another gift is their internationalism, a sense of being connected with other Salvationists around the globe. And another very practical gift is the contribution of the Salvation Army bands. These often play a significant role in ecumenical celebrations.

iii) Gifts from other churches

Question: *What examples would you see of gifts your church has gained from its engagement with other churches?*

All the interviewees noted the value and benefit of ecumenical engagement to their own denomination. Remarks included: "this keeps on bringing up examples where we can learn from others"; "we encourage our members to become involved ecumenically"; "all these different gifts make us aware of the Holy Spirit blowing where it will"; "a small church benefits greatly from ecumenical engagement – it gains a broader perspective"; "helped us rediscover our shared history and roots". This was not just "rose-tinted" ecumenism. Each interviewee acknowledged key areas of

---

[17] Interview: Idris Jones, 19 June 2009.

[18] Lex orandi, lex credendi: the law of prayer is the law of belief. How a person or community worships shows what they really believe, and can influence or shape what they believe, about God.

[19] Interview: Mario Conti, 16 June 2009.

[20] Interview: Robert McIntyre, 8 July 2009.

division and even tension among or between churches. But, these issues were not the focus of the exercise.

Idris spoke of the Presbyterian churches' emphasis on the Word and how that has encouraged the Scottish Episcopal Church to take preaching very seriously: especially in providing good training for relevant and understandable preaching. He recognised the gift of the Second Vatican Council of the Roman Catholic Church. Pope John XXIII's initiative gave the challenge and freedom for all churches which think of themselves within the catholic tradition to explore new expressions of the life of the church.

Robert focussed on the gifts the Salvation Army has received through the experience of the liturgy in other churches. The Army is a non-sacramental church and does not have a set structure for worship. The service depends on the person leading. The Army has gained from experiencing the music, ritual, style and academic expertise of other churches. For example, the SEC liturgy offers a much more structured, biblically based, thematic preaching style. It can also be very meaningful to participate appropriately in Holy Communion in another church.

Mario recognised the deep faith of the other churches. He reflected on the close cooperation of clergy and laity in the Church of Scotland, especially in the working of the General Assembly. He had recently represented the Catholic Bishops at the General Assembly and had felt most welcome and free to contribute to the debate – a sign of how far our churches have travelled together. The SEC also provides a key role for the laity in church decision making. Mario recognises a level of closeness with the SEC in elements of its episcopal structure and sacramental life.

He admired the devotion to the sacred Scriptures in the evangelical churches. This has helped develop an understanding that Scripture and Tradition are not two sources, but one. He also admired the sense of community and devotion in the Methodist Church; and the sense of community, of togetherness, in the Religious Society of Friends, which is a non-structured body.

Douglas and Andrew greatly appreciated that engagement with other churches has helped a small denomination to overcome, to some extent, the temptation to be inward-looking or separatist. In very practical terms, as a small denomination, the UF has gained from the expertise of other churches in training for ministry. Local ecumenism and joint services with the CofS have helped considerably to heal old bitternesses and attitudes dating as far back as 1929. Key to the improving situation has been the building up of good personal relationships at the local and national level. The warm welcome given today to ecumenical visitors to the UF General Assembly bears witness to this.

Sheilagh identified the most obvious gift gained by the Church of Scotland from its ecumenical engagement as being in terms of worship. The CofS now enjoys more diversity and richness in liturgical material and worship, for example: congregational participation in responses, readings and intercessions; new hymns; the use of visuals, including candles. The church has learned to recover elements of its history from before the Reformation: elements that were perhaps abandoned for being "Catholic and not us".

Ecumenical engagement has taught the CofS to be less arrogant and more sensitive to, more respectful of, other churches, especially the smaller denominations. The church has learned to listen to their voices, to allow their voices to be heard. From the SEC and Methodist Church, the CofS has learned something about collaborative ministry. From the RC and SEC traditions, it has rediscovered the saints – the idea of the Communion of Saints was dear to Calvin.

All the churches have learned unwritten ecumenical protocols, like: agreeing to recognise differences of opinions between churches and not commenting on them in the public arena.

iv) Obstacles on our ecumenical journey

Question: *What would you see, particularly in Scotland, as the main obstacles that we face on the road towards the goal of the "Full Visible Unity of the One Church of Jesus Christ"?*

This question generated some quite intense feedback, reflecting both institutional teaching and personal feelings. Some familiar major issues were identified by several people, particularly regarding sharing communion; ministry and authority; and, moral and ethical questions. Other responses were more particular to denominations.

The aim of "Full Visible Unity" is rooted in Jesus' prayer for his followers "May they all be one" (John 17:21). Our churches have committed themselves to this. However, do our churches and our members see this a realistic aim or only as a distant aspiration? What might it mean? It does appear to seek some kind of relational or structural unity, but uniformity does not seem to be what is desired. The concept of the "one, true church" poses problems. One person commented that, since the great schism between East and West in the 12th century, no one church could claim to be the "one, true" church.

There are some key, possibly intractable, theological, doctrinal and ecclesiological differences among and between our churches. Our inability to share communion came up strongly in this regard. There are related issues of recognition, or non-recognition, of the ordained ministry and the validity of sacraments in other churches. Indeed, there are different understandings of what it means to be "church". For example, there was a question as to whether the Salvation Army is considered to be a "church". There are underlying serious issues of control or power. The intractability, this unwillingness to compromise or change, is evident at both structural and individual church member level.

There are increasing difficulties over moral and ethical questions. From one perspective there is a concern over the loss of traditional values; from another the fear of being swamped by a more liberal church; from another an appeal to learn to live with diversity. Many of these issues are not resolvable within a simply Scottish context. There are wider contexts within denominations and across the world church.

Specifically within the Scottish experience, there is a fear in some smaller churches that ecumenical engagement might lead to loss of identity or even of extinction. The term "bishop" carries problematic historical baggage and has confounded attempts towards unity even in recent times.[21] Scotland is still affected by sectarianism, the deep suspicion and antagonism towards other communities. We have made significant progress in recent years, but in some parts of the country it doesn't take much to bring sectarian attitudes to the surface.

The ecumenical frustrations and historical hurts felt among our churches were very much to the fore in the responses to this question. At the same time, interviewees were talking out of a perspective of hope. Their comments included: "We have come a long way in the last 20-30 years"; "There is already significant unity... in faith, in ideas, in baptism"; "Things that are thought of as inimical are not necessarily in opposition"; "I don't ever see us as the 'one church', i.e. all doing the same thing. I think there is a value in difference"; "There is a need for recognition of the presence and action of the Holy Spirit in other traditions."

v) Opportunities on our ecumenical journey

Question: *Again, particularly in Scotland, what would you see as the main opportunities available to our churches in reaching towards this goal (Full Visible Unity)?*

Everyone spoke here of their positive experience of developments in ecumenical work and relationships in Scotland within our lifetimes. They commented both on the national level, with ACTS and CTBI, and at the level of local churches together. ACTS is a "good news" story for the churches in Scotland, bringing benefits to the participants through the work of commissions and projects. Relationships are healthy: robust enough to allow some discussion of the more "neuralgic" issues.[22] The smaller

---

[21] For example: SCIFU (the Scottish Church Initiative for Union). Working from 1996 to 2003, SCIFU was a dialogue among the Church of Scotland, Methodist Church, Scottish Episcopal Church and the United Reformed Church. The United Free Church and Roman Catholic Church were observers. In 2003, the Church of Scotland decided not to proceed and that particular initiative ceased. Since then, the SEC, Methodists and URC have continued a joint dialogue, known as "EMU". They were expected to sign a Covenant in 2010.

[22] "Neuralgic" issues include, for example: shared Eucharist and responses to some contemporary moral or ethical questions. Many ecumenists feel that more

churches feel respected, listened to and empowered within the new structure of ACTS.

Local "Churches Together" initiatives have deepened knowledge of and relationships with one another at the grassroots level. There has been a growth in ecumenical services and of churches working together on social or local issues. Clergy are often invited to speak in other churches. People see more clearly the witness of good living among other Christians. Church leaders are often seen in the public arena standing together to address society or the Government on issues of common concern, for example: climate change or Trident.

There is already a degree of unity among the churches in terms of their common Baptism, unity in the Spirit, and recognition of Jesus as Lord and Saviour. Existing significant ecumenical initiatives could be taken further. In February 2006, the Joint Commission on Doctrine of the Church of Scotland and the Roman Catholic Church in Scotland issued a document on Baptism and Justification. Recognising our common Baptism may have implications in other areas of church life, including the Eucharist. This could be a fruitful area for further theological discussion.

The conversation among the Scottish Episcopal, Methodist and United Reformed Churches (EMU) was expected to lead to the signing of a Covenant in 2010. A Covenant agreement already exists between the United Free Church and the Church of Scotland. The United Reformed Church was held up as a practical and successful example of how different traditions can come together into one united body.[23]

Practical opportunities clearly lie in developing further relationships, common worship and joint action among our churches. Perhaps churches could make more use of shared worship space, even if they may not yet fully share worship. Churches can work together on fresh initiatives in church development or Christian outreach, e.g.: the Church of Scotland "Future Focus" programme. They may also engage in social service to the local community, e.g. homeless or refugees. Local and national ecumenical bodies can play a significant part in supporting and resourcing such activity. One person commented that the concept of "Receptive Ecumenism" may help churches approach difficult ecumenical issues in fresh ways.

---

theological reflection and discussion need to be done on such issues at all levels of ecumenical encounter. Recently, the ACTS Church Life Network discussed the quality of our churches' commitment to ecumenism; and, its Faith Studies Network discussed reactions to the Roman Catholic Statement "Responses to Some Questions regarding Certain Aspects of the Doctrine on the Church" (Rome, 29 June 2007) and, on another occasion, explored "End of Life" issues.

[23] The United Reformed Church was created in 1972 with the union of the Presbyterian Church of England and the Congregational Church of England and Wales. They were later joined by the Reformed Association of Churches of Christ (1981) and the Congregational Union of Scotland (2003).

vi) Gift of the Scottish Experience

Question: *Reflecting on our experience as churches here in Scotland, what ecumenical insights / lessons might we have to share with the world church?*

Historically, Scotland has experienced difficult ecumenical relations, both between Reformed and Catholic traditions and also within the Reformed tradition. That has changed over recent years. Praying together, working together and learning to accept one another has helped all our churches move forwards. We have made progress in friendship and engagement together. Good relations are important at both the institutional and personal levels.

Currently, as in many parts of the world, Scotland is undergoing some kind of re-ordering of ecumenical commitments, activity and expectations. The ecumenical vision needs to be caught afresh in each generation. So, structures have to keep changing. One person observed, "Scotland is a natural laboratory for the ecumenical movement: it can allow experiments. No one church dominates." Another commented, "Full Visible Unity is not just 'organisational synergy'. You can be diverse and yet have a sense of being together. It requires people working together at the local level, getting to know one another, from the ground up."

In recent years, the Scottish Churches have chosen to operate on a "churches together" model rather than a "council of churches" one.[24] This is manifested in the new governance structures of ACTS,[25] where each of the nine member churches holds one equal vote and the Board of Trustees is designed to optimise the involvement all the churches. ACTS Associated Ecumenical Groups and Working Parties are drawn from those churches that choose to be involved in the particular piece of work. The smaller churches genuinely feel that their contribution is respected and listened to. Many local church together groups operate a similar relational system.

---

[24] There is an interesting and subtle difference between a Churches Council model and a Churches Together one. Under the Council model, churches came together to decide how to carry out tasks on behalf of member churches. However, it was felt that sometimes this left ecumenical enthusiasts too much scope to set the agenda – not always to one that church leadership would like. Under a Churches Together model, like ACTS, churches work together where there is consensus; and, church leaders tend to play a more prominent part in decision-making. Some people think this diminishes the ecumenical body's capacity to be a "thorn in the flesh" of the churches, its ability to spur churches along the road towards unity. Currently, ACTS prefers to see itself as a service agency rather than a thorn. As it says in the constitution: ACTS has no agenda apart from the Churches. See further Stephen Smyth, "Ecumenism Today – Scotland and the Wider World", The Glasgow Newman Association Lecture, 22 Feb 2008.
[25] ACTS has been reorganised as a "Company limited by Guarantee". The Company"s "Memorandum and Articles of Association" were approved on 8 Sept 2008.

It is felt that the structure works so well because the churches are committed to making it work: they send key people to participate at all levels. The one drawback is that it is perhaps not quite so easy to challenge another church where there are areas of difficulty. The challenge to us all is simply to keep working at it.

vii) A special gift from the Scottish experience

Question: *Might there be a special gift from our experience? If so, what might it be?*

The wide responses to this question can be grouped under four main themes.

Our understanding of our current context: ecumenism seems to be in a bit of a melting pot at present. No one church has all the answers – or, indeed, all the wisdom or resources. There is a real sense of us all being in this together – even if it is partly due to a sense of necessity. Many people simply feel "at home" in their own tradition. It is not only a matter of doctrine or principle: it is also about emotional and relational aspects of our lives.

Our commitment and perseverance: we must hold on to the vision that inspires us. This is a journey to be travelled. But, we need to hold on to the dream. It may take a long time and there may be many setbacks on the journey. We need to be prepared to keep at it.

Our appreciation of the importance of relationships: a lot of progress has depended on us developing good relationships among our churches. Individuals and personalities play an important part in this. We have experienced the value of partnership, among and beyond the churches, including working with the government and local authorities to address social issues e.g. sectarianism. We need openness to change, openness to challenge from each other and from society.

A reminder of the call to Mission: how can we make the Gospel accessible to all those people in our society who are seeking something spiritual? How can we unlock all of our rich traditions? How can we live in celebratory mode with all those who would respond to the Gospel?

Reflecting on the Interviews

For me, carrying out these interviews has been like walking on holy ground. It was uplifting for me to hear, one-to-one, the love these committed ecumenists have for their own communities and traditions and the respect they have for those of others. In Scotland, relationships among key church personnel are generally warm and healthy.

Interviewees found the idea of "founding charism" interesting and the perspectives of "receptive ecumenism" and "identifying gifts" very helpful. They were generous in their comments on one another's traditions. All recognise the presence and work of the Holy Spirit in the other. At the same time, these were not rose-tinted-spectacles conversations. People also shared occasional criticisms, frustrations and hurts regarding other traditions, but these were not the main focus of the exercise.

The interviewees recognised that, in Scotland, there are particular historical difficulties and some major theological or doctrinal differences among the churches. But, there was little attention given to any "clash of ecclesiologies" between the Presbyterian and Episcopal traditions. This is perhaps a hopeful sign of growing mutual respect or, perhaps something that needs following up in other studies.

There is also a recognition that the ecumenical movement is going through a period of transition, or re-ordering, at every level: global, national and local. While there is some disappointment at what has not yet been achieved, people affirm that, in our lifetimes, so much has changed for the better.

At the Receptive Ecumenism conference in Durham in 2009, many contributors spoke of the current slowness, uncertainty or disappointment in ecumenical developments. Donald Bolen commented, "While much ecumenical work proceeds quietly ahead, hopes of major steps towards full visible unity have greatly diminished in recent years."[26] He also quoted Cardinal Kasper speaking of "the shifting ecumenical landscape" and calling for "new ideas, strategies, projects and initiatives which would faithfully and creatively move us forward in the search for unity among Christians." Bolen finds his own focus moving away from the international dialogues towards regional and local encounters. The insights of "ecumenism of life" or "spiritual ecumenism" seem to represent developments that are more relational than structural. Jeff Astley considered ecumenism as a learning process.[27] He focussed on the relational values of critical openness, hospitality, friendliness and healing hurts. He spoke of the need for ecumenical "teachers" to help in the process. I found an interesting resonance here with the old Celtic tradition of the Soul Friend, the Anam Cara, who acts as mentor, sounding-board,

---

[26] Donald Bolen, "Reconciling Paths: Ecumenical Learning, Conversing and Deepening Fundamental Human Experience", Conference: Receptive Ecumenism and Ecclesial Learning: Learning to Be Church Together", Ushaw College, Durham, 11-15 January 2009. Mgr Donald Bolen, holds the Nash Chair of Religion, Campion College, University of Regina, Canada; and is a former staff member of the Pontifical Council for Promoting Christian Unity, Vatican City.
[27] Jeff Astley, "What Prevents Christian Churches from Learning?", Conference: Receptive Ecumenism and Ecclesial Learning: Learning to Be Church Together", Ushaw College, Durham, 11-15 January 2009. Prof Jeff Astley is Director of the North of England Institute for Christian Education, St Chad"s College, Durham.

and healthy critic.[28] Might that be a healthy role to encourage among our churches: acting as a "Critical Friend" one to another?

Structural initiatives seem to have taken us only so far. There seems to be a move away from multi-lateral to bi-lateral dialogues. The emphasis may be shifting, but we need both. Bi-lateral statements or agreements will need to be "received" by other ecumenical partners. Rusch points to a way forward when he talks of "differentiated consensus", where there is fundamental agreement on a topic and a noting of differences which do not challenge the fundamental agreement; and "differentiated participation" in the working out of such agreements.[29]

In all this, there is clearly a desire for more focussed ecumenical engagement and action at the level of local congregations, rather than just the wider global and more institutional level.

I sometimes think of this tension as being between "big" and "small" ecumenism. Big ecumenism takes place at the level of church institutions, structures and leadership, in theological and doctrinal exploration and debate, and in major inter-church initiatives. Small ecumenism happens at the level of local congregations, clergy groups and neighbour to neighbour. It tends to be more direct and practical, expressing itself in worship and social action. Of course, for the good of all, we need both. The institutional needs to listen to the frustrations and insights of the grassroots. Otherwise it runs the risk of being too theoretical, heady, and perhaps even arid. The local needs to remain grounded in participants' doctrine and tradition. Otherwise it can become somewhat cosy or facile, ignoring significant issues.

Perhaps we are entering a new phase of our ecumenical journey, one that is more relational and requires different skills to negotiate. Here, we might appreciate afresh the charisms and values in our different traditions, for example: both faithful and ever-reforming; the inter-relation of clergy and laity, and with society and culture; love of Scripture, and liturgy, and tradition; the desire for unity in diversity; commitment and perseverance. At the same time, we probably need to spend more time exploring the difficult issues of doctrine and ecclesiology – a space of "hard" ecumenism.

Light on the Path

This exercise proved to be very affirmative of ACTS and of the way our member churches have chosen to relate and work together. ACTS takes the "churches together" model very seriously. Coming out of a difficult

---

[28] For an insightful reflection on the historical and possible contemporary roles of the "Soul-Friend", or "Anam Cara," see Ian Bradley, *Colonies of Heaven – Celtic Models for Today's Church* (London: Darton, Longman and Todd Ltd, 2000), 101ff.

[29] William G. Rusch, *Ecumenical Reception – Its Challenge and Opportunity* (Grand Rapids: Wm B Eerdmans, 2007), 124, 130.

historical and religious context, the churches in Scotland have made considerable progress in knowledge of, respect for, and cooperation with one another. In many ways, ACTS member churches have responded well to the challenge of the Swanwick Declaration (1987) to move "from cooperation to commitment".[30] Our experience shows that difficult history can be overcome.

There is a real challenge as to how the "big" ecumenism at the national level best relates to and serves the "small" ecumenism at the local and congregational level. This is, and has to be, a major concern for ACTS and our member churches.

Looking to the future: along with many of their contemporaries, the six committed ecumenists who were interviewed for this study have brought our churches a considerable way along the ecumenical road. But, four of these six are in the process of retiring from full time ministry. This provides our churches and ecumenical activists with another challenge: how to ensure that the story and lessons of our ecumenical pilgrimage so far are known by the upcoming generations in our churches.

Is Full Visible Unity possible? Probably not in our lifetime, nor in the foreseeable future. But, we believe that the work of Christian Unity is God's initiative, a gift to the church in our time. There is a strong feeling that, whatever shape Christian unity takes, it will include the ability to live with appropriate diversity.[31] It will also achieve the goal of full unity in the Eucharist. In Durham, Kasper re-iterated: "Ultimately it is not we, but the Spirit of God alone, who can create unity. Therefore, in the tradition of Paul Couturier, we can say that spiritual ecumenism is the soul of the ecumenical movement. That encompasses prayer, conversion, and self-sanctification. Spiritual Ecumenism also makes it clear that we should not be satisfied with such intermediate goals as better mutual awareness, cooperation, and peaceful coexistence. The goal of ecumenism is the shared celebration of the one Eucharist, partaking in the one bread and the one chalice (1 Cor 10:17)."[32] Full Visible Unity must remain the goal of our endeavours as churches together.

---

[30] The Swanwick Declaration, 1987. "It is our conviction that, as a matter of policy at all levels and in all places, our churches must now move from co-operation to clear commitment to each other, in search of the unity for which Christ prayed and in common evangelism and service of the world." See: *The Next Steps for Churches Together in Pilgrimage: Including Definitive Proposals for Ecumenical Instruments* (London: British Council of Churches and the Catholic Truth Society for the Inter-Church Process, 1989).

[31] One person used the image of a salad bowl. The best salad is the one which has the most different ingredients and where each ingredient retains its own characteristics. It is the richness of the "difference together" that makes the best salad. "What we want is salad, not stew", he said.

[32] Walter Kasper, *"Credo Unam Sanctam Ecclesiam* – The Relationship Between the Catholic and Protestant Principles in Fundamental Ecclesiology", in Murray, *Receptive Ecumenism*, 85.

The process of Receptive Ecumenism offers us a very relational approach to deepening dialogue and respect. Moving from the mindset of "What do they have to learn from us?" towards "What might we have to learn from them?" requires a certain humility and openness. Reception "is not a mere exchange of ideas. Rather, churches receive, in a most profound sense of that word, insights of the Christian faith and life from other churches. This process of reception may take years."[33] It is not necessarily the case that the gift we identify in the other will be missing within one's own tradition. Rather, their witness of this gift might encourage us to strengthen that gift in our own community. This kind of dialogue and exchange depends on sound knowledge and good relationships, at both the institutional and personal levels.

While the term "receptive ecumenism" may be new, the lived experience of it is familiar to ecumenical activists – as is clear in the lives of my six interviewees. In Scotland, there has been lots of groundwork in this regard. ACTS is but one of many good examples of local and national initiatives, projects and cooperation. The fruit of this is clearly visible in the quality of relationships among the churches and the diminishment of old prejudices. A major challenge is how to build on the groundwork and "receive" the gifts and insights of this experience into our churches.

Perhaps, too, we need to create more opportunities for our members to engage in some "hard" ecumenism: bringing people together for theological reflection and discussion, to explore, in depth, the important and sometimes "neuralgic" issues that continue to obstruct the path towards unity.

The idea of "founding charism" offers the churches a fresh lens through which to explore their histories and identities, and to help understand and respect difference. The focus is on discovering the founding principles or vision of a community. This may help us heal some ecumenical hurts and offences. History has moved on: our understandings may have changed, and issues may no longer have the critical and divisive nature they once had. Some issues may, of course, remain intractable, but, I am convinced, our churches will become closer in the exploration. We have an opportunity to explore in a new way the inspirations of each others' Presbyterian, Episcopal and Non-Conformist traditions. Another challenge is to develop nationally and locally the everyday skills and practices that increase and deepen ecumenical knowledge and relationships. This "spiritual ecumenism" can be summed up quite simply: we must pray more and do more – together.

What might Scotland's experience have to say to the wider church? First, our ecumenical journey is rooted in the particular history and context of our people, good and bad. Second, we have come a long way; we need to

---

[33] William G. Rusch, "The International Lutheran-Roman Catholic Dialogue – An Example of Ecclesial Learning and Ecumenical Reception", in Murray, *Receptive Ecumenism*, 12.

persevere and to hold on to the vision. Third, relationships are key, both at the personal and the structural levels; and, we have already gained much from one another, for example in liturgical enrichment. Fourth, we are reminded that our common call is a call to Mission. Finally, as was evident in each of the interviews, despite the difficulties, we in Scotland feel a sense of hope for the ecumenical journey ahead.

I finish with two final reflections. First, when talking of their ecumenical experience most of our interviewees used images of pilgrimage and spoke of the need for perseverance on this important journey. Second, at the 3rd European Ecumenical Assembly in Sibiu, 2007, Metropolitan Kirill encouraged us on the road by quoting St Augustine: "in essential things, unity; in nonessential things, diversity; and, in all things, charity."[34]

Perseverance to continue on this pilgrimage, and a reminder of the core virtue of charity. This sounds like a good set of signposts for the way ahead on our ecumenical journey.

---

[34] Originally from St Augustine. Quoted by Metropolitan Kirill, then of Smolensk and Kaliningrad, in his address "The Light of Christ and the Church", 3rd European Ecumenical Assembly, Sibiu, Romania, 5 September 2007.

Internationalism and Scottish Missionary Thought

Chris Wigglesworth

Introduction

This chapter seeks to show that internationalism, meaning the belief that nations of the world should work for greater mutual understanding and co-operation, has from early in the nineteenth century, increasingly influenced Scottish thinking and action on mission, with a corresponding decline in imperialist and isolationist attitudes. The 1910 Edinburgh Conference was significant in this process. This has important implications for 2010 mission thinking, especially in relations between Christianity and Islam, at a time when religion is a major aspect of globalised society.

"Scottish Internationalism": A Useful Category for Considering Scottish Mission.

Though not a common theme in discussions of Scottish Protestant missionary life, internationalism is a significant concept in assessing missionary contributions to Scottish identity, and equally to future mission thinking. "Internationalism" is a concept that grew in use through the nineteenth century. The *Oxford English Dictionary* defines it as: "international character or spirit; the principle of community of interests or action between different nations"; and *Webster's New International English Dictionary* as: "international character, principles, interests, or outlook". Chambers' expands this to "the attitude of favouring the common interests of all nations".[1]

The present First Minister, Alex Salmond, has asserted: "Scotland requires to rediscover the sense of internationalism which once defined our nation", and his predecessor, Jack McConnell, said much the same.[2] It is true that for many Scots the word "international" first calls to mind Murrayfield and rugby, yet the basic definition is "a person belonging to two different nations" (*Oxford English Dictionary*), which describes those many Scots who have gone overseas as emigrants, soldiers, explorers, engineers, doctors and surgeons, nurses, colonial officials, diplomats, traders, free-booters, and missionaries, and who grew to champion the culture of their new home. That is sharpened by a further *Webster*

---

[1] Oxford English Dictionary; Webster New International English Dictionary.
[2] Alex Salmond, Speech to Scottish Parliament, 11 July 2007; Jack McConnell, Speech to Scottish Parliament, 9 June 2003.

definition: "a person having relations with or obligations to more than one nation".

My own impression, as a Sassenach drawn to Scotland for a "proper" theological education five decades ago, was of a nation with a reputation for international sympathies. I recalled this when listening in 2008 to the reminiscences of the distinguished Asian Scot, Bashir Mann. He has written recently of early days in India and recalled Westerners' colonialist attitudes: "there were exceptions of course and the Scots rated very high in these exceptions. They were friendly and gregarious, not as overbearing and lordly as their English cousins."[3]

This internationalist tradition in Scottish life and culture is certainly part of a much wider ethos. Wikipedia's current articles on " internationalism" distinguish two streams from the nineteenth century onwards: proletarian and liberal internationalism.[4] The former is epitomised by the Marxist *Internationale* anthem and the International Working Men's Association, and the latter by Gladstone, the British Liberal Party and support for Free Trade. While there are such distinct emphases in the fields of politics and economics, Scottish internationalism includes the full breadth of social life, encompassing the diversity of cultural, religious and environmental concerns, as well as the political and the economic. Scots poets from Robert Burns -"A man's a man" – to Hamish Henderson – "The Freedom Come-All-Ye", with its "great glen o' the warld" – have celebrated global humanity. It is important to do justice to this attitude, while at the same time drawing attention to the specific Christian elements contributed by Scottish missionaries.

Scottish internationalism has included a substantial mission element. Though neglected in cultural studies, and viewed with mixed feelings in church circles, it featured until very recently on Scottish banknotes, with their depiction of Mary Slessor and David Livingstone. The many biographers of these iconic Scots and their less celebrated colleagues provide ample details to illustrate how Scottish Christian men and women gained a reputation for working all over the world preaching and teaching the Christian message, at the same time as exploring, translating, starting a wide range of educational institutions for girls and women, as well as for boys and for men. They engaged in the earliest medical work in rural and urban areas, worked for famine relief and for agricultural improvement, for engineering projects and for technical training. The *Dictionary of Scottish Church History and Theology* and the *Dictionary of National Biography*

---

[3] Bashir Mann, *The Thistle and the Crescent* (Glendaruel: Argyll, 2008), 53. See also his earlier comments in *The New Scots* (Edinburgh , John Donald 1992) – "a friendly and tolerant nation" 202, and on St Giles' Cathedral's positive attitudes to Muslims in 1991, 206.

[4] www.wikipedia.com

provide many of the other names, only a few of which can be mentioned below.[5]

Being sent on a mission means going somewhere else. This implies crossing frontiers and exploring new cultures in pioneering ventures. This is not to deny that for many there was a relation with "the spirit of Empire", especially in what is called the "high empire period", roughly 1880 to 1920.[6] In the inevitable reaction to the misdeeds of excessive patriotism in the past, the relationship of mission with imperialism has rightly been exposed and criticised from many quarters, but there was also a steady stream of men and women in Christian mission who opposed colonial and narrow settler interests. One of the earliest examples was John Philip (1775-1851), as demonstrated by John McCracken.[7]

A case can be made for an inverse relationship within church and mission circles, and in wider society, between an increasing internationalist spirit and a declining attachment to the interests of empire. A defining moment and an abiding image of this spirit was the Edinburgh *Make Poverty History* march, in July 2005. Nearly a quarter of a million people assembled on the Meadows and marched round the Castle in a peaceful demonstration of international concern about Third World debt, the need for more and better aid, and the importance of Fair Trade. This exemplified the popular support for internationalist values, the central place of a Christian world-view, and equally the wide range of movements with overlapping international concerns. The broad alliance of interests echoed the coalitions of the anti-slavery campaigns at the start of the nineteenth century. That march made the link to another important issue in mission, that of inter-dependence. The reality of globalisation requires that mission will have to be re-defined in the context of increasing global interdependence. Christian mission has to be holistic in responding to the interlocking economic, environmental, cultural, political and religious realities, all of which are facing the impact of globalisation. Another way of expressing this is to state that there are even more reasons today for mission to be inclusive. The implications are enormous.

---

[5] Nigel M. de S. Cameron ed., *Dictionary of Scottish Church History and Theology* (Edinburgh: T. & T. Clark, 1993); H.C.G. Matthew & Brian Harrison ed., *Dictionary of National Biography*, Vols. 1-60 (Oxford: Oxford University Press, 2004).

[6] See Torben Christensen and William R. Hutchison ed., *Missionary Ideologies in the Imperialist Era 1880-1920* (Arhus, Denmark: Aros, 1982), 163.

[7] McCracken, 'Andrew Ross and the Radical Strand in Scotland's Missionary Tradition', this volume, 84-90; see also Andrew C. Ross, *John Philip, 1775-1851:Missions, Race and Politics in South Africa* (Aberdeen: Aberdeen University Press, 1985).

Missionaries and the Growth of Internationalism

From Scottish missionaries there has been a continuous flow of information and exhortation, of financial appeals for gifts of money and goods, but there has also been a growing recognition of a debt to be repaid and of challenges to the way of life in the West. The evidence for this growing internationalist Scottish mission understanding is found in significant names and places in nineteenth century Protestant mission history, long before Edinburgh 1910. Those leading that conference were highly significant in spelling out this understanding, but they were not its originators.

Some of the appeals made at the close of the eighteenth century for overseas mission were from the very same people who urged the ending of the slave trade. The coalitions developed in that campaign contributed to the growing international interests amongst churches, and in particular amongst students concerned about mission. John Erskine (1721-1803), famed for his contribution to the 1796 Church of Scotland General Assembly debate on mission, was an abolitionist. Jamaica was at the heart of that issue and Jamaican mission links with the Calabar mission in West Africa, see below, were one part of a complex and growing struggle against colonialism and for the cause of humanity. Hope Waddell (1804-1895) spent twenty years in Jamaica before moving to eastern Nigeria.[8]

Alexander Duff (1806-78) sailed to Calcutta in 1830, on a Christian mission which included a challenge to India's casteism with its evil of untouchability. He was an enthusiast for education with the aim of forming a comprehensive world-view different to that prevalent in India. John Wilson (1804-75) and his equally renowned wife, Margaret Bayne (1798-1835), in Mumbai from 1829, had a similar approach but she concentrated on the critically important girls and women's education.[9] These pioneers had a comprehensive, holistic approach to their witness, built on education and translation work, which is usually regarded as characteristic of nineteenth century Scottish missionaries. Their approach, however, was

---

[8] See Elizabeth G.K. Hewat, *Vision and Achievement 1796-1956: A History of the Foreign Missions of the Churches united in the Church of Scotland* (London: Thomas Nelson, 1960), 18; A.C. Ross, "Anti-slavery" in Cameron, *Dictionary of Scottish Church History and Theology* , 18-19; and Iain Whyte, *Scotland and the Abolition of Black Slavery, 1756-1838* (Edinburgh: Edinburgh University Press, 2006), 72, 213-24. Whyte's concluding sentence suggests wider issues: "In spite of heavy commercial pressures and strong resistance from certain quarters to abolition, a small nation whose own history was bedevilled by internal fractures and an endemic lack of self-confidence was nevertheless able to make a significant contribution to the long struggle against one of the greatest crimes against humanity." 255.

[9] See Lesley Orr Macdonald, *A Unique and Glorious Mission: Women and Presbyterianism in Scotland 1830-1930* (Edinburgh: John Donald, 2000), 111-12 for Margaret Bayne; also Hewat, *Vision and Achievement,* 43-53.

even wider than that, as even a cursory look at their biographies will show. The biographical dictionary label, "missionary" or "educationalist" conceals the breadth of their interests and the international range of their concerns about long-term change in cultural and economic, as much as religious, conditions. An important part of this was the missionary response to recurrent famine conditions, for example in Rajasthan during 1868-70, which kept economic issues on the mission agenda. Duff's early nineteenth century challenges were renewed in the concern for the inter-dependence of "home" and "foreign" mission shown in the life of Norman MacLeod (1812-72), who was equally concerned for women's education in India and working class savings banks in Glasgow.[10]

Duff and his Indian contemporaries influenced early Scottish mission work in South Africa, notably in Lovedale, where William Govan (1804-75) sought their advice in 1841, when starting what developed as a broad liberal, technical and educational community. It was in South Africa that John Philip had already by 1821 become convinced that fundamental reform of governmental policy was necessary if Christian mission was to flourish and he developed an anti-imperialist approach to mission, retiring there in 1847.[11] Later on, in 1876, another Scot, John Mackenzie (1835-99) took the lead there in this combination of missionary endeavour and commitment to humanitarian justice. But already Dr Jane Waterston (1843-1931), a name not sufficiently celebrated in the mission tradition, was a pioneer educationalist and doctor for women. Serving first, from 1866, in Lovedale, she then, in order to work in a rural area, qualified in medicine (one of the first Scots women to do so) in 1878 – no easy matter in Victorian Britain. She was in at the start of the Livingstonia mission in Malawi where she was critical of Robert Laws' paternalism. Waterston went on to work on her own in Cape Town from 1883 until 1931, as an outstanding physician honoured for her commitment to social and political issues.[12]

In West Africa, the famous Calabar mission began in 1846 through a Jamaican and slave emancipation connection. The importance to mission of economic trading relations continued that link throughout the century. Cultural and economic changes as an intrinsic component of educational and medical work were seen to be as important as evangelistic preaching.

For Central Africa, centred in what later became Malawi, the same comprehensive approach characterised the women and men who established Livingstonia and Blantyre. Agricultural improvement and the use of appropriate technology as well as medical and educational work laid holistic mission foundations, which meant that as political change became

---

[10] See G. Wareing, "MacLeod, Norman", in Cameron, *Dictionary of Scottish Church History and Theology*, 532-33.
[11] See A.C. Ross, "Philip, John", in Cameron, *Dictionary of Scottish Church History and Theology*, 656.
[12] Macdonald, *A Unique and Glorious Mission,* 120, 133-6.

more and more important, the Church had a critical role across the region. There may have been mixed motives in the opposition to Portuguese expansion but criticism of the ensuing protectorate supports the view that there was real concern for the rights of the people. Andrew Walls has suggested that this comprehensive approach may not have been typical of general British or European mission in the "high" imperial, missionary period, starting around 1880.[13] Whether this is true or not, it characterised Scottish mission. In his detailed article on "Missions" in the *Dictionary of Scottish Church History and Theology*, Walls summarises the fascinating complexity and diversity of nineteenth century Scottish overseas mission and its many connections with English and other missions.[14] But equally he evidences the far from deferential attitude of many Scottish missionaries to the imperial project. This had its continuing impact in the twentieth century, as did the characteristic enthusiastic student concern for justice as well as compassion in addressing human material and spiritual need. The Scots contribution, through Henry Drummond, Donald Fraser, Oldham, and many others, to the Christian student movement and foreign mission is also brought out in Robin Boyd's recent book.[15]

Lesslie Newbigin was surely thinking of such examples when he observed a recurring trend towards a holistic mission approach, pointing out that missionaries often started off with a desire to concentrate on "pure evangelism", only to be compelled by circumstances and "the simple logic of the gospel" to engage with the needs of the whole person and the community, which involves economic and international issues.[16]

That sense of mutual inter-dependence, with its internationalist rationale, shows equally in the developing nineteenth century perception of mission training needs. Women were perhaps quicker to realise this. As mentioned above, Jane Waterston acted on it, then Annie Small (1857-1945) and Catherine Forrester-Paton (1855-1914) with their training of women missionaries, in advance of any for men. They laid an emphasis on "culture and faiths in the other countries in which they would work."

As Mary Levison recently observed, it was sociology "in its infancy".[17] The strategy of reaching Muslim women through their needs in "zenanas"

---

[13] Andrew F. Walls, "British Missions", in Christensen & Hutchison, *Missionary Ideologies in the Imperialist Era,* 163.
[14] Andrew F. Walls, "Missions" in Cameron, *Dictionary of Scottish Church History and Theology* , 567-94.
[15] Robin Boyd, *The Witness of the Student Christian Movement* (London: SPCK, 2007), chapter 1. See also Clifton Phillips, "Changing Attitudes in the Student Volunteer Movement in Great Britain and North America 1886-1928", in Christensen and Hutchison, *Missionary Ideologies in the Imperialist Era,* 131-45.
[16] Lesslie Newbigin, *The Open Secret (*London: SPCK, 1978), 102-3.
[17] Isabel Lusk (Mary Levison), *A Throughly Furnished Woman: Annie Small and the Training of Women Missionaries* (Edinburgh, St Colm's, 1994), 14. See also

(the Persian and Indian term for "harems") may have started with a totally critical view of the status of women yet it began the effort to understand and engage in dialogue about culture and religions. Annie Small's little book about Islam, and each of those on the other world faiths show a real concern for the actual needs and character of the women.

Of course, the majority of church-goers were not much concerned. Andrew Walls observed that overseas mission has always been peripheral to the Scottish churches' priorities.[18] Compare the 1910 comment of David Watson (1859-1943), the home mission pioneer of social criticism: "Christianity has been frankly excluded as inapplicable and unworkable... in social, political and international relations".[19] Both have been the case, so that while there was a growing sense of Scottish internationalism at the 1910 Conference, much of it was on the edge of or outside the Scottish churches.

Kenneth Ross' chapter has provided ample evidence of the Scottish contribution to the 1910 Conference itself.[20] It included an insistence that mission be internationalist in a variety of ways. The best evidence of this can be found in the contribution of its secretary, J. H. Oldham (1874-1969).[21] The fact that Oldham also became secretary of the all-important Continuation Committee of the Conference ensured a significant on-going influence for Scots, reinforced by his editorship of the *International Review of Missions*, started in 1912, and in founding the International Missionary Council. Those two titles signify the wide acceptance of the internationalist ethos.

Three of the many other Scots associated with 1910 are important in demonstrating essential evidence of internationalism. A.G. Hogg (1875-1954), J.N. Farquhar (1861-1929), and Nicol Macnicol (1870-1952) all pioneered a learning attitude to other religions.[22] This contrasted with the establishment view of committee conveners – see below on James Ogilvie.

A.H. Small, *Letters to Missionary Friend* (Edinburgh: Macniven and Wallace, 1908); and Macdonald, *A Unique and Glorious Mission.*

[18] Walls, "Missions", 573.

[19] Cit. Donald C. Smith, *Passive Obedience and Prophetic Protest* (New York: Peter Lang, 1987), 330.

[20] Ross, 'The World Missionary Conference 1910: Its Scottish Provenance', this volume, 38-56; see also D. F. Wright, "World Missionary Conference", in Cameron, *Dictionary of Scottish Church History and Theology* , 893-94.

[21] See Keith Clements' very full discussion in his biography of Oldham, *Faith on the Frontier* (Edinburgh: T&T Clark, 1999). See also Katherine Bliss, revised Andrew Porter, "Oldham, Joseph Houldsworth (1874-1969)" in *Dictionary of National Biography*, Vol. 41, 692-94; A.C. Ross, "Oldham, Joseph Houldsworth" in Cameron, *Dictionary of Scottish Church History and Theology* , 633; and Andrew Morton, "J.H. Oldham", in Nansie Blackie ed., *A Time for Trumpets: Scottish Church Movers and Shakers* (Edinburgh, St Andrew Press, 2005), 3-16.

[22] See J.N. Farquhar, *The Crown of Hinduism* (London and Edinburgh: Oxford University Press, 1913); Nicol MacNicol, *Indian Theism* (London: Oxford

To some extent after 1910 divide-and-rule competition in mission gave way to co-existence, termed "comity of mission", which slowly led on to co-operation. Early on some had the realisation that "mission at home and abroad is one", though it was only spelt out much later, for example, at the New Delhi Assembly of the World Council of Churches in 1961.

The danger of Christian triumphalism in plans for "the evangelisation of the world in this generation", evident at the 1910 Conference, was chastened by the "Great" War of 1914-18, at least to the extent that much mission became rather less nationalistic and Eurocentric in its planning. Katherine Bliss commented on how Oldham, "as the servant of all missions and especially of those hardest hit by the war [ww1], tried to keep the spirit of internationalism alive".[23] In particular, his efforts in getting the Allied authorities to deal more justly with German missions, especially in Africa, but also in Asia and the Pacific, were important. However, this period also made clear how the increasing relative influence of North American churches paralleled the changing balance of power in the world and perhaps heralded new forms of economic colonialism.

Several qualifications have to be made to this picture of growing internationalism.

Firstly, in the Middle East, European colonialist and Zionist issues complicated Christian mission, as they still do. Former President George W Bush drew on the jingoistic Jerusalem 1917 writings of the Scottish evangelical, Oswald Chambers, after the September 2001 atrocity.

Second, the Evangelical split from the mainstream among students around 1910 led to some lost momentum in the awareness of social issues – as revealed in attitudes to independence movements, eg, Indian nationalism. On this, the sociologist, David Moberg, has pointed out that for a long time Evangelicals were wary of new social issues, and took longer to accept their importance for the mission of the church.[24]

Robin Boyd notes that Evangelicals have often ignored the 1910 Conference.[25] However, honesty also requires the recognition that the lofty words at international gatherings were rarely acted on in denominational actions on the ground. The 1910 Conference may have focussed a vision, but it was often narrowly expressed subsequently, side-tracked by internal Christian and denomination power-struggles. It is salutary to note that the 1910 Conference is also not mentioned by Elizabeth Hewat.

University Press,1915), and to some extent in its earlier form, A.G. Hogg, *The Christian Message to the Hindu* (London: SCM,1947), were all definitive contributions which emerged from the conference. The preparatory papers for Commission IV were in the main more traditional.

[23] Bliss and Porter, "Oldham", 693.

[24] David Moberg, *The Great Reversal: Evanglism and Social Concern* (London: Scripture Union, 1973), 40-42.

[25] Boyd, *The Witness of the Student Christian Movement*, 13.

From Scots in India in that period the contrasted international attitudes of Nicol Macnicol, mentioned earlier, and James Ogilvie are significant. Ogilvie (1860-1926) was on the Continuation Committee and an influential Church of Scotland foreign mission committee convener from 1909 to 1925. As a mission scholar Macnicol, writing in 1922 was sympathetic to young Indian Christian identification with nationalist hopes.[26] Ogilvie, on the other hand, with a Madras Scots' chaplain background, could write in 1924 of "criticisms of Empire", about an "unpleasing element in 'Young India'". This was "nationalist fervour", not "we may reasonably hope, a permanent feature in the life of Christian India"![27]

So it is hardly surprising that the churches officially took little notice of the wider growth of internationalism. As far as Scottish internationalism in the Indian subcontinent is concerned, the liberal stream can be represented by Patrick Geddes (1854-1932), sociologist and town-planning pioneer. His time in India and his relationship with Rabindranath Tagore (1861-1941) is described in Bashabi Fraser's editing of their correspondence.[28] India affords many examples of the indirect ways in which the spirit of Christ influenced changes in society even when church and mission organisations have hardly realised the fact, a point clearly made by M.M. Thomas in his *The Acknowledged Christ of the Indian Renaissance,* where he brings out "the many levels of faith-response to Christ outside of Christianity".[29]

Mission and the Need for Peace Among the Religions

Few would dispute that internationalism has an even greater importance for the mission of the Church today. In conclusion some suggestions are made, in the hope that they will be useful, amongst other things, for the Edinburgh 2010 mission agenda.

---

[26] See Nicol MacNicol, "Indian Christianity and Some Notable Indian Christians", *International Review of Missions*, Vol. IX (1920), pp 214-28. This article includes consideration of K.T. Paul and S.K. Datta with the eminent Christians, Pandita Ramabai, Narayan Tilak and Sadhu Sunder Singh; see also Nicol MacNicol, *The Making of Modern India* (London: Oxford University Press,1924).

[27] James Ogilvie, *Our Empire's Debt to Missions* (London: Hodder and Stoughton, 1924), p188-9. It is tempting to observe that Ogilvie's contemporary on the home mission side, John Whyte (1867-1951) was noted for his hostility to the Irish, suggesting that the church mainstream lived in the past! It also has to be observed that too often overseas issues in the Church of Scotland were divided between, and sometimes treated differently by the Church and Nation Committee and the Foreign Mission Committee from 1919 onwards, to their mutual loss. To start with the former committee had an "Empire Problems" section, however, by 1945, its "International Affairs" had a very different approach.

[28] Bashabi Fraser ed., *A Meeting of Two Minds* (Edinburgh: Word Power 2005).

[29] M.M. Thomas, *The Acknowledged Christ of the Indian Renaissance* (Madras: Christian Literature Society, 1969).

Internationalism considered from a Christian mission perspective is about glorifying God through seeking the common good among the peoples of the nations, in the name and spirit of Jesus Christ. At this time of intensified global interdependence it is impossible to separate out the needs of oppressed fellow Christian believers from the rights of the poor of the earth. The mass of suffering humanity is deeply affected by three major, inter-connected global issues. Two are well publicised and attract the support of many people of good will: environmental problems, and economic inequality.

Few groups, other than those connected with far right United States fundamentalism, and their parallels in other religions, reject the challenges posed by climate change and by poverty. Those who are convinced they will be "raptured" believe themselves to be immune to problems of heat and hunger. Everyone else surely can support such appeals as Hans Küng's call for a Global Ethic.[30]

But as Küng recognises, there is a third problem, that of peace between faith groups. Commission Four at Edinburgh 1910 was perhaps starting to recognise the growing importance of other religions. Significantly it is the one issue where the mainline inter-governmental and voluntary institutions are starting to look to the Churches and other religions for more of a lead, rather than simply valuing support on such matters as carbon footprints, fair-trade and the myriads of urgent related economic and environmental issues. In a recent major Oxfam report on poverty and scarcity, its compiler, Duncan Green, states: "Perhaps the most powerful force in shaping attitudes and beliefs is religion".[31] So today Mission has to give serious attention to the need for Peace among the religions. In particular there is a strong case for seeing at the heart of this concern the practical relationship between Christianity and Islam.

Like Edinburgh 1910, Edinburgh 2010 included a commission on "The Missionary Message in relation to Non-Christian Religions". It is now given the more friendly title "Christian mission among other faiths".[32] But serious consideration has to be given to the concern raised by Küng and many others that there will be no peace in the world without peace between the religions, and in particular peace between Islam and Christianity. In fact "Mission" still means "crusade" more often than "dialogue". A hundred years ago at Edinburgh the very idea of any dialogue with followers of other religions, based on an interest in their beliefs, was regarded with deep suspicion. As noted above, Annie Small was a pioneer in insisting that missionaries should be prepared to be interested in the beliefs of others.

---

[30] See most recently Hans Küng, *Islam: Past, Present and Future* (Oxford: One World, 2007).

[31] Duncan Green, *From Poverty to Power: How Active Citizens and Effective States can Change the World* (Oxford: Oxfam International, 2008).

[32] See Daryl Balia and Kirsteen Kim eds., *Edinburgh 2010: Witnessing to Christ Today* (Oxford: Regnum, 2010), 34-60.

It is about Internationalism and Religions globally that our distance from 1910 is greatest. It is true that Commission IV of Edinburgh 1910 is still instructive for the 2010 agenda. David S. Cairns' and Annie Small's concerns, and the fact that the first issue of the *International Review of Missions* in 1912 started with both a justification for an international approach by the editor, J.H. Oldham, and an article on Mission and Islam should alert us. But there is grave underestimation of the particular urgency as to what is meant about Mission and Muslims. First, globalisation makes our lives inseparable from people of a faith almost as numerous and international as ours. Secondly, the fact that Islam came six hundred years after Christ indicates the limitations of evolutionary approaches like that of A.G. Hogg, a correspondent of Edinburgh 1910's Commission IV. The contemporary significance of the complex European history of Muslims is not recognised by British Christians. Our disastrous contemporary political and economic relationship with the Middle East, from Israel to Pakistan, is over-influenced by economic ideology, by oil prices, and equally by millennial fantasies about the Holy Land. Such things prevent genuine relationships with most Muslims here and in North America.

In 1993, the Church of Scotland General Assembly received a Board of World Mission and Unity report on "Mission and Evangelism in a Multifaith Society and in a Multifaith World".[33] Its Secretary well recalls the two years' work and its stormy reception in some evangelical circles! That report is still one of the few attempts to provide some practical help and basic theological reflection, but sixteen years on it is essential that Christian mission is clear about its relationship to Islam, otherwise it will degenerate into propaganda and spin.

Christian-Muslim relations globally are toxic, to borrow the current financial term. But there are hopeful signs and missiologists should take a close interest in recent initiatives. "A Common Word" from an international group of Muslim leaders and scholars is very slowly evoking a Christian response, as it was meant to.[34] For example, Rowan Williams' comments need priority attention in the preparation for 2010.[35]

In Scotland, David Kerr and before him W. Montgomery Watt were eminent scholars who were ahead of the churches in seeking positive relations between Muslims and Christians.[36] But there is still a truly

---

[33] *Reports to the General Assembly of the Church of Scotland, 1993* (Edinburgh: Church of Scotland, 1993), 569-591.

[34] See www.acommonword.com.

[35] Rowan Williams, *A Common Word for the Common Good* (Canterbury: Church of England, 2008).

[36] Professor Kerr who founded the Birmingham Centre for the Study of Islam and Christian-Muslim Relations in 1976 was Professor of Christianity in the Non-Western World at the University of Edinburgh from 1995 to 2005. Professor Watt, called "the last Orientalist", published internationally renowned works on

alarming degree of ignorance in Christian circles about almost all aspects of Islam, apart from some of the skeletons in its cupboard, and aspects of international violence in relation to the Muslim world.

If mutual respect in dialogue can be more widely established, many important discoveries are likely to shape Christian mission. The more Christians and Muslims discover how much common ground is shared the more opportunities there will be for a joint prophetic witness. The centrality of God and the reality of human accountability to God could challenge global societies in a new way.

In the current crisis of international finance there is a new opportunity for Christians and Muslims in all walks of life to share ideas and seek common causes, especially about reducing poverty, and on stewardship of the environment. Christians may need to listen to hard truths on interest, usury and speculation, with questions about the real value of assets and the sharing of risk. The march to "make poverty history" focussed on Debt, yet now debt is haunting the world. Islamic thinkers have much to offer – the prohibition on "riba", or usury, links with the injustice of odious debts and the folly or greed of easy credit. There is an emphasis on the sharing of risk between lender and borrower. Michael Taylor has begun to open these concerns for Christian ethics.[37]

At the same time, there are issues where Christians may have something of a challenge to Islam in return, so long as we do this with more humility, and after better listening than appears to come naturally to missiologists. There is legitimate concern about the position of women in majority Muslim countries. Historical interest in Annie Small's indignation about Islam's treatment of women has contemporary equivalents, for example, yet these must be qualified by an informed discussion of recent contributions by Muslim women in particular.[38] And on the place of women in religion and society we need to recall the chequered history of the Church, and contemporary struggles, not least in the Catholic and Orthodox churches. The same is true on wider sexuality questions. An equally important area where open discussion on a basis of mutual respect is important relates to the nature of democracy, including reciprocal rights for believers in such countries as Saudi Arabia or Pakistan.

Conclusion

Examples have been provided of Scottish Protestant missionary activity responding to increasing international inter-dependence. This suggests that

---

Muhammed. Neither man was taken sufficiently seriously by the churches over their concerns for a genuine meeting of Muslim and Christian minds.

[37] Michael Taylor, *Border Crossings: Exploring Social Theology in Christianity and Islam* (Prague: International Baptist Theological Seminary, 2006), 66ff.

[38] For example, Leila Ahmed, *Women and Gender in Islam: Historical Roots of a Modern Debate* (Yale: Yale University Press, 1992).

for Christian mission to be authentic in the context of the three global challenges of poverty, environmental threat and religious conflict, it should recognise that a co-operative approach to religion is the right way ahead. There is as much of the way, the truth and the life of Jesus Christ outwith the Church as there is within its institutions. In particular, Christianity and Islam have to grow to accept their mutual responsibilities in the complex interdependence of the world today.

CONCLUSION

In a small book published just over one hundred years ago, David S. Cairns, Professor of Systematic Theology at the United Free Church of Scotland College in Aberdeen and Chairman of the influential Commission IV on "The Missionary Message in relation to Non-Christian Religions" at the Edinburgh 1910 World Missionary Conference, argued that there are three features which distinguish the Scottish contribution to the modern missionary movement.[1] By way of conclusion to the essays assembled in this book, it may be observed that Cairns' three features continue to make their mark. To these will be added three further features which stand out perhaps no less strongly.

Social Vision

The first feature discerned by Cairns was the extent to which Scottish missionary engagement was driven by a vision of social transformation. Without compromising the place of personal conversion and church growth in Christian mission, the Scottish endeavour was inspired by a vision of "…a legislative and economic order of Society which shall be in accordance with the mind of Christ."[2] "All down through Scottish history," as Cairns read it, "has gone this theocratic inspiration which it derived from Geneva." This Calvinist legacy, sometimes described as the "Godly Commonwealth", has nurtured a communitarian vision in Scotland which continues to distinguish its political life. Surveying the early years of the Scottish Parliament, restored in 1999, Graham Blount comments that "… a legacy of 'cultural Presbyterianism', in the form of a commitment to social justice, is at the heart of the parliament's and perhaps the nation's agenda…"[3]

When Scots, inspired by faith, applied themselves to missionary engagement in Asia, Africa and elsewhere, it is perhaps little surprise that social justice was high on their agenda. John McCracken's essay, with its consideration of four great Scottish missionaries in southern Africa, their combined work spanning almost 200 years, brings this into focus. No wonder that Thabo Mbeki, when he addressed the Scottish Parliament as President of South Africa in June 2001, devoted so much of his speech to paying tribute to what the Scottish missionary contribution had meant for

---

[1] David S. Cairns, *The Vocation of Scotland in View of her Religious Heritage* (London: SCM, 1911). See further this volume, 29-37, 100-101.
[2] Cairns, *Vocation of Scotland*, 22.
[3] Graham K. Blount, "A New Voice in a New Land?", in William Storrar and Peter Donald eds., *God in Society: Doing Social Theology in Scotland Today* (Edinburgh: St Andrew Press, 2003), 47.

the resistance of racism and the advance of social justice in southern Africa.[4]

The approach of Scottish missionaries in southern Africa was influenced by that of their compatriots in India who held out against any tendency to concentrate exclusively on individual conversion in favour of a strategy which aimed to influence the entire community, indeed the entire nation, over an extended period of time. The passion for this big social vision was perhaps never better expressed than in the attempts of the aged William Miller to lobby the Edinburgh 1910 World Missionary Conference in favour of an approach to mission which aimed at the "Christianisation" of the entire community. A vision of the kingdom of God coming to expression in the life of the community runs as a continuous thread through the story of Scottish missionary engagement around the world.

Ecclesial Commitment

The second strong feature discerned by David Cairns was the prominence of the church in Scottish missionary thinking. As he wrote, employing the military metaphor which was popular at the time: "I praise God for the great free lances of the Spirit, whom he has given to the world all down through history, to widen its thinking and to ennoble its aspirations, but the conquest of the world for Christ will never be made by the free lances but by the regular army, the Church which Christ founded and against which the gates of hell shall not prevail."[5] It can be argued that Cairns rather underestimated the role of the "free lances" in the missionary enterprise. Rose Dowsett's chapter opens up a whole sector where missionary work was only loosely connected with formal church structures. Even when the connection was there, forthright missionaries were often uncomfortably related to the church bodies to which they were responsible.

Nonetheless, compared with the situation in many other countries where missionary societies were separate from the regular life of the church, in the Scottish Presbyterian churches a sustained effort was made to integrate overseas mission work into the mainstream life of the church. As Dugald Mackichan observed:

> If it be true, as has sometimes been said, that in proportion to their membership and their resources the Scottish Churches have a larger place in the missionary world than most other churches, with the exception of the Moravian Church, this is to be attributed not to superiority in spirituality and devotion to their Lord, but largely to the place which they have been led to give to Missions in the scheme of Church life and to the facilities which their ecclesiastical organization has provided for the realisation of their ideal. Once its Foreign Mission had secured this place *within* the Church of Scotland

---

[4] See *Scotland: A Global Connection Strategy* (Edinburgh: Scottish Executive, 2001), 5.

[5] Cairns, *Vocation of Scotland*, 28-29.

there was ready to hand the organization which was needed for enlisting the aid of its members in the near and remote parts of the land.[6]

It has to be acknowledged that this was an ideal which was never completely fulfilled. The sobering judgement of Andrew F. Walls has met with wry recognition from those with worldwide mission closest to their hearts: "While the Scottish perception of missions has sometimes (not always) been a high one, it is hard to escape the conclusion that the missionary project, whether forwarded by the abundance of the rich or the tithes of the poor, was always a peripheral one, always on the edge of the home church's vision, always the direct concern of the few."[7] However, even if the ideal was often frustrated by the inability or unwillingness of the home church to take the missionary project into its core self-understanding, those who served overseas as missionaries had a very strong church consciousness. As concluded in the chapter above, they "took the church seriously, both the Church which sent them and, where they found one, that into which they became integrated".[8]

Intellectual Quality

The third distinguishing feature identified by Cairns was that "Scotland has always loved strong thinking in religion and she loves it still."[9] Few nations have had such a passionate commitment to the development of education, at all levels, over such a long period of time as is the case with Scotland. When this was translated into the missionary enterprise, it resulted in intellectual formation being given a central place. Alexander Duff in Calcutta, John Wilson in Bombay and William Miller at Madras were outstanding leaders in this field. Institutions such as Lovedale in South Africa's Eastern Cape, the Hope Waddell Institution at Calabar in Nigeria and the Overtoun Institution at Livingstonia in northern Malawi were responsible for the intellectual formation of the future leaders of these nations – something often acknowledged with gratitude.

Many of the missionaries who served were children of the Scottish Enlightenment just as much as of Scottish traditions of faith. This meant that they took an intellectual approach to their task. James Legge in China or J.N. Farquhar and A.G. Hogg in India were leading figures, on any reckoning, in opening up critical debate on the understanding of Christian faith required by the cultures and contexts in which it was taking root in

---

[6] Dugald Mackichan, *The Missionary Ideal in the Scottish Churches* (London: Hodder & Stoughton, 1927), 101.
[7] A.F. Walls, "Missions", in Nigel M. de S. Cameron ed. *Dictionary of Scottish Church History and Theology* (Edinburgh: T. & T. Clark, 1993), 573.
[8] Ross and Wilkie, 'Edinburgh 1910 and Scottish Experience of Serving in Mission 1950-2000', this volume, 104.
[9] Cairns, *Vocation of Scotland*, 33-34.

Asia. For a broad intellectual engagement with the missionary movement as a whole, probably the outstanding figure in the 20th century was J.H. Oldham. At the beginning of the 21st century, no interpreter of the significance of the missionary movement has greater influence than Andrew F. Walls.

If Scotland made a disproportionate contribution to the worldwide missionary movement, it is probably in its intellectual dimension that this is most clearly apparent. In assessing the influence of its Scottish provenance on the Edinburgh 1910 World Missionary Conference it is notable that one of the most innovative features of the Conference was the engagement of leading theologians in its counsels and debates. This intellectual quality is one of the threads which runs through Scottish involvement in the worldwide missionary movement right up to the present day.

Extensive Engagement

It would be remiss to conclude this book without acknowledging the extent of the Scottish engagement in worldwide mission which it has illustrated. It is, purposely, a "broad brush" kind of book which rarely enters far into the detail of particular missionary projects. Nevertheless, even by way of passing allusion, it demonstrates the wide extent of Scottish missionary engagement. When the three major Presbyterian churches in Scotland were re-united as the Church of Scotland in 1929, the Church magazine commented on the work of the Foreign Mission Department that its work, "...dazzles one by its magnitude. Scarcely possible is it for an ordinary mind to keep track of it all."[10] The way in which work was taken forward during the 20th century is revealed by the chapter by Kenneth Ross and James Wilkie with its contributions featuring Argentina, Bhutan, Belgium, France, the Netherlands, Ghana, Hong Kong, India, Israel/Palestine, Jamaica, Kenya, Madagascar, Malawi, Nigeria, Pakistan, South Africa, and Zambia. Rose Dowsett's chapter draws our attention to Scots who served in China, Indonesia and Thailand as well as Australia and New Zealand.

Time and space forbade any justice being done to such revered pioneers as John G. Paton to whose work the origin of the church in Vanuatu (New Hebrides) may be traced,[11] William and Isabella Carslaw whose 37 years at Dhour El Choueir did much to lay the foundations of the Reformed Church in Lebanon, or Robert and Sarah Kalley whose work was seminal for the emergence of Presbyterianism in Brazil.[12] No mention has been made of George Turner of Samoa, John Mackenzie of Botswana, James Chalmers of

---

[10] Cit. Elizabeth A.C. Walls, *Pages of Life* (Edinburgh: Church of Scotland Board of World Mission and Unity, 1987), 21.
[11] See James Paton ed., *John G. Paton, D.D., Missionary in the New Hebrides: An Autobiography* Vols I and II (London: Hodder & Stoughton, 1889).
[12] See William B. Forsyth, *The Wolf from Scotland: The Story of Robert Reid Kalley – Pioneer Missionary* (Darlington: Evangelical Press, 1988).

Papua New Guinea or James Gilmour of Mongolia, each a missionary of enormous significance in their chosen sphere. An even greater scale of omission comes into view when consideration is given to Scots who have participated in Roman Catholic missionary work. The structure of international missionary orders through which much of the Roman Catholic missionary endeavour is channelled makes it harder to trace the outline of a specifically national effort. Nonetheless this certainly exists and there is a hidden but important history which largely remains to be written. Should the time come when the totality of Scottish participation in the modern missionary movement is readily appreciated, its sheer extent will be one of the most striking features.

Taking the Long View

A perennial debate in regard to missionary strategy concerns the level of priority to be attached to short-term gains which are relatively easily attainable as opposed to working for results which will be apparent only in the longer term but which might have higher and more enduring quality. The default Scottish position in any such debate is to look to having impact which will be demonstrated in the longer term.

Dugald Mackichen observed that: "There is a quality of mind to which Lord Bacon has given the name 'longanimity'. He finds it in those who are prepared to work towards a distant goal, the attainment of which is ultimate, not immediate. In facing the problem of the Christianization of India the Church of Christ may find room for the exercise of this mental quality."[13] As the first large "mission field" with which Scottish missionaries were substantially engaged, India cast a long shadow across the entire enterprise. This may help to explain the inclination to the long view which runs through the thinking of many Scottish missionaries.

National Identity and Global Outlook

The final strand to be considered is the balance struck between a strong sense of national identity, on the one hand, and a highly global outlook on the other. The establishment of the SSPCK in 1709, which may be taken as marking the beginning of the Scottish missionary movement, came just two years after the Union of the Parliaments in 1707. During three hundred years when Scottish identity was very much at stake, the missionary movement proved to be one outlet through which it could be expressed. Esther Breitenbach, in her chapter, indicates the extent to which the missionary movement fostered a source of national pride in Scotland and played its part in the construction of Scottish identity.

---

[13] Mackichen, *The Missionary Ideal*, 167.

On the other hand, it is in the nature of the missionary movement that it is anything but parochial. One outcome of the missionary movement was the strongly ecumenical vision which took root in Scotland and is considered in its contemporary manifestation by Stephen Smyth in his chapter. This shows both how Scotland has been influenced by the ecumenical movement and how it has contributed to it. Chris Wigglesworth, in his chapter, traces ways in which the missionary movement proved to be a seedbed of internationalism. It apparently had a capacity both express Scottish identity and to foster an internationalist outlook. John McCracken's analysis of a succession of Scottish missionaries to Africa notes that they "combined a sensitivity to global events and intellectual influences with a profound sense of Scottishness".[14] The perspectives offered in this book suggest that this may be regarded as characteristic of the movement as a whole.

The Surprise Factor

Despite what its aficionados might hope, the reality is that the Scottish missionary movement was rather a fringe affair. To those outside the church constituency it was a source of puzzlement or embarrassment, the more so in the recent age of post-colonial guilt. Even within the churches which provided its support base, it was often a marginal band of enthusiasts who kept the flag flying for the missionary movement. Most leaders and members were preoccupied with local concerns. Little did they dream of the outcome which has been sketched by Andrew Walls:

> Few in ecclesiastical leadership had the remotest idea that the so often struggling movement was to be instrumental in the transformation of the demographic and cultural composition of the Christian church. A movement that arose in the heart of Christendom helped Christianity to survive the death of Christendom. A project that was soaked in the Enlightenment helped produce a Christianity whose strength now lies in its independence from the Enlightenment. An expression of Christianity that arose from interaction with deep currents of European culture helped to foster a Christianity that will depend for its future on its critical interaction with the ancient cultures of Africa and Asia.[15]

In this extraordinary transformation the Scottish missionary movement played no small part. Were its contribution to be characterised, among its leading features would be social vision, ecclesial commitment, intellectual quality, extensive engagement, an inclination to the long view, and a balance struck between national identity and global outlook. Insofar as these characteristics help to explain the impact it has had, they merit

---

[14] McCracken, 'Andrew Ross and the Radical Strand in Scotland's Missionary Tradition', this volume, 84.
[15] Andrew F. Walls, *The Cross-Cultural Process in Christian History* (Edinburgh: T.&T. Clark & New York: Orbis, 2002), 235.

consideration by all who take responsibility for the ongoing development of Christian mission.

BIBLIOGRAPHY

Primary Sources

A Short History of Glasgow City Mission, Centenary Report, 1926.

ACTS (Action of Churches Together in Scotland). *Memorandum and Articles of Association.* 8 September 2008.

Andrew Ross to George Macleod, 17 March 1959, Macleod of Fuinary Papers, National Library of Scotland Acc. 9084/68.

Ashcroft, Tony. "Roots and Fruits – Madagascar." Paper presented to "Roots and Fruits" conference, Glasgow, 25 April 2009.

Astley, Jeff. "What Prevents Christian Churches from Learning?" "Receptive Ecumenism and Ecclesial Learning: Learning to Be Church Together" Conference, Ushaw College, Durham, 11-15 January 2009.

Berkeley, John and Muriel. "Roots and Fruits." Paper presented to "Roots and Fruits" conference, Glasgow, 25 April 2009.

Bible Training Institute Annual Report for 1908-9.

Bolen, Donald. "Reconciling Paths: Ecumenical Learning, Conversing and Deepening Fundamental Human Experience." "Receptive Ecumenism and Ecclesial Learning: Learning to Be Church Together" Conference, Ushaw College, Durham, 11-15 January 2009.

Brown, Janet. "Reflections on Time Spent in Pakistan." Paper presented to "Roots and Fruits" conference, Glasgow, 25 April 2009.

Calvert, Robert. "Scots International Church, Rotterdam." Paper presented to "Roots and Fruits" conference, Glasgow, 25 April 2009.

Campbell, Laurie. "Roots and Fruits – Kenya." Paper presented to "Roots and Fruits" conference, Glasgow, 25 April 2009.

China's Millions, November 1900.

The Next Steps for Churches Together in Pilgrimage: Including Definitive Proposals for Ecumenical Instruments. London: British Council of Churches and the Catholic Truth Society for the Inter-Church Process, 1989.

Dodman, Roy and Jane. "Roots and Fruits: The Jamaican Experience." Paper presented to "Roots and Fruits" conference, Glasgow, 25 April 2009.

Hepburn, Anne. "Roots and Fruits – Malawi 1950-1966." Paper presented to "Roots and Fruits" conference, Glasgow, 25 April 2009.

[Heron, Robert.] *Account of the Proceedings and Debate in the General Assembly of the Church of Scotland respecting the Propagation of the Gospel to the Heathen...* Edinburgh: Lawrie, 1796.

Hulbert, Alastair. "Mission to Structures and Ideologies." Paper presented to "Roots and Fruits" conference, Glasgow, 25 April 2009.

Jeffrey, Carol. "Gold Coast / Ghana: A Reflection." Paper presented to "Roots and Fruits" conference, Glasgow, 25 April 2009.

Jeffrey, Eric W.S. "Roots and Fruits – Northern Malawi." Paper presented to "Roots and Fruits" conference, Glasgow, 25 April 2009.

Kerr, Elspeth. "Roots and Fruits – Israel/Palestine." Paper presented to "Roots and Fruits" conference, Glasgow, 25 April 2009.

MacGregor, Margaret S. "Roots and Fruits: Bengal." Paper presented to "Roots and Fruits" conference, Glasgow, 25 April 2009.

Mackenzie, Bill. "Lubwa, Northern Rhodesia/Zambia." Paper presented to "Roots and Fruits" conference, Glasgow, 25 April 2009.

Mackenzie, Murdoch and Anne. "Roots and Fruits: Madras, India, 1966-1978." Paper presented to "Roots and Fruits" conference, Glasgow, 25 April 2009.

Macrae, Norman C. "But Why Edinburgh?" Paper presented to "Roots and Fruits" conference, Glasgow, 25 April 2009.

Minutes of the Annual Business Meetings of the Bible Training Institute, 1893 and 1895.

Moir, Ian. "Roots and Fruits: South Africa." Paper presented to "Roots and Fruits" conference, Glasgow, 25 April 2009.

Morton, Alasdair. "Zambia." Paper presented to "Roots and Fruits" conference, Glasgow, 25 April 2009.

Morton, Colin. "Roots and Fruits: Israel/Palestine." Paper presented to "Roots and Fruits" conference, Glasgow, 25 April 2009.

Musgrave, Joan and Clarence. "Roots and Fruits – Zambia." Paper presented to "Roots and Fruits" conference, Glasgow, 25 April 2009.

New Directions, Presbyterian Church of Queensland magazine, 12/5 (Oct/Nov 2008).

New Edinburgh Almanac, 1873.

Paton, Molly. "My Ghanaian Experience." Paper presented to "Roots and Fruits" conference, Glasgow, 25 April 2009.

Perfectae Caritatis (Decree on the Up-to-Date Renewal of Religious Life). Austin Flannery ed. *Vatican Council II – The Conciliar and Post Conciliar Documents.* Leominster: Fowler Wright, 1980.

Proceedings and Debates of the General Assembly of the Free Church of Scotland, 1890. Edinburgh: Lorimer and Gillies; London: James Nisbet, 1890.

Queensland Baptist, December 1923.

Report of the Foreign Mission Committee. *Reports on the Schemes of the Church of Scotland, 1890.* Edinburgh: William Blackwood and Sons, 1890.

Report of the Foreign Mission Committee. *Reports on the Schemes of the Church of Scotland, 1910.* Edinburgh: William Blackwood and Sons, 1910.

Report of the Board of World Mission and Unity. *Reports to the General Assembly of the Church of Scotland, 1993.* Edinburgh: Church of Scotland, 1993.

Tenth Report on Foreign Mission (for 1909). *Reports to the General Assembly of the United Free Church of Scotland,* 1910. Edinburgh: United Free Church of Scotland, 1910.

Ritchie, James Mcl. "South Arabia Mission in Sheikh Othman, a Township in Aden Colony." Paper presented to "Roots and Fruits" conference, Glasgow, 25 April 2009.

"Roll of Missionaries from Scotland, 1829-1900." *Proceedings and Debates of the General Assembly of the Free Church of Scotland, Held at Edinburgh, May 1900.* Edinburgh: Lorimer and Gillies; London: James Nisbet, 1900.

Scotland: A Global Connection Strategy, Edinburgh: Scottish Executive, 2001.

Scottish Missionary and Philanthropic Register, 1826.

Smyth, Stephen. "Ecumenism Today – Scotland and the Wider World." The Glasgow Newman Association Lecture, 22 February 2008.

Stone, Vernon. "Reflections on Malawi 1949-56 and Zambia 1956-67." Paper presented to "Roots and Fruits" conference, Glasgow, 25 April 2009.

Taylor, Howard. "Malawi 1965-81." Paper presented to "Roots and Fruits" conference, Glasgow, 25 April 2009.

The Scots Confession 1560. Edited by G D Henderson, together with a rendering into modern English by James Bulloch. Edinburgh: St Andrew Press, 1960.

United Free Church of Scotland: Statement of Principles.

Report on Foreign Missions for 1890. *The Proceedings of the Synod of the United Presbyterian Church, May 1891.* Edinburgh, United Presbyterian Church, 1891.

Ut Unum Sint – On Commitment to Ecumenism. Papal Encyclical. Rome, May 1995, art. 77.

Wallace, Dorothy. "Darjeeling, Eastern Himalaya Diocese, Church of North India." Paper presented to "Roots and Fruits" conference, Glasgow, 25 April 2009.

Wigglesworth, Chris. "Western India, the Church and I." Paper presented to "Roots and Fruits" conference, Glasgow, 25 April 2009.

World Council of Churches. "Called to Be One." Document of 9th Assembly of WCC, Porto Allegre, Brazil, 2006.

"World Missionary Conference" [by a Contributor]. *The Scotsman,* 15 June 1910.

World Missionary Conference 1910. *Monthly News Sheet.*

World Missionary Conference, 1910. Commission I – Responses to Questionnaire, manuscripts held by The Burke Library at Union Theological Seminary in the City of New York, Columbia University Libraries.

World Missionary Conference, 1910. Commission IV – Responses to Questionnaire, manuscripts held by the Centre for the Study of World Christianity, University of Edinburgh.

World Missionary Conference, 1910. *Cooperation and the Promotion of Unity.* Report of Commission VIII. Edinburgh & London: Oliphant, Anderson & Ferrier; New York, Chicago and Toronto: Fleming H. Revell, 1910.

World Missionary Conference, 1910. *Education in Relation to the Christianization of National Life.* Report of Commission III. Edinburgh & London: Oliphant, Anderson & Ferrier; New York, Chicago and Toronto: Fleming H. Revell, 1910.

World Missionary Conference, 1910. *Missions and Governments.* Report of Commission VII. Edinburgh & London: Oliphant, Anderson & Ferrier; New York, Chicago and Toronto: Fleming H. Revell, 1910.

World Missionary Conference, 1910. *Statement of Aims and Plans.*

World Missionary Conference, 1910. *Statistical Atlas of Christian Missions.* Edinburgh: World Missionary Conference, 1910.

World Missionary Conference, 1910. *The Church in the Mission Field.* Report of Commission II, Edinburgh & London: Oliphant, Anderson & Ferrier; New York, Chicago, and Toronto: Fleming H. Revell, 1910.

World Missionary Conference, 1910. *The History and Records of the Conference.* Edinburgh & London: Oliphant, Anderson & Ferrier; New York, Chicago and Toronto: Fleming H. Revell, 1910.

World Missionary Conference, 1910. *The Missionary Message in Relation to Non-Christian Religions.* Report of Commission IV. Edinburgh & London: Oliphant, Anderson & Ferrier; New York, Chicago and Toronto: Fleming H. Revell, 1910.

World Missionary Conference, 1910. *The Preparation of Missionaries*, (also titled *The Training of Teachers*). Report of Commission V. Edinburgh & London: Oliphant, Anderson & Ferrier; New York, Chicago and Toronto: Fleming H. Revell, 1910.

Secondary Sources

Ahmed, Leila. *Women and Gender in Islam: Historical Roots of a Modern Debate.* Yale: Yale University Press, 1992.

An Account of the Rise, Constitution and Management of the Society in Scotland for Propagating Christian Knowledge. Edinburgh: William Brown, 1720.

Anderson, Gerald H. ed. *Biographical Dictionary of Christian Missions.* Grand Rapids: Eerdmans, 1999.

Ansdell, Douglas. *The People of the Great Faith: The Highland Church 1690-1900.* Stornoway: Acair, 1998.

Arnot, Frederick S. *Bible and Garenganze; or Four Years Further Work in Central Africa.* London: J.E. Hawkins, 1893.

Arnot, Frederick S. *Garenganze: or, Seven Years' Pioneer Mission Work in Central Africa.* London: J.E. Hawkins, 1889.

Arnot, Frederick S. *Missionary Travels in Central Africa.* With an introduction by W.H. Bennet. Bath: Echoes of Service, 1914.

Baillie, John. "Kennedy, Harry Angus Alexander."*Dictionary of National Biography 1931-1940.* Ed. L.G. Wickham Legg. London: Oxford University Press, 1949, pp. 504-505.

Balia, Daryl and Kirsteen Kim Eds. *Edinburgh 2010: Witnessing to Christ Today.* Oxford: Regnum, 2010.

Banerjea, K.M. *Dialogues on the Hindu Philosophy.* Calcutta: Thacker, Spink & Co: 1861.

Bebbington, D.W. "Balfour of Burleigh, Lord." Nigel M. de S. Cameron Ed., *Dictionary of Scottish Church History and Theology.* Edinburgh: T. & T. Clark, 1993, p. 53.

Bell, George K. A. *Randall Davidson: Archbishop of Canterbury.* 3rd ed. London: Oxford University Press, 1952.

Bliss, Katherine, revised Andrew Porter. "Oldham, Joseph Houldsworth (1874-1969)." *Dictionary of National Biography*, Vol. 41, pp. 692-94.

Blount, Graham K. "A New Voice in a New Land?" William Storrar and Peter Donald Ed. *God in Society: Doing Social Theology in Scotland Today.* Edinburgh: St Andrew Press, 2003, pp. 36-49.

Bolink, Peter. *Towards Church Union in Zambia: Church Union Efforts in Central Africa.* Franeker, Netherlands: Wever, 1967.

[Bonar, Andrew A. and Robert Murray McCheyne]. *Narrative of a Mission of Inquiry to the Jews from the Church of Scotland in 1839.* Edinburgh: William Whyte, 1843.

Boorman, Howard L. Ed. *Biographical Dictionary of Republican China.* New York: Columbia University Press, 1964.

Boyd, Robin. *The Witness of the Student Christian Movement.* London: SPCK, 2007.

Bradley, Ian. *Colonies of Heaven – Celtic Models for Today's Church.* London: Darton, Longman and Todd Ltd, 2000.

Brooks, Joanna ed. *Collected Writings of Samson Occom, Mohegan: Leadership and Literature in 18th Century Native America.* New York: Oxford University Press, 2006.

Brown, Sheana. *Rough Diamond: the Life Story of Bill Gilvear.* Fearn: Christian Focus, 1996.

Brown, Stewart J. "William Robertson, Early Orientalism and the Historical Disquisition on India." *Scottish Historical Review,* Vol. 88 (2009), pp. 289–312.

Brown, Stewart J. and David Fergusson. "The Rev Andrew Ross: Missionary and Church Historian." *The Independent,* 3 September 2008.

Brown, Stewart J. *Providence and Empire: Religion, Politics and Society in the United Kingdom, 1815-1914.* Harlow: Pearson/Longman, 2008.

Brown, William. *History of the Propagation of Christianity among the Heathen since the Reformation.* 2nd ed., Edinburgh: Fullarton, 1823.

Brunton, Henry. *Grammar and Vocabulary of the Susoo Language.* Edinburgh: J. Ritchie, 1802.

Bryce, James. *Sketch of Native Education in India under the Superintendence of the Church of Scotland; with remarks on character and condition of the Hindus as they bear on the question of conversion to Christianity.* London: W.H. Allen and Edinburgh: Blackwood, 1839.

Buchan, James. *Capital of the Mind: How Edinburgh Changed the World.* London: John Murray, 2003.

Buchanan, Claudius. *Christian Researches in Asia, with notices on the translation of the Scriptures into the Oriental languages.* 5th ed. London: Cadell and Davies, 1812.

Buchanan, Claudius. *Colonial Ecclesiastical Establishment, being a brief view of the state of the colonies of Great Britain and of the Asiatic Empire, humbly submitted to the consideration of the Imperial Parliament.* London: Cadell and Davies, 1812.

Buchanan, Claudius. *Memoir of the Expediency of an Ecclesiastical Establishment for British India: both as the means of perpetuating the Christian religion amongst our own countrymen and as a foundation for the ultimate civilization of the Natives.* London: Cadell and Davies, 1805.

Burns, Islay. *Memoir of the Rev William C. Burns, Missionary to China from the English Presbyterian Church.* London: James Nisbet 1870; reprinted Stoke-on-Trent: Tentmaker, 2006.

Cairns, David S. *Life and Times of Alexander Robertson MacEwen.* London: Hodder & Stoughton, 1925.

Cairns, David S. *The Vocation of Scotland in View of her Religious Heritage.* London: SCM, 1911.

Calder, James M. *Scotland's March Past: The Share of Scottish Churches in The London Missionary Society.* London: The Livingstone Press, 1945.

Cameron, Nigel M. de S. Ed. *Dictionary of Scottish Church History and Theology.* Edinburgh: T. & T. Clark, 1993.

Chalmers, James. *His Autobiography and Letters.* With a supplementary chapter by A.I. Johnston. London: Religious Tract Society, 1914.

Chalmers, J.A. *Tiyo Soga: A Page of Missionary History.* Edinburgh: Elliot, 1873.

Chambers, Don. "The Church of Scotland's nineteenth century Foreign Mission Scheme: Evangelical or Moderate revival?" *Journal of Religious History* 9/2 (1976), pp. 115-138.

Choi, Sung-il. "John Ross (1842-1915) and the Korean Protestant Church." Ph.D. thesis, University of Edinburgh, 1992.

Christianity in India: proceedings of a public meeting held at Exeter Hall to consider the future relations of the British government to religion in India. London: Reed and Parden, 1858.

Christie, Dugald. *Thirty Years in Moukden: Being the Experience of Dugald Christie.* Edited by his wife [Iza Christie]. London: Constable, 1912.

Christie, Mrs Dugald. *Dugald Christie of Manchuria, Pioneer and Medical Missionary: The Story of a Life with a Purpose.* London: J. Clarke, [1932].

Clarke, W.K. Lowther. *A History of the SPCK.* London: SPCK, 1959.

Clements, Keith. *Faith on the Frontier: A Life of J.H. Oldham.* Edinburgh: T. & T. Clark; Geneva: WCC, 1999.

Conference on Missions held in 1860 in Liverpool. Edited by the Secretaries of the Conference. London: Nisbet, 1860.

Cox, James L. "The Development of A.G. Hogg's Theology in Relation to Non-Christian Faith: Its Significance for the Tambaram Meeting of the International Missionary Council 1938." Ph.D. thesis, University of Aberdeen, 1977.

Cox, Jeffrey. *Imperial Fault Lines: Christianity and Colonial Power in India, 1818-1940.* Stanford, CA: Stanford University Press, 2002.

Cracknell, Kenneth. *Justice, Courtesy and Love: Theologians and Missionaries Encountering World Religions 1846-1914.* London: Epworth Press, 1995.

Crawford, Dan. *Back to the Long Grass: My Link with Livingstone.* London: Hodder and Stoughton, 1923.

Crawford, Dan. *Thinking Black: 22 Years Without a Break in the Long Grass of Central Africa.* London: Hodder and Stoughton, 1912.

Daniel, W. Harrison. "Patterns of Mission Preaching: The Representation of the Christian Message and the Efik Response in the Scottish Calabar Mission, Nigeria, 1846-1900." Ph.D. thesis, University of Edinburgh, 1993.

David Cairns: An Autobiography, Some Recollections of a Long Life and Selected Letters. Edited by his Son and Daughter with a Memoir by D.M. Baillie. London: SCM, 1950.

Davidson, Allan K. *Evangelicals and Attitudes to India, 1785-1813: Missions, Publicity and Claudius Buchanan.* Abingdon, Berks: Sutton Courtenay Press, 1990.

Day, Lal Behari. *Recollections of Alexander Duff DD LLD, and of the Mission College which he Founded in Calcutta.* London: T. Nelson & Sons, 1879.

De Gruchè, Kingston. *Dr D. Duncan Main of Hangchow, who is known in China as Dr Apricot of Heaven Below.* London: Marshall, Morgan and Scott, 1930.

De Kock, Leon. *Civilising Barbarians: Missionary Narrative and African Textual Response in Nineteenth Century South Africa.* Johannesburg: Witwatersrand University Press, 1996.

Debenham, Frank. *Nyasaland: Land of the Lake.* London, HMSO, 1955.

Dickson, Mora. *The Inseparable Grief: Margaret Cargill of Fiji.* London: Dobson, 1976.

Dow, Derek Alexander . "Domestic Response and Reaction to the Foreign Missionary Enterprises of the Principal Scottish Presbyterian Churches, 1873-1929." Ph.D. thesis, Edinburgh University, 1977.

Duff, Alexander. *A New Era of the English Language and English Literature in India; or, An exposition of the late Governor-General's last edict.* Edinburgh: John Johnstone, 1837.

Duff, Alexander. *India and Indian Missions.* Edinburgh: John Johnstone, 1840.

Duff, Alexander. *Missions the Chief End of the Christian Church; also the qualifications, duties, and trials of an Indian missionary.* Edinburgh: John Johnstone, 1839.

Duff, Alexander. *Vindication of the Church of Scotland's India Missions, being the substance of an address, delivered before the General Assembly of the Church...* Edinburgh: John Johnstone 1837.

Duncan, Graham A. *Lovedale: Coercive Agency.* Pietermaritzburg: Cluster Publications, 2003.

Edwards, Jonathan. *The Works of Jonathan Edwards Vol. 5: Apocalyptic Writings.* Ed. Stephen J. Stein. New Haven CT: Yale University Press, 1977.

Edwards, Jonathan. *The Works of Jonathan Edwards Vol. 7: The Life of David Brainerd.* Ed. Norman Pettit. New Haven CT: Yale University Press, 1984.

Elphick, Richard. *Equality of Believers: Protestant Missionaries and the Racial Politics of South Africa.* Charlottesville: University of Virginia Press, 2012.

Every-Clayton, Joyce E. Winifred. "The Legacy of Robert Reid Kalley." *International Bulletin of Missionary Research,* Vol. 26/3 (2002), pp. 123-127.

Extracts of Letters from the Rev. John Paterson and the Rev. Ebenezer Henderson during their respective tours through the East Sea provinces of Russia, Sweden, Denmark, Jutland, Holstein, Swedish Pomerania etc, to promote the objects of the British and Foreign Bible Society. London: Tilling and Hughes, 1817.

Fairbank, John K. "Assignment for the '70s." *American Historical Review,* 74/3 (1969), pp. 861-79.

Farquhar, J.N. *Gita and Gospel.* Madras: Christian Literature Society 1917.

Farquhar, J.N. *Outline of the Religious Literature of India.* London: Oxford University Press, 1920.

Farquhar, J.N. *Modern Religious Movements in India.* London: Macmillan, 1915.

Farquhar, J.N. *The Crown of Hinduism.* London: Oxford University Press, 1913.

Fawcett, Arthur. *The Cambuslang Revival of the Eighteenth Century.* London: Banner of Truth, 1971.

Fiedler, Klaus. *The Story of Faith Missions.* Oxford: Regnum, 1996.

Forrester, D.B. "Macnicol, Nicol." Nigel M. de S. Cameron Ed., *Dictionary of Scottish Church History and Theology.* Edinburgh: T. & T. Clark, 1993, p. 535.

Forrester, D.B. "Miller, William." Nigel M. de S. Cameron Ed., *Dictionary of Scottish Church History and Theology.* Edinburgh: T. & T. Clark, 1993, pp. 564-65.

Forsyth, William B. *The Wolf from Scotland: The Story of Robert Reid Kalley – Pioneer Missionary.* Darlington: Evangelical Press, 1988.

Foster, John. "A Scottish Contributor to the Missionary Awakening: Robert Millar of Paisley." *International Review of Missions* Vol. 37 (1948), pp. 138-145.

Foster, John. "The Bicentenary of Jonathan Edwards' *Humble Attempt.*" *International Review of Missions* Vol. 37/4 (1948), pp. 375-381.

Fraser, Bashabi Ed. *A Meeting of Two Minds.* Edinburgh: Word Power, 2005.

Friesen, J. Stanley. *Missionary Responses to Tribal Religions at Edinburgh, 1910.* New York et al: Peter Lang, 1996.

Fry, Michael. *The Scottish Empire.* Edinburgh: Tuckwell Press & Birlinn, 2001.

Frykenberg, Robert Eric. *Christianity in India from the Beginnings to the Present.* Oxford: Oxford University Press, 2008.

Fulton, Austin. *Through Earthquake, Wind and Fire: Church and Mission in Manchuria, 1867-1950.* Edinburgh: St Andrew Press, 1967.

Gairdner, W.H.T. *Edinburgh 1910: An Account and Interpretation of the World Missionary Conference*. Edinburgh & London: Oliphant, Anderson & Ferrier; New York, Chicago and Toronto: Fleming H. Revell, 1910.

Gilmour, James. *James Gilmour of Mongolia: His Letters, Diaries and Reports*. Edited and arranged by Richard Lovett. London: Religious Tract Society, 1895.

Gilmour, James. *More about the Mongols*. Selected and arranged from the Diaries and Reports of James Gilmour by Richard Lovett. London: Religious Tract Society, 1893.

Giradot, Norman J. *The Victorian Translation of China: James Legge's Oriental Pilgrimage*. Berkeley: University of California Press, 2002.

Gordon, James M. *James Denney (1856-1917): An Intellectual and Contextual Biography*. Milton Keynes: Paternoster, 2006.

Gray, Nathan Philip. "A Publick Benefite:" the Charitable and Religious Origins of the Society in Scotland for Promoting Christian Knowledge, 1695-1715". Ph.D. thesis, University of Glasgow, 2011.

Grayson, James H. *John Ross: First Missionary to Korea*. Published in Korean, *Na Yohan: Han'gug-ui ch'ot son'gyo-sa*. Taegu: Kyemyŏng University Press, 1982.

Green, Duncan. *From Poverty to Power: How Active Citizens and Effective States can Change the World*. Oxford: Oxfam International, 2008.

Hackett, Rosalind. *Religion in Calabar: The Religious Life and History of a Nigerian Town*. Berlin and New York: Mouton de Gruyter, 1989.

Hall, Catherine. *Civilising Subjects: Metropole and Colony in the English Imagination 1830-1867*. Cambridge: Polity Press, 2002.

Harrison, Alexina Mackay. *A.M. Mackay: Pioneer Missionary of the Church Missionary Society to Uganda*. London: Hodder & Stoughton, 1890.

Hastings, Adrian. *The Church in Africa 1450-1950*. Oxford: Clarendon Press, 1994.

Herman, Arthur. *How the Scots Invented the Modern World: The True Story of How Western Europe's Poorest Nation Created Our World and Everything in It*. New York: Crown Publishers, 2001.

Hetherwick, Alexander. *The Romance of Blantyre: How Livingstone's Dream Came True*. London: James Clarke, no date. [1931].

Hewat, Elizabeth G.K. *Vision and Achievement 1796-1956, A History of the Foreign Missions of the Churches United in the Church of Scotland*. London: Thomas Nelson, 1960.

Hitchen, J.M. "Training Tamate: Formation of the Nineteenth Century Missionary Worldview: the Case of James Chalmers." Ph.D. thesis, University of Aberdeen, 1984.

Hogg, A.G. *Christ's Message of the Kingdom: A Course of Daily Study for Private Students and Bible Circles*. Edinburgh: T. and T. Clark, 1911.

Hogg, A.G. *Karma and Redemption: An Essay Toward the Interpretation of Hinduism and the Restatement of Christianity*. London: Christian Literature Society for India, 1910.

Hogg, A.G. *The Christian Message to the Hindu*. London: SCM, 1947.

Hogg, Rena L. *Master-Builder on the Nile; Being a Record of the Life and Aims of John Hogg, DD, a Christian Missionary*. Pittsburgh: United Presbyterian Board of Publication, 1934.

Hopkins, C. Howard. *John R. Mott 1865-1955: A Biography*. Geneva and Grand Rapids: WCC and Eerdmans, 1979.

Hood, George A. *Mission Accomplished? The English Presbyterian Mission in Lintung, South China*. Frankfurt: Peter Lang, 1986.

Hood, George A. *Neither Bang nor Whimper: The End of a Missionary Era in China.* Singapore: Presbyterian Church of Singapore, [1990].

Ingham, Kenneth. *Reformers in India: An Account of the Work of Christian Missionaries on Behalf of Social Reform.* Cambridge: Cambridge University Press, 1956.

Inglis, John. *Bible Illustrations from the New Hebrides, with Notices of the Progress of the Mission.* London: Nelson, 1990.

Ion, A. Hamish. *The Cross and the Rising Sun, Vol. 1, The Canadian Protestant Missionary Movement in the Japanese Empire, 1872-1931.* Waterloo Ont.: Wilfred Laurier University Press, 2009.

Ion, A. Hamish. *The Cross and the Rising Sun, Vol. 2, The British Protestant Missionary Movement in Japan, Korea and Taiwan, 1865-1945.* Waterloo Ont.: Wilfred Laurier University Press, 1993.

Johnson, Todd M. and Kenneth R. Ross ed. *Atlas of Global Christianity 1910-2010.* Edinburgh: Edinburgh University Press, 2009.

Johnston, Geoffrey. *Of God and Maxim Guns: Presbyterianism in Nigeria 1846-1946.* Waterloo Ont.: Wilfred Laurier University Press, 1988.

Jones, E. Stanley. *The Christ of the Indian Road.* London; Hodder & Stoughton, 1925.

Jones, M.V. "The Sad and Curious Story of Karass, 1802-1835." *Oxford Slavonic Papers* No. 8 (1975), pp. 53-81.

Kalapati, Joshua and Ambrose Jeyasekaran. *Life and Legacy of Madras Christian College (1837-1978).* Chennai: Zha Communications, 2010.

Kalapati, Joshua. *Dr S. Radhakrishnan and Christianity: an Introduction to Hindu-Christian Apologetics.* Delhi: ISPCK 2002.

Kandaswamy, O. Chetty. *Dr. William Miller.* Madras: Christian Literature Society, 1924.

Kasper, Walter. *A Handbook of Spiritual Ecumenism.* New York: New City Press, 2007.

Kasper, Walter. "*Credo Unam Sanctam Ecclesiam* – The Relationship Between the Catholic and Protestant Principles in Fundamental Ecclesiology." Paul Murray Ed. *Receptive Ecumenism and the Call to Catholic Learning – Exploring a Way for Contemporary Ecumenism.* Oxford: Oxford University Press, 2008, pp. 78-88.

Kerr, David A. and Kenneth R. Ross Eds. *Edinburgh 2010: Mission Then and Now.* Oxford: Regnum, 2009.

Kessler, J.B.A. *A Study of the Older Protestant Churches in Peru and Chile.* Goes, Netherlands: Oosterbaan en Le Cointre, 1957.

Kovacs, Abraham. *A History of the Free Church of Scotland's Mission to the Jews in Budapest, and its Impact on the Reformed Church of Hungary.* Frankfurt: Peter Lang, 2006.

Küng, Hans. *Islam: Past, Present and Future.* Oxford: One World, 2007.

Langridge, A.K. *John G. Paton: Later Years and Farewell.* London: Hodder and Stoughton, 1910.

Launhardt, Johannes. *Evangelicals in Addis Ababa (1919-1991): with special reference to the Ethiopian Church Mekane Yesus and the Addis Ababa Synod.* Berlin, Hamburg and Munster: LIT Verlag, 2005.

Laird, Michael A. *Missions and Education in Bengal 1793-1897.* Oxford: Clarendon Press, 1972.

Laws, Robert. *Reminiscences of Livingstonia.* Edinburgh & London: Oliver & Boyd, 1934.

Livingstone, David. *Missionary Travels and Researches in South Africa.* London: John Murray 1857.

Livingstone, W.P. *The White Queen of Okoyong.* London: Hodder and Stoughton, c. 1919.

Lovett, Richard. *History of the London Missionary Society 1795-1895.* Vol. 1. London: Henry Frowde, 1899.

Low, D.A. "Alexander Mackay." *Makerere Journal* Vol. 2 (1959), 50-56.

Lowe, John. *Medical Missions, Their Place and Power.* London: T. Fisher Unwin, 1886.

[Lowe, John] *Medical Missions as Illustrated by Some Letters and Notices of the late Dr Elmslie.* Edinburgh: Edinburgh Medical Missionary Society, 1874.

Lusk, Isabel. *"A Throughly Furnished Woman": Annie Small and the Training of Women Missionaries.* Edinburgh: St Colm's, 1994.

Lyon, David H.S. *In Pursuit of a Vision: the Story of the Church of Scotland's Developing Relationship with the Churches Emerging from the Missionary Movement in the Twenty-five years from 1947 to 1972.* Edinburgh: St Andrew Press, 1998.

McCracken, John. *A History of Malawi 1859-1966.* Rochester NY: James Currey, 2012.

McCracken, John. *Politics and Christianity in Malawi 1875-1940: the Impact of the Livingstonia Mission in the Northern Province.* Cambridge: Cambridge University Press, 1977; 3rd edn., Zomba: Kachere, 2008.

MacInnes, John. *The Evangelical Movement in the Highlands of Scotland, 1688-1800.* Aberdeen: Aberdeen University Press, 1951.

Macintosh, Hamish. *Robert Laws: Servant of Africa.* Edinburgh: Handsel Press, 1993.

Mackay, John A. *The Other Spanish Christ: A Study in the Spiritual History of Spain and South America.* New York: Macmillan 1932.

MacKenzie, John. "David Livingstone: the Construction of the Myth." Graham Walker and Tom Gallagher Eds. *Sermons and Battle Hymns: Protestant Culture in Modern Scotland.* Edinburgh: Edinburgh University Press, 1990.

Mackichan, Dugald. *The Missionary Ideal in the Scottish Churches.* London: Hodder & Stoughton, 1927.

Mackie, Robert C. *Layman Extraordinary.* London: Hodder & Stoughton, 1965.

Maclean, Marjory. "Historical Paper from the Church of Scotland: The 1921 Settlement and the 1929 Union." Report of Committee on Ecumenical Relations, Appendix IX. *Reports to the 2005 General Assembly of the Church of Scotland.* Edinburgh: Church of Scotland, 2005, pp. 26/46-26/51.

MacNicol, Nicol. "Indian Christianity and Some Notable Indian Christians." *International Review of Missions,* Vol. IX (1920), pp 214-28.

MacNicol, Nicol. *Indian Theism.* London: Oxford University Press, 1915.

MacNicol, Nicol. *The Making of Modern India.* London: Oxford University Press, 1924.

Macpherson, G. *Life of Lal Behari Dey: Convert, Pastor, Professor and Author.* Edinburgh: T. & T. Clark, 1900.

Macpherson, R. *The Presbyterian Church in Kenya: An Account of the Origins and Growth of the Presbyterian Church of East Africa.* Nairobi: Presbyterian Church of East Africa, 1973.

Mair, Alexander Mair. *Unforgettable: Memories of China and Scotland.* London: Epworth Press, 1967.

Mann, Bashir. *The New Scots.* Edinburgh , John Donald 1992.

Mann, Bashir. *The Thistle and the Crescent.* Glendaruel: Argyll, 2008.

Martin, Hugh. *Beginning at Edinburgh: A Jubilee Assessment of the World Missionary Conference 1910.* London: Edinburgh House Press, 1960.

Mason, J.C.S. *The Moravian Church and the Missionary Awakening in England.* Woodbridge, Suffolk: Boydell Press for Royal Historical Society, 2001.

Matthew, H.C.G. and Brian Harrison Eds. *Dictionary of National Biography*, Vols. 1-60. Oxford: Oxford University Press, 2004.

Maxwell, Ian. "Alexander Duff and the Theological and Philosophical Background to the General Assembly's Mission to Calcutta." Ph.D. thesis, University of Edinburgh, 1998.

Meek, Donald E. "Gaelic Bible, Revival and Mission: Spiritual Rebirth of the Nineteenth Century Highlands". In James Kirk ed., *The Church in the Highlands.* Edinburgh: Scottish Church History Society, 1998, pp. 114-145.

Metzger, John Mackay. *The Hand and the Road: the Life and Times of John A. Mackay.* Louisville KY: Westminster John Knox Press, 2010.

Millar, Robert. *The History of the Propagation of Christianity and the Overthrow of Paganism, wherein the Christian religion is confirmed, the rise and progress of heathenish idolatry is considered, the overthrow of paganism and the spreading of Christianity in the several ages of the New Testament Church are explained, the present state of the heathens is enquired into and methods for their conversion offered.* Edinburgh, 1723; 2nd ed. London, 1726.

Miller, William. *Scottish Missions in India: Two Lectures.* Edinburgh: Elliot, 1868.

Mitchell, William. "Diego Thomson: Precursor de la Traducción Bíblica en la Época Moderna." *La Biblia en las Américas* Vol. 48/4 (1993), pp. 21-23.

Mitchell, William. "James Thomson and Bible Translation in the Andean Languages." *The Bible Translator Technical Papers* Vol. 41/3 (July 1990), pp. 341-45.

Moberg, David. *The Great Reversal: Evangelism and Social Concern.* London: Scripture Union, 1973.

Monahan, C.H. *The Lepers of Dichpalli,* London: Methodist Book Room, no date.

Morton, Andrew. "J.H. Oldham." Nansie Blackie Ed. *A Time for Trumpets: Scottish Church Movers and Shakers.* Edinburgh, St Andrew Press, 2005, pp. 3-16.

Muller, Max F. *Essays on the Science of Religion.* New York: Charles Scribner's Sons, 1871.

Muller, Max F. *Introduction to the Science of Religion.* London: Longmans, 1882 [1873].

Murray, Paul. "Receptive Ecumenism and Catholic Learning – Establishing the Agenda." Paul Murray Ed. *Receptive Ecumenism and the Call to Catholic Learning – Exploring a Way for Contemporary Ecumenism.* Oxford: Oxford University Press, 2008, pp. 5-25.

Myklebust, Olav Guttorm. *The Study of Missions in Theological Education: an historical enquiry into the place of world evangelization in Western Protestant ministerial training, with particular reference to Alexander Duff's chair of Evangelistic Theology.* Vols. 1 and 2. Oslo: Forlaget Land og Kirke, 1955 and 1957.

Nauroji , Dhanjibhai. *From Zoroaster to Christ: An Autobiographical Sketch of the Rev Dhanjibhai Nauroji the first modern convert from the Zoroastrian religion.* Edinburgh: Oliphant, Anderson & Ferrier, 1909.

Newbigin, Lesslie. *The Open Secret.* London: SPCK, 1978.

Nolan, Albert. *God in South Africa: Challenge of the Gospel.* London: Catholic Institute for International Relations, 1988.

Oak, Sung-Deuk. *The Making of Korean Christianity.* Waco TX: Baylor University Press, 2013.

O'Connor, Daniel. *Three Centuries of Mission: the United Society for the Propagation of the Gospel, 1701-2000.* London and New York: Continuum, 2000.

Oddie, Geoffrey A. *Popular Religion, Elites and Reform: Hook-swinging and its Prohibition in Colonial India.* New Delhi: Manohar, 1996.

Ogilvie, James. *Our Empire's Debt to Missions.* London: Hodder and Stoughton, 1924.

Oldham, J.H. "Reflections on Edinburgh 1910." *Religion in Life.* Vol. XXIX (1959-60), pp. 329-38.

Oliphant, Margaret. "The Missionary Explorer." *Blackwood"s Magazine* (April 1858).

Oliver, Roland. *Sir Harry Johnston and the Scramble for Africa.* London, Chatto & Windus, 1959.

Orr Macdonald, Lesley. *A Unique and Glorious Mission: Women and Presbyterianism in Scotland.* Edinburgh: John Donald, 2000.

Osborne, F.J. and G.D. Johnston. *Coastlands and Islands: First Thoughts on Caribbean Church History.* Kingston, Jamaica: United Theological College of the West Indies, 1972.

Padwick, Constance E. *Temple Gairdner of Cairo.* London: SPCK, 1929.

Palsetia, J.S. "Parsi and Hindu Traditional and Nontraditional Responses to Christian Conversion in Bombay 1839-1843." *Journal of the American Academy of Religion* Vol. 74/3 (2006), pp. 615-645.

Paton, James Ed. *John G. Paton, D.D., Missionary in the New Hebrides: An Autobiography.* Vols. I and II. London: Hodder & Stoughton, 1889.

Pfister, Lauren F. *Striving for the "Whole Duty of Man": James Legge and the Scottish Protestant Encounter with China. Assessing Confluences in Scottish Nonconformism, Chinese Missionary Scholarship, Victorian Sinology, and Chinese Protestantism.* Vols. 1 and 2. Frankfurt: Peter Lang, 2004.

Philip, T.V. *Krishna Mohan Banerjea: Christian Apologist.* Madras: Christian Literature Society, 1982.

Phillips, Clifton. "Changing Attitudes in the Student Volunteer Movement in Great Britain and North America 1886-1928." Torben Christensen and William R. Hutchison Eds. *Missionary Ideologies in the Imperialist Era: 1880-1920.* Arhus, Denmark: Aros, 1982, pp. 131-45.

Piggin, Stuart and John Roxborogh. *The St Andrews Seven: The Finest Flowering of Missionary Zeal in Scottish History.* Edinburgh: Banner of Truth, 1985.

Prior, Katherine. "Fraser, Sir Andrew Henderson Leith." H.C.G. Matthew and Brian Harrison Ed. *Oxford Dictionary of National Biography*, Vol. 20 (Oxford: Oxford University Press, 2004), pp. 822-23.

Pritchard, John. *Methodists and their Missionary Societies.* Farnham, Surrey: Ashgate, 2014.

Rawlins, Clive L. Ed. *The Diaries of William Paterson Paterson*. Edinburgh: Faith and Life, 1987.

Ritchie, Bruce. "The Missionary Theology of Robert Moffat of Kuruman." Ph.D. thesis, University of Malawi, 2006.

Ritchie, J.M. *The Church of Scotland South Arabia Mission founded by Ion Keith-Falconer's Vision,* Stoke-on-Trent: Tentmaker, 2006.

Roberson, Rusty. "Scottish Missions and Religious Enlightenment in Colonial America: the SSPCK in Transatlantic Context". Ph.D. thesis, University of Edinburgh, 2012.

Roberts, A.D. *A History of the Bemba: Political Growth and Change in North-Eastern Zambia before 1900*. London: Longman, 1973.

Robertson, William. *An Historical Disquisition concerning the Knowledge which the Ancients had of India, and the progress of trade in that country prior to the discovery of the passage to it by the Cape of Good Hope; with an appendix containing observations on the civil polity - the laws and judicial processes - the arts – the sciences - and the religious beliefs of the Indians*. London, 1701.

Robertson, William. *The Situation of the World at the Time of Christ's Appearance and its connection with the success of his religion considered*. Edinburgh, 1755.

Rooy, S.H. *The Theology of Missions in the Puritan Tradition*. Grand Rapids: Eerdmans, 1965.

Ross, A.C. "Anti-slavery." Nigel M. de S. Cameron Ed. *Dictionary of Scottish Church History and Theology*. Edinburgh: T. & T. Clark, 1993, pp. 18-19.

Ross, Andrew C. *Blantyre Mission and the Making of Modern Malawi*. Blantyre, Malawi: CLAIM, 1996.

Ross, Andrew C. *Colonialism to Cabinet Crisis: A Political History of Malawi*. Zomba: Kachere Series, 2009.

Ross, Andrew. *David Livingstone: Mission and Empire*. London: Hambledon Continuum, 2006.

Ross, Andrew. *John Philip (1775-1851): Missions, Race and Politics in South Africa*. Aberdeen: Aberdeen University Press, 1986.

Ross, A.C. "Oldham, Joseph Houldsworth." Nigel M. de S. Cameron Ed. *Dictionary of Scottish Church History and Theology*. Edinburgh: T. & T. Clark, 1993, p. 633.

Ross, A.C. "Philip, John" Nigel M. de S. Cameron Ed. *Dictionary of Scottish Church History and Theology*. Edinburgh: T. & T. Clark, 1993, p. 656.

Ross, Andrew. "Scotland and Malawi, 1859-1964." Stewart J. Brown and George Newlands Eds. *Scottish Christianity in the Modern World*. Edinburgh: T & T Clark, 2000, pp. 283-309.

Ross, Andrew C. "Scottish Missionary Concern 1874-1914: A Golden Era?" *Scottish Historical Review,* Vol. 51 (1972), pp. 52-72.

Ross, Andrew C. "The African – A Child or a Man." In Eric Stokes and Richard Brown Eds., *The Zambesian Past: Studies in Central African History*. Manchester, Manchester University Press, 1966, pp. 332-51.

Ross, Kenneth R. "Andrew Ross: CCAP Minister, Church Historian and Social Activist." *Religion in Malawi* Vol. 15 (2008-09), pp. 43-45.

Ross, Kenneth R. "Crisis and Identity: Presbyterian Ecclesiology in Southern Malawi 1891-1993." *Missionalia*, Vol. 25/ 3 (1997), pp. 375-91.

Ross, K.R. "Denney, James." In Nigel M. de S. Cameron Ed. *Dictionary of Scottish Church History and Theology*. Edinburgh: T. & T. Clark, 1993, p. 240.

Ross, Kenneth R. "James Dougall 1896-1980: Architect of Scottish Post-War Foreign Mission Policy." *Records of the Scottish Church History Society*, Vol. XXXVII (2007), pp. 183-206.

Ross, Kenneth R. *Malawi and Scotland: Together in the Talking Place since 1859.* Mzuzu: Mzuni Press, 2013.

Ross, Kenneth R. *Presbyterian Theology and Participatory Democracy.* Edinburgh: St Andrew Press 1993.

Ross, Kenneth. "Serving by Going: The Missionary Call Then and Now." David Wright and David Stay Eds. *Serving the Word of God.* Edinburgh: Rutherford House, 2002, pp. 117-130.

Ross, Kenneth R. and David A. Kerr. "The Commissions After a Century." In David A. Kerr and Kenneth R. Ross Eds. *Edinburgh 2010: Mission Then and Now.* Oxford: Regnum, 2009, pp. 307-317.

Rouse, Ruth and Stephen C. Neill, Eds. *A History of the Ecumenical Movement, 1517-1948.* Vol. I. London: SPCK, 1967.

Roy, Ram Mohun. *The Precepts of Jesus: the Guide to Peace and Happiness, extracted from the New Testament ascribed to the four evangelists.* Calcutta: Unitarian Press, 1924.

Rusch, William G. *Ecumenical Reception – Its Challenge and Opportunity.* Grand Rapids: Wm B Eerdmans, 2007.

Rusch, William G. "The International Lutheran-Roman Catholic Dialogue – An Example of Ecclesial Learning and Ecumenical Reception." Paul Murray Ed. *Receptive Ecumenism and the Call to Catholic Learning – Exploring a Way for Contemporary Ecumenism.* Oxford: Oxford University Press, 2008, pp. 149-159.

Sanders, J. Oswald. *Prayer Power Unlimited.* Grand Rapids: Discovery House Publishers, 1979.

Szasz, Margaret Connell. *Scottish Highlands and Native Americans: Indigenous Education in the Eighteenth Century.* Norman, OK: University of Oklahoma Press, 2007.

Schneiders, Sandra. *Finding the Treasure – Locating Catholic Religious Life in a New Ecclesial and Cultural Context.* Mahwah, NJ: Paulist Press, 2000.

Scrimgeour, A.D. "Historical Paper from the United Free Church: 1929 – As the Continuers Saw It." Report of Committee on Ecumenical Relations, Appendix 1X. *Reports to the 2005 General Assembly of the Church of Scotland.* Edinburgh: Church of Scotland, 2005, pp. 26/52-26/54.

Sefton, Henry R. "The Scotch Society in the American Colonies in the Eighteenth Century." *Scottish Church History Society Records*, Vol. XVII (1972), pp. 169-84.

Sharpe, Eric J. "A.G. Hogg 1875-1954: The Christian Message to the Hindu." Gerald H. Anderson, Robert T. Coote, Norman A. Horner & James M. Phillips Eds. *Mission Legacies: Biographical Studies of Leaders of the Modern Missionary Movement.* New York: Orbis, 1994, pp. 330-38.

Sharpe, Eric J. *Alfred George Hogg 1875-1954: An Intellectual Biography.* Chennai: Christian Literature Society, 1999.

Sharpe, Eric J. *J.N. Farquhar: A Memoir.* Calcutta: YMCA, 1963.

Sharpe, Eric J. "J.N. Farquhar 1861-1929." In Gerald H. Anderson, Robert T. Coote, Norman A. Horner & James M. Phillips Eds. *Mission Legacies: Biographical Studies of Leaders of the Modern Missionary Movement.* New York: Orbis, 1994, pp. 290-96.

Sharpe, Eric J. *"Not to Destroy but to Fulfil": The Contribution of J.N. Farquhar to Protestant Missionary Thought in India before 1914.* Studia Missionalia Upsaliensia & Lund: C.W.K. Gleerup, 1965.

Sharpe, Eric J. Ed. *The Theology of A.G. Hogg.* Bangalore: CISRS and Madras: CLS, 1971.

Shepperson, George. "David Livingstone the Scot." *Scottish Historical Review,* Vol. 39 (1969), pp. 113-21.

Sillery, Anthony. *John Mackenzie of Bechuanaland, 1835-1899: A Study in Humanitarian Imperialism.* Cape Town: A.A. Balkema, 1971.

Signs of the Spirit. Geneva: World Council of Churches, 1991.

Sinclair, E. *The Wee Man with the Big Heart: The Story of the Life of Matthew Sinclair and of the United Pentecostal Mission.* Kilsyth: United Pentecostal Mission, 1973.

Singh, Behari Lal. *Leading Incidents Connected with a Missionary Tour in the Gangetic Districts of Bengal.* Calcutta: J. Thomas, 1853.

Small, A.H. *Letters to Missionary Friends.* Edinburgh: Macniven and Wallace, 1908.

Smith, David. "Junction or Terminus? Christianity in the West at the Dawn of the Third Millennium." In Timothy Yates Ed. *Mission – An Invitation to God's Future.* Calver: Cliff College, 2000, pp. 85-98.

Smith, Donald C. *Passive Obedience and Prophetic Protest.* New York: Peter Lang, 1987.

Smith, George. *The Life of Alexander Duff.* London: Hodder and Stoughton, 1881.

Smith, George. *The Life of John Wilson, DD, FRS.* London: John Murray, 1878.

Smith, Noel. *The Presbyterian Church of Ghana, 1835-1960.* Accra: Ghana Universities Press, 1966.

Smith, Sydney. "Indian Missions." *Edinburgh Review,* 12 (1806), pp. 151-81.

Stanley, Brian. *A History of the Baptist Missionary Society, 1792-1992.* Edinburgh: T and T Clark, 1992.

Stanley, Brian. "Church, State, and the Hierarchy of 'Civilization': The Making of the 'Missions and Governments' Report at the World Missionary Conference, Edinburgh 1910." In Andrew Porter Ed. *The Imperial Horizons of British Protestant Missions, 1880-1914.* Cambridge and Grand Rapids: Eerdmans, 2003, pp. 58-84.

Stanley, Brian. "Scotland and the World Missionary Conference, Edinburgh 1910." *Records of the Scottish Church History Society*, Vol. XLI (2012), pp. 113-132.

Stanley, Brian. *The World Missionary Conference, Edinburgh 1910.* Grand Rapids and Cambridge: Eerdmans, 2009.

Stock, Eugene. *A Short Handbook of Missions.* London: Longmans, 1904.

Taylor, John Randolph. *God Loves Like That! The Theology of James Denney.* London: SCM, 1962.

Taylor, Michael. *Border Crossings: Exploring Social Theology in Christianity and Islam.* Prague: International Baptist Theological Seminary, 2006.

Thomas, M.M. *The Acknowledged Christ of the Indian Renaissance.* Madras: Christian Literature Society, 1969.

Thompson, T. Jack. *Christianity in Northern Malawi: Donald Fraser's Missionary Methods and Ngoni Culture.* Leiden: E.J. Brill, 1995.

van der Bent, Ans J. "Ecumenical Conferences." Nicholas Lossky et al Eds. *Dictionary of the Ecumenical Movement.* Geneva and Grand Rapids: WCC and Eerdmans, 1991, pp. 325-336.

Vickers, John A. *Thomas Coke, Apostle of Methodism*. London: Epworth Press, 1969.

Wainwright, Geoffrey. *Lesslie Newbigin: A Theological Life*. Oxford: Oxford University Press, 2000.

Walls, Andrew F. "British Missions." Torben Christensen and William R. Hutchison Eds. *Missionary Ideologies in the Imperialist Era: 1880-1920*. Arhus, Denmark: Aros, 1982, pp. 159-165.

Walls, Andrew F. "Christie, Dugald." In Gerald H. Anderson ed., *Biographical Dictionary of Christian Missions*. Grand Rapids: Eerdmans, 1999, p. 134.

Walls, Andrew F. "Distinguished Visitors: Tiyo Soga and Lal Behari Singh in Europe and at Home." In Judith Becker and Brian Stanley Ed. *Europe as the Other: External Perspectives on European Christianity*. Goettingen: Vandenhoek & Ruprecht, forthcoming.

Walls, A.F. "Farquhar, John Nicol", Nigel M. de S. Cameron Ed. *Dictionary of Scottish Church History and Theology*. Edinburgh: T. & T. Clark, 1993, p. 315.

Walls, Andrew F. "Missiological Education in Historical Perspective." In J. Dudley Woodberry, Charles Van Engen and E.J. Elliston Ed. *Missiological Education for the 21st Century: the Book, the Circle and the Sandals. Essays in honor of Paul E. Pierson*. Maryknoll NY: Orbis, 1996, pp. 11-22.

Walls, A. F. "Missions." Nigel M. de S. Cameron Ed. *Dictionary of Scottish Church History and Theology*. Edinburgh: T. & T. Clark, 1993, pp. 567-94.

Walls, Andrew F. *The Cross-Cultural Process in Christian History*. Maryknoll NY: Orbis & Edinburgh T. & T. Clark, 2002.

Walls, Andrew F. *The Missionary Movement in Christian History*. Marynoll NY: Orbis & Edinburgh T. & T. Clark, 1996.

Walls, Andrew F. "West African Languages and Christian Proclamation: The Early Years." *Bible Translator Technical Papers* Vol. 55/3 (2004), pp. 389-400.

Walls, Elizabeth A.C. *Pages of Life*. Edinburgh: Church of Scotland Board of World Mission and Unity, 1987.

Wareing, G. "MacLeod, Norman." Nigel M. de S. Cameron Ed. *Dictionary of Scottish Church History and Theology*. Edinburgh: T. & T. Clark, 1993, pp. 532-33.

Watt, Hugh. "Moderator, Rax me that Bible." *Scottish Church History Society Records*. Vol. X (1950), p. 54.

Weir, R.W. *Foreign Missions of the Church of Scotland*. Edinburgh: R & R Clark, 1900.

Whyte, Iain. *Scotland and the Abolition of Black Slavery, 1756-1838*. Edinburgh: Edinburgh University Press, 2006.

Williams, Donovan Ed. *The Journal and Selected Writings of the Rev Tiyo Soga*. Cape Town: Balkema for Rhodes University, 1983.

Williams, Donovan. *Ufumdisi: A Biography of Tiyo Soga*. Alice: Lovedale Press, 1978.

Williams, Rowan. *A Common Word for the Common Good*. Canterbury: Church of England, 2008.

Wilson, John. *Memoir of Margaret Wilson*. Edinburgh: John Johnstone, and London: Whittaker and Co and J. Nisbet and Co, 1838.

Wright, D. F. "World Missionary Conference." In Nigel M. de S. Cameron Ed. *Dictionary of Scottish Church History and Theology*. Edinburgh: T. & T. Clark, 1993, pp. 893-94.

Yates, Timothy. *Christian Mission in the Twentieth Century*. Cambridge: Cambridge University Press, 1994.

Yates, T.E. "Edinburgh Revisited: Edinburgh 1910 to Melbourne 1980." *The Churchman*, Vol. 94/2 (1980), pp. 145-155.

Youngson, John F.W. *Forty Years of the Punjab Mission of the Church of Scotland 1855-1895*. Edinburgh: R. & R. Clark, 1896.

LIST OF CONTRIBUTORS

Esther Breitenbach is Honorary Research Fellow in the School of History, Classics and Archaeology, University of Edinburgh. She has written widely on women in Scotland, and has also researched the impact of participation in the British empire on Scottish society. Among her publications are *Empire and Scottish Society: the Impact of Foreign Missions at Home, c. 1790- c. 1914* (Edinburgh: Edinburgh University Press, 2009) and *Scottish Women: A Documentary History, 1780-1914* (Edinburgh: Edinburgh University Press, 2013), co-edited with Linda Fleming, S. Karly Kehoe and Lesley Orr.

Rose Dowsett has been a member of OMF International since 1969, and with husband Dick has served in Asia and the UK. She taught Church History and Missiology at the Bible Training Institute/ Glasgow Bible College, now International Christian College, for 18 years. Though theoretically now retired, she is still active in global mission networks, as a writer, researcher, and international speaker. She represented World Evangelical Alliance on the Edinburgh 2010 Council. Among her recent publications are *Global Mission: Reflections & Case Studies in Contextualisation for the Whole Church* (2011) and *The Cape Town Commitment: Study Edition* (2012).

John McCracken is Honorary Senior Research Fellow at the University of Stirling where he taught for many years. He has also taught at the University of Dar es Salaam and at Chancellor College, University of Malawi, where he was Professor of History, 1980 to 1983 and Visiting Professor, 2008. He is a Past President of the African Studies Association from whom he received the award of Distinguished Africanist in 2008. Among his publications are *Politics and Christianity in Malawi* (3rd edition 2009) and *A History of Malawi, 1859-1966* (2012).

Stephen Smyth was General Secretary of ACTS from 2007 to 2014 and helped coordinate the engagement of the Churches in Scotland with Edinburgh 2010. He is a member of the Marist Brothers, a Roman Catholic Religious Congregation. He has wide experience of teaching at secondary and adult levels and group facilitation. For seven years he was Ecumenical Officer for Glasgow Churches Together and is a member of an ecumenical Contextual Bible Study Group. He has published poetry and written hymn lyrics.

Kenneth R. Ross is Church of Scotland parish minister at Netherlorn in Argyll, Honorary Fellow of Edinburgh University School of Divinity and

Chair of the Scotland Malawi Partnership. He has also served as Professor of Theology at the University of Malawi and General Secretary of the Church of Scotland Board of World Mission. From 2001 to 2009 he chaired the Towards 2010 Council which prepared for the centenary of the Edinburgh 1910 World Missionary Conference and organized the conference series on which this book is based. His publications include the *Atlas of Global Christianity* (2009) and *Mission Spirituality and Authentic Discipleship* (2013).

Andrew F. Walls is Professor Emeritus of the Study of Christianity in the Non-Western World at the University of Edinburgh. Having earlier worked in Sierra Leone and Nigeria, he is now a regular visiting Professor at the Akrofi-Christaller Institute of Theology, Mission and Culture in Ghana. He was founding editor of the *Journal of Religion in Africa*, founding General Secretary of the International Association for Mission Studies, and founding Director of the Scottish Institute for Missionary Studies. He is the author of *The Missionary Movement in Christian History: Studies in the Transmission of Faith* (1996).

Chris Wigglesworth trained in geology and theology before serving as a Church of Scotland mission partner in western India where he completed highly acclaimed water engineering projects as well as contributing in a variety of ways to the work of the Church of North India. He later lectured in Practical Theology at the University of Aberdeen before being appointed General Secretary of the Church of Scotland Board of World Mission and Unity. He is currently Vice-Convener of the Kirk's Church and Society Council with particular interest in water resources and Muslim-Christian relations.

Jim Wilkie trained as a Minister with the Church of Scotland and worked in rural mission in Zambia with the United Church of Zambia and as an ecumenical university chaplain. In London he served the British Council of Churches on issues to do with Africa and World Mission. From 1984 until he retired in 1998 he was the Africa Secretary of his Church's Board of World Mission based in Edinburgh. His early experience of mission in rural Africa was published in the *International Review of Missions* in July 1965.

INDEX

REGNUM EDINBURGH CENTENARY SERIES

David A. Kerr, Kenneth R. Ross (Eds)
Mission Then and Now
2009 / 978-1-870345-73-6 / 343pp (paperback)
2009 / 978-1-870345-76-7 / 343pp (hardback)

Daryl M. Balia, Kirsteen Kim (Eds)
Witnessing to Christ Today
2010 / 978-1-870345-77-4 / 301pp (hardback)

Claudia Währisch-Oblau, Fidon Mwombeki (Eds)
Mission Continues
Global Impulses for the 21st Century
2010 / 978-1-870345-82-8 / 271pp (hardback)

Brian Woolnough and Wonsuk Ma (Eds)
Holistic Mission
God's Plan for God's People
2010 / 978-1-870345-85-9 / 268pp (hardback)

Kirsteen Kim and Andrew Anderson (Eds)
Mission Today and Tomorrow
2010 / 978-1-870345-91-0 / 450pp (hardback)

Tormod Engelsviken, Erling Lundeby and Dagfinn Solheim (Eds)
The Church Going Glocal
Mission and Globalisation
2011 / 978-1-870345-93-4 / 262pp (hardback)

Marina Ngurusangzeli Behera (Ed)
Interfaith Relations after One Hundred Years
Christian Mission among Other Faiths
2011 / 978-1-870345-96-5 / 338pp (hardback)

Lalsangkima Pachuau and Knud Jørgensen (Eds)
Witnessing to Christ in a Pluralistic Age
Christian Mission among Other Faiths
2011 / 978-1-870345-95-8 / 277pp (hardback)

Beth Snodderly and A Scott Moreau (Eds)
Evangelical Frontier Mission
Perspectives on the Global Progress of the Gospel
2011 / 978-1-870345-98-9 / 312pp (hardback)

Rolv Olsen (Ed)
Mission and Postmodernities
2011 / 978-1-870345-97-2 / 279pp (hardback)

Cathy Ross (Ed)
Life-Widening Mission
2012 / 978-1-908355-00-3 / 163pp (hardback)

Beate Fagerli, Knud Jørgensen, Rolv Olsen, Kari Storstein Haug and
Knut Tveitereid (Eds)
A Learning Missional Church
Reflections from Young Missiologists
2012 / 978-1-908355-01-0 / 218pp (hardback)

Emma Wild-Wood & Peniel Rajkumar (Eds)
Foundations for Mission
2012 / 978-1-908355-12-6 / 309pp (hardback)

Wonsuk Ma & Kenneth R Ross (Eds)
Mission Spirituality and Authentic Discipleship
2013 / 978-1-908355-24-9 / 248pp (hardback)

Stephen B Bevans (Ed)
A Century of Catholic Mission
2013 / 978-1-908355-14-0 / 337pp (hardback)

Robert Schreiter & Knud Jørgensen (Eds)
Mission as Ministry of Reconcilation
2013 / 978-1-908355-26-3 / 382pp (hardback)

Petros Vassiliadis, Editor
Orthodox Perspectives on Mission
2013 / 978-1908355-25-6 / 262pp (hardback)
Orthodox Perspectives on Mission is both a humble tribute to some great Orthodox theologians, who in the past have provided substantial contribution to contemporary missiological and ecumenical discussions, and an Orthodox input to the upcoming 2013 Busan WCC General Assembly. The collected volume is divided into two parts: Part I: The Orthodox Heritage consists of Orthodox missiological contributions of the past, whereas Part II includes all the papers presented in the Plenary of the recent Edinburgh 2010 conference, as well as the short studies and contributions prepared, during the Edinburgh 2010 on going study process.

Pauline Hoggarth, Fergus MacDonald,
Bill Mitchell & Knud Jørgensen, Editors
Bible in Mission "
2013 / 978-1908355-42-3 / 317pp (hardback)
To the authors of Bible in Mission, the Bible is the book of life, and mission is life in the Word. This core reality cuts across the diversity of contexts and hermeneutical strategies represented in these essays. The authors are committed to the boundary-crossings that characterize contemporary mission – and each sees the Bible as foundational to the missio Dei, to God's work in the world.

Wonsuk Ma, Veli-Matti Kärkkäinen
& J Kwabena Asamoah
Pentecostal Mission and Global Christianity
*2014 / 978-1908355-43-0 / 397pp (*hardback)

Although Pentecostalism worldwide represent the most rapidly growing missionary movement in Christian history, only recently scholars from within and outside the movement have begun academic reflection on the mission. This volume represents the coming of age of emerging scholarship of various aspects of the Pentecostal mission, including theological, historical, strategic, and practical aspects.

Afe Adogame, Janice McLean & Anderson Jeremiah, Editors
Engaging the World
Christian Communities in Contemporary Global Societies
*2014 / 978-1908355-21-8 / 235pp (*hardback)

Engaging the World deals with the lived experiences and expressions of Christians in diverse communities across the globe. Christian communities do not live in a vacuum but in complex, diverse social-cultural contexts; within wider communities of different faith and social realities. Power, identity and community are key issues in considering Christian communities in contemporary contexts.

Peniel Jesudason Rufus Rajkumar, Joseph Prabhakar Dayam
& IP Asheervadham, Editors
Mission At and From the Margins
Patterns, Protagonists and Perspectives
*2014 / 978-1908355-13-3 / 283pp (*hardback)

Mission At and From the Margins: Patterns, Protagonists and Perspectives revisits the 'hi-stories' of Mission from the 'bottom up' paying critical attention to people, perspectives and patterns that have often been elided in the construction of mission history. Focusing on the mission story of Christian churches in the South Indian state of Abdhra Pradesh this collection of essays ushers its readers to re-shape their understanding of the landscape of mission history by drawing their attention to the silences and absences within pre-dominant historical accounts.

REGNUM STUDIES IN GLOBAL CHRISTIANITY

David Emmanuel Singh (Ed)
Jesus and the Cross
Reflections of Christians from Islamic Contexts
2008 / 978-1-870345-65-1 / 226pp

Sung-wook Hong
Naming God in Korea
The Case of Protestant Christianity
2008 / 978-1-870345-66-8 / 170pp (hardback)

Hubert van Beek (Ed)
Revisioning Christian Unity
The Global Christian Forum
2009 / 978-1-870345-74-3 / 288pp (hardback)

Young-hoon Lee
The Holy Spirit Movement in Korea
Its Historical and Theological Development
2009 / 978-1-870345-67-5 / 174pp (hardback)

Paul Hang-Sik Cho
Eschatology and Ecology
Experiences of the Korean Church
2010 / 978-1-870345-75-0 / 260pp (hardback)

Dietrich Werner, David Esterline, Namsoon Kang, Joshva Raja (Eds)
The Handbook of Theological Education in World Christianity
Theological Perspectives, Ecumenical Trends, Regional Surveys
2010 / 978-1-870345-80-0 / 759pp

David Emmanuel Singh & Bernard C Farr (Eds)
Christianity and Education
Shaping of Christian Context in Thinking
2010 / 978-1-870345-81-1 / 374pp

J.Andrew Kirk
Civilisations in Conflict?
Islam, the West and Christian Faith
2011 / 978-1-870345-87-3 / 205pp

David Emmanuel Singh (Ed)
Jesus and the Incarnation
Reflections of Christians from Islamic Contexts
2011 / 978-1-870345-90-3 / 245pp

Ivan M Satyavrata
God Has Not left Himself Without Witness
2011 / 978-1-870345-79-8 / 264pp

Bal Krishna Sharma
From this World to the Next
Christian Identity and Funerary Rites in Nepal
2013 / 978-1-908355-08-9 / 238pp

J Kwabena Asamoah-Gyada
Contemporary Pentecostal Christianity
Interpretations from an African Context
2013 / 978-1-908355-07-2 / 194pp

David Emmanuel Singh and Bernard C Farr (Eds)
The Bible and Christian Ethics
2013 / 978-1-908355-20-1 / 217pp

Martin Allaby
Inequality, Corruption and the Church
Challenges & Opportunities in the Global Church
2013 / 978-1-908355-16-4 / 228pp

Paul Alexander and Al Tizon (Eds)
Following Jesus
Journeys in Radical Discipleship – Essays in Honor of Ronald J Sider
2013 / 978-1-908355-27-0 / 228pp

Cawley Bolt
Reluctant or Radical Revolutionaries?
Evangelical Missionaries and Afro-Jamaican Character, 1834-1870
2013 / 978-1-908355-18-8 / 287pp
This study is based on extensive research that challenges traditional ways of understanding some evangelical missionaries of nineteenth century Jamaica and calls for revision of those views. It highlights the strength and character of persons facing various challenges of life in their effort to be faithful to the guiding principles of their existence.

Isabel Apawo Phiri & Dietrich Werner (Eds)
Handbook of Theological Education in Africa
2013 / 978-1-908355-45-4 / 1110pp
The *Handbook of Theological Education in Africa* is a wake-up call for African churches to give proper prominence to theological education institutions and their programmes which serve them. It is unique, comprehensive and ambitious in its aim and scope.

Hope Antone, Wati Longchar, Hyunju Bae, Huang Po Ho, Dietrich Werner (Eds)
Asian Handbook for Theological Education and Ecumenism
2013 / 978-1-908355-30-0 / 675pp (hardback)
This impressive and comprehensive book focuses on key resources for teaching Christian unity and common witness in Asian contexts. It is a collection of articles that reflects the ongoing 'double wrestle' with the texts of biblical tradition as well as with contemporary contexts. It signals an investment towards the future of the ecumenical movement in Asia.

Bernhard Reitsma
The God of My Enemy
The Middle East and the Nature of God
2014 / 978-1-908355-50-8 / 206pp
The establishment of the State of Israel in 1948 for the Church in the West has been the starting point of a rediscovery of its own roots. In the Middle East the effect has been exactly the opposite: Christians have become estranged from their Old Testament roots, because they have been expelled from their land exactly because of an appeal to the Old Testament. The concept of Israel changed from a nation in the Bible, with which they could associate, to an economic, political and military power that was against them

Pantelis Kalaitzidis, Thomas Fitzgerald, Cyril Hovorun, Aikaterini Pekridou,
Nikolaos Asproulis, Dietrich Werner & Guy Liagre (Eds)
Orthodox Handbook on Ecumenism
Resources for Theological Education
2014 / 978-1-908355-44-7 / 962pp (hardback)
We highly recommend the publication of this new *Orthodox Handbook* for Teaching Ecumenism edited by a group of orthodox theologians in collaboration with WCC/ETE Program, the Conference of European Churches, Volos Academy for Theological Studies in Greece, and Holy Cross Greek Orthodox School of Theology in Brookline, Massachusetts.

Myung Sung-Hoon, Hong Young-Gi (Eds)
Charis and Charisma
David Yonggi Cho and the Growth of Yoido Full Gospel Church
2003 / 978-1870345-45-3 / 218pp

Samuel Jayakumar
Mission Reader
Historical Models for Wholistic Mission in the Indian Context
2003 / 1-870345-42-8 / 250pp
(Published jointly with ISPCK)

Bob Robinson
Christians Meeting Hindus
An Analysis and Theological Critique of the Hindu-Christian Encounter in India
2004 / 987-1870345-39-2 / 392pp

Gene Early
Leadership Expectations
How Executive Expectations are Created and Used in a Non-Profit Setting
2005 / 1-870345-30-9 / 276pp

Tharcisse Gatwa
The Churches and Ethnic Ideology in the Rwandan Crises 1900-1994
2005 / 978-1870345-24-8 / 300pp
(Reprinted 2011)

Julie Ma
Mission Possible
Biblical Strategies for Reaching the Lost
2005 / 978-1870345-37-8 / 142pp

I. Mark Beaumont
Christology in Dialogue with Muslims
A Critical Analysis of Christian Presentations of Christ for Muslims
from the Ninth and Twentieth Centuries
2005 / 978-1870345-46-0 / 227pp

Thomas Czövek,
Three Seasons of Charismatic Leadership
A Literary-Critical and Theological Interpretation of the Narrative of
Saul, David and Solomon
2006 / 978-1870345-48-4 / 272pp

Richard Burgess
Nigeria's Christian Revolution
The Civil War Revival and Its Pentecostal Progeny (1967-2006)
2008 / 978-1-870345-63-7 / 347pp

David Emmanuel Singh & Bernard C Farr (Eds)
Christianity and Cultures
Shaping Christian Thinking in Context
2008 / 978-1-870345-69-9 / 271pp

Tormod Engelsviken, Ernst Harbakk, Rolv Olsen, Thor Strandenæs (Eds)
Mission to the World
Communicating the Gospel in the 21st Century:
Essays in Honour of Knud Jørgensen
2008 / 978-1-870345-64-4 / 472pp (hardback)

Al Tizon
Transformation after Lausanne
Radical Evangelical Mission in Global-Local Perspective
2008 / 978-1-870345-68-2 / 281pp

Bambang Budijanto
Values and Participation
Development in Rural Indonesia
2009 / 978-1-870345-70-4 / 237pp

Alan R. Johnson
Leadership in a Slum
A Bangkok Case Study
2009 / 978-1-870345-71-2 / 238pp

Titre Ande
Leadership and Authority
Bula Matari and Life - Community Ecclesiology in Congo
2010 / 978-1-870345-72-9 / 189pp

Frank Kwesi Adams
Odwira and the Gospel
A Study of the Asante Odwira Festival and its Significance for Christianity in Ghana
2010 /978-1-870345-59-0 / 232pp

Bruce Carlton
Strategy Coordinator
Changing the Course of Southern Baptist Missions
2010 / 978-1-870345-78-1 / 273pp

Julie Ma & Wonsuk Ma
Mission in the Spirit:
Towards a Pentecostal/Charismatic Missiology
2010 / 978-1-870345-84-2 / 312pp

Allan Anderson, Edmond Tang (Eds)
Asian and Pentecostal
The Charismatic Face of Christianity in Asia
2011 / 978-1870345-94-1 / 500pp
(Revised Edition)

S. Hun Kim & Wonsuk Ma (Eds)
Korean Diaspora and Christian Mission
2011 / 978-1-870345-89-7 / 301pp (hardback)

Jin Huat Tan
Planting an Indigenous Church
The Case of the Borneo Evangelical Mission
2011 / 978-1-870345-99-6 / 343pp

Bill Prevette
Child, Church and Compassion
Towards Child Theology in Romania
2012 / 978-1-908355-03-4 / 382pp

Samuel Cyuma
Picking up the Pieces
The Church and Conflict Resolution in South Africa and Rwanda
2012 / 978-1-908355-02-7 / 373pp

Peter Rowan
Proclaiming the Peacemaker
The Malaysian Church as an Agent of Reconciliation in a Multicultural Society
2012 / 978-1-908355-05-8 / 268pp

Edward Ontita
Resources and Opportunity
The Architecture of Livelihoods in Rural Kenya
2012 / 978-1-908355-04-1 / 328pp

Kathryn Kraft
Searching for Heaven in the Real World
A Sociological Discussion of Conversion in the Arab World
2012 / 978-1-908355-15-7 / 142pp

Wessley Lukose
Contextual Missiology of the Spirit
Pentecostalism in Rajasthan, India
2013 / 978-1-908355-09-6 / 256pp

Paul M Miller
Evangelical Mission in Co-operation with Catholics
A Study of Evangelical Tensions
2013 / 978-1-908355-17-1 / 291pp

Alemayehu Mekonnen
Culture Change in Ethiopia
An Evangelical Perspective
2013 / 978-1-908355-39-3 / 199pp

This book addresses the causes and consequences of culture change in Ethiopia, from Haile Selassie to the present, based on thorough academic research. Although written from an evangelical perspective, this book invites Ethiopians from all religions, ideological, and ethnic backgrounds to reflect on their past, to analyse their present and to engage in unity with diversity to face the future.

Godwin Lekundayo
The Cosmic Christ
Towards Effective Mission Among the Maasai
2013 / 978-1-908355-28- 7 / 259 pp

This book reveals a complex interaction between the Christian gospel brought by western missionaries and the nomadic Massai culture of Tanzania ... an important insider's voice courageously questioning the approach to condemn some critical Maasai practices, particularly polygamy, and its missionary consequences. This is a rare study from a Maasai Christian leader.

Philippe Ouedraogo
Female Education and Mission
A Burkina Faso Experience
2014 / 978-1-908355-11-9 / 263pp

This volume is the result of six years research in 'Overcoming Obstacles to Female Education in Burkina Faso'. It narrates how Christians and religious groups can speed up female education and contribute to the socio-economic growth of Burkina Faso. Religious culture and traditions were seen as a problem to female education. However, the evidence from this research shows that Christianity is also part of the solution to a quality female education, thus a key factor of socio economic growth of the country.

Haw Yung
Mangoes or Bananas?
The Quest for an Authentic Asian Christian Theology
(Second Edition)
2014 / 978-1-908355-47-8 / 232pp

Over the past few decades there has been a growing awareness of the need for contextual theologies throughout Asia. But how genuinely contextual are these? Based on the premise that theology and mission are inseparable, the author applies four missiological criteria to representative examples of Protestant Asian writings to assess their adequacy or otherwise as contextual theologies.

Daniel Taichoul Yang
Called Out for Witness
The Missionary Journey of Grace Korean Church
2014 / 978-1-908355-49-2 / 167pp

This book investigates the theological motivation for GKC's missions: Reformed theology, Presbyterian theology, and mission theology. The book also shows the extent of the church's mission engagement by continents. Finally, the book turns its attention to the future with an evaluation of the church's missionary journey.

REGNUM RESOURCES FOR MISSION

Knud Jørgensen
Equipping for Service
Christian Leadership in Church and Society
2012 / 978-1-908355-06-5 / 150pp

Mary Miller
What does Love have to do with Leadership?
2013 / 978-1-908355-10-2 / 100pp

Mary Miller (Ed)
Faces of Holistic Mission
Stories of the OCMS Family
2013 / 978-1-908355-32-4 / 104pp

David Cranston and Ruth Padilla DeBorst (Eds)
Mission as Transformation
Learning from Catalysts
2013 / 978-1-908355-34-8 / 77pp

This book is the product of the first Stott-Bediako Forum, held in 2012 with the title *Portraits of Catalysts*. Its aim was to learn from the stories of Christian leaders whose lives and work have served as catalysts for transformation as each, in his or her particular way, facilitated the intersection between the Good News of Jesus Christ and the context in which they lived, in particular amongst people who are suffering.

Brian Woolnough (Ed)
Good News from Africa
Community Transformation Through the Church
2013 / 978-1-908355-33-1 / 123pp

This book discusses how sustainable, holistic, community development can be, and is being, achieved through the work of the local church. Leading African development practitioners describe different aspects of development through their own experience.

Makonen Getu (Ed)
Transforming Microfinance
A Christian Approach
2013 / 978-1-908355-31-7 / 264pp

"This book highlights the important role that Christian-based organisations bring to the delivery of financial services for the poor. It is times, significant and important and deserves a wide circulation".

Lord Carey of Clifton, former Archbishop of Canterbury

Jonathan Ingleby, Tan Kand San, Tan Loun Ling, (Eds)
Contextualisation & Mission Training
Engaging Asia's Religious Worlds
2013 / 978-1-908355-40-9 / 109pp

Contextualisation & Mission Training, offers "contextual frameworks" and "explorations" in order to enhance deeper engagement with the complexity of Asian social, cultural and religious systems.

On Eagle's Wings
Models in Mentoring
2013 / 978-1-908355-46-1 / 105pp
David Cranston writes unashamedly as a Christian for whom no account of mentoring would be complete without placing it in the biggest context of all – that of the relationship between humans and God.

John Lennox, Professor of Mathematics, University of Oxford
Fellow in Mathematics and Philosophy of Science

GENERAL REGNUM TITLES

Vinay Samuel, Chris Sugden (Eds)
The Church in Response to Human Need
1987 / 1870345045 / xii+268pp

Philip Sampson, Vinay Samuel, Chris Sugden (Eds)
Faith and Modernity
Essays in modernity and post-modernity
1994 / 1870345177 / 352pp

Klaus Fiedler
The Story of Faith Missions
1994 / 0745926878 / 428pp

Douglas Peterson
Not by Might nor by Power
A Pentecostal Theology of Social Concern in Latin America
1996 / 1870345207 / xvi+260pp

David Gitari
In Season and Out of Season
Sermons to a Nation
1996 / 1870345118 / 155pp

David. W. Virtue
A Vision of Hope
The Story of Samuel Habib
1996 / 1870345169 / xiv+137pp

Everett A Wilson
Strategy of the Spirit
J.Philip Hogan and the Growth of the Assemblies of God Worldwide, 1960 - 1990
1997 /1870345231/214

Murray Dempster, Byron Klaus, Douglas Petersen (Eds)
The Globalization of Pentecostalism
A Religion Made to Travel
1999 / 1870345290 / xvii+406pp

Peter Johnson, Chris Sugden (Eds)
Markets, Fair Trade and the Kingdom of God
Essays to Celebrate Traidcraft's 21st Birthday
2001 / 1870345193 / xii+155pp

Robert Hillman, Coral Chamberlain, Linda Harding
Healing & Wholeness
Reflections on the Healing Ministry
2002 / 978-1- 870345-35- 4 / xvii+283pp

David Bussau, Russell Mask
Christian Microenterprise Development
An Introduction
2003 / 1870345282 / xiii+142pp

David Singh
Sainthood and Revelatory Discourse
An Examination of the Basis for the Authority of Bayan in Mahdawi Islam
2003 / 8172147285 / xxiv+485pp

REGNUM AFRICA TITLES

Kwame Bediako
Jesus in Africa, The Christian Gospel in African History and Experience
(2000) (Theological Reflections from the South series)
SECOND EDITION FORTHCOMING 2013

Mercy Amba Oduyoye
Beads and Strands, Reflections of an African Woman on Christianity in Africa
(Theological Reflections from the South series)
2002 / 1-870345-41-X / 114pp

Kä Mana
Christians and Churches of Africa Envisioning the Future, Salvation in Christ and the Building of a new African Society
(Theological Reflections from the South series)
2002 / 1-870345-27-4 / 119pp

Ype Schaaf
On Their Way Rejoicing, The History and Role of the Bible in Africa
2002 / 1-870345-35-9 / 252pp

E.A.W. Engmann
Kpawo-Kpawo Toi Kpawo – Vol. 1, Adesai, Oboade, Lalai, Ajenui ke Shwemoi (Folklore of the Ga People)
(Gbotsui Series - Indigenous Sources of Knowledge in Ghanaian Languages)
2009 / 978-9988-1-2296-6 / 70pp

Philip Tetteh Laryea
Yesu Homowo Nuntso (Jesus, Lord of Homowo)
(Nyamedua series in Mother-tongue Theology)
(reprinted 2011) / 1-870345-54-1 / 176pp

E.A.W. Engmann
Kpawo-Kpawo Toi Kpawo – Vol. 2, Kusumii (Folklore of the Ga People)
(Gbotsui Series - Indigenous Sources of Knowledge in Ghanaian Languages)
2012 / 978-9988-1-2294-2, 186pp

Philip T. Laryea
Ephraim Amu: Nationalist, Poet and Theologian (1899–1995)
2012 / 978-9988-1-2293-5, 425pp

Jon P. Kirby
The Power and the Glory, Popular Christianity in Northern Ghana
(Trends in African Christianity Series)
2012 / 978-9988-1-2295-9, 350pp

For the up-to-date listing of the Regnum books visit www.ocms.ac.uk/regnum

Regnum Books International
Regnum is an Imprint of The Oxford Centre for Mission Studies
St. Philip and St. James Church
Woodstock Road
Oxford, OX2 6HR

regnum